Transcendence and Collective Psychology

Darren Kelsey

Transcendence and Collective Psychology

Cosmic Minds, Mystical Wisdom and the Work of Richard Rohr

palgrave
macmillan

Darren Kelsey
School of Arts & Cultures
Newcastle University
Newcastle-Upon-Tyne, UK

ISBN 978-3-032-09494-0 ISBN 978-3-032-09495-7 (eBook)
https://doi.org/10.1007/978-3-032-09495-7

This Palgrave Macmillan imprint is published by the registered company Springer Nature Switzerland AG.
The registered company address is: Gewerbestrasse 11, 6330 Cham, Switzerland

God is holy and happy. God is not an actual person, it's the spirit inside of us.
—Daisy Kelsey

Science without religion is lame, religion without science is blind.
—Albert Einstein

The cosmos is within us. We are made of star-stuff. We are a way for the universe to know itself.
—Carl Sagan

In loving memory of Deacon Peter Lavery

Preface: For the Seekers and Sceptics

This book begins with a tension—between the grounded and the floating, the rational and the irrational, the scientific and the sacred. It's a tension I've lived personally, wrestled with intellectually, and followed intuitively through the winding paths of modern life. And if you're holding this book, I imagine some part of you lives in that same in-between space: curious, uncertain, and hungry for more than the flat explanations we're so often offered about what it means to be human.

As someone who has always been fascinated by the roles of stories in our lives, there are so many questions that motivated the research for this book.

What kinds of stories do we need now—not just to make sense of life, but to save it? What narratives can move us beyond mere survival and toward a deeper sense of purpose? What questions must we ask—not simply to find answers, but to unlock new possibilities? What ways of meaning-making help us not just endure turbulent times, but grow, flourish, and thrive within them? What myths and messages can connect us—not only to what lies beyond in this wondrous cosmos, but to the deeper truth that we already belong to it? What does it mean to tell stories that awaken us—not to the past we've inherited, but to the futures we imagine and build together?

In a world overwhelmed by distraction and division, perhaps the crisis we face isn't about broken minds, but broken stories—a lack of imagination about who we are, what we all have in common, what we're here for, and what lies beyond our current understanding of reality.

Over the past decade, I've been circling this concern from multiple directions—through the lens of political and cultural storytelling, the challenges of collective psychology, the rise of self-help consumerism in a noisy digital world, and more recently, the quiet return of mysticism in a (post)secular culture. Mysticism here is not as superstition, not as nostalgia, but as a rigorous, felt, lived response to a world too often stripped of those universal meanings that connect us as humans.

This book, the second in a trilogy on collective psychology, attempts to trace that response across three tangled terrains: mystical theology, anomalous experiences, and the evolution of consciousness.

Here, you'll meet a Franciscan friar whose teachings dissolve the old binary between science and religion. You'll encounter people who claim to have seen beyond death, touched the limits of the mind on psychedelics, or glimpsed otherworldly craft in the sky. You'll also meet the thinkers—psychologists, mystics, scientists, and visionaries—who have dared to ask whether these strange experiences might be telling us something about what it means to be fully human.

This is not a book of answers, but of possibilities and tackling some of the seemingly impossible topics of our times.

Following the spirit of Jeff Kripal's *Superhumanities*, I believe we need to re-enchant our disciplines—not by abandoning rigor, and not by avoiding the pursuit of social justice, but by expanding what our pursuit of justice and rigor allows us to explore in our humanness. The humanities are, at their core, about being human. But what if being human has always been something more? Something porous, with universal and collective potentials, and always mysteriously unfinished?

My aim is to chart a path between the sacred and the secular without collapsing one into the other. To take seriously what our mystical traditions and arcane experiences have long told us: that consciousness is not merely a by-product of brain activity, but part of a deeper unfolding mystery that we're only beginning to glimpse.

The terrain of this book may feel uncomfortable at times. It should. Transcendence, by definition, stretches us. But if we're willing to sit with the discomfort, a new kind of horizon opens—one that holds space for psychology and divinity, science and wonder, intellect and intuition.

This book is for anyone who has ever felt the pull of something beyond, even if they couldn't name it. For those who have found the church both wounding and healing. For those who trust science but suspect it's not the whole story. For those who are ready to explore the mystical not as an escape from reality, but as a deeper descent into it.

We are not separate from the mysteries we study. We are entangled in them. And maybe, just maybe, we were never meant to solve them entirely—but to be changed by them. Be ready to be changed.

Newcastle-Upon-Tyne, UK Darren Kelsey

Acknowledgements

Monica and Daisy, you are the best. Nothing would be possible without you. And I would never have found God without your love and grace.

To Mum, Dad, Nan, Ian, and the rest of the Kelsey-Ansell and Thompson-Rochford mobs, thank you!

To the Whitten and McKenna families: your presence in our lives has been a gift beyond words.

In terms of colleagues, first things first: *don't forget Katy McDonald*, as I embarrassingly did last time. Katy has been a constant and patient friend throughout my academic journey. Sometimes we take the best people for granted, but not this time, thank you!

I will resist the temptation to list every colleague and friend who needs thanking. The truth is, there are simply too many, and I am blessed to work and live alongside such generous, inspiring, supportive, and funny people. Peers, mentors, advisors, and lifelong friends from all parts of my wonderful life—you all deserve my deepest gratitude, and you know who you are.

The same goes for those of you in the parish of St Joseph's, Birtley—thank you. Deacon Peter Lavery is deeply missed and deserves all the love in the world for the countless lives he touched within and beyond our parish. My thanks also to Pauline Lavery, for her support in the parish and for the love and guidance she shared with Peter on the Journey of Faith, from which so many of us have benefited.

I must also thank St Benet's Catholic Primary School and Catherine Young for leading such a phenomenal team of staff. Daisy has attended a school that shows what education should be like for all our children:

unconditionally kind, loving, fun, and inspiring—even if you do struggle with the audio-visual equipment during Mass.

To every kind person I have ever met, and equally to every person who has challenged, upset, or disappointed me (and vice versa): we all populate each other's lives, and we are all on the same journey. Thank you. God bless, and peace be with you.

Daisy Kelsey, Alice Thompson, and Emily Thompson, we are the dream team. No adults, just kids! Skibidi. Slay. Rizz.
😊

Competing Interests The author has no competing interests to declare that are relevant to the content of this manuscript.

Ethics Approval The author declares that this manuscript does not include primary studies involving animals.

Contents

CHAPTER 1

Introduction: From the Porch to the Cross

In 2022, I published *Storytelling and Collective Psychology: Ancient Wisdom, Modern Life, and the Work of Derren Brown.*[1] My aim was to escape the messiness of modern life and the mixed messages of self-help hacks and gimmicks by returning to the ancient Athenian marketplace—the Stoa Poikile—a painted porch where Stoic philosophers once taught the people of Athens. Stoicism, a street philosophy, guided individuals in turbulent times to live well and manage their thoughts and actions to reduce inner disturbance (See Brown 2016, Kelsey, 2021, Aurelius 2006).

That book was a personal endeavour with collective insights, reflecting on my journey through therapy for anxiety and a serendipitous discovery of Stoic philosophy via the work of Derren Brown. This latest project picks up from where that one left off—in terms of my personal journey and its seamless connection with my research and teaching on collective psychology.

While recounting a personal journey through therapy, my earlier research traced Stoic philosophy into modern psychology, highlighting its influence on Cognitive Behavioural Therapy (CBT) and its resonance in popular culture. I also outlined practical applications of Stoicism in daily life, showing how it could enhance mental wellbeing both individually and collectively.

However, I never identified as "a Stoic." Rather, I sought to share those personal insights and expand Stoicism's relevance through analysis

D. Kelsey, *Transcendence and Collective Psychology*,
https://doi.org/10.1007/978-3-032-09495-7_1

of data relating to collective psychology, personal development, political discourse, and popular culture. While this was a rewarding project and personal journey, I never believed Stoicism held all the answers to my existential questions, especially as my mental health improved and I became more resilient in daily life.[2]

Beyond Stoicism

Stoicism became a useful philosophical and psychological framework for navigating life's challenges. My research showed how Stoic philosophy extended beyond personal development into timely realms of collective psychology and public discourse. Yet, while working on that project, I began to realise that Stoicism wasn't offering the answers to many of my deeper existential curiosities. After finishing that book, I found myself drawn to explore connections between Stoicism and other belief systems.

I was particularly struck when I read Kevin Vost's *The Porch and the Cross*.[3] Vost explores the similarities between Stoicism and Christianity—two traditions I had long sensed could be compatible. At the time, I was an atheist who was beginning to flirt with agnosticism while often attending Catholic Mass with my wife and daughter who are both Catholic.[4]

When I noticed similarities between Stoic virtues and Christian teachings, I experienced a metaphorical and psychological resonance in biblical stories, sermons, and the communal rituals of Mass. Given my research and teaching on collective psychology and mythology, I found myself increasingly compelled by the visceral yearning and embodied resonance I experienced in church.

Massimo Pigliucci, a popular scholar of modern Stoicism, makes the point that Stoicism can be practised by atheists and theists alike.[5] Although there are clear differences between Stoicism and Christianity, both traditions share a commitment to virtue, humility, and service to a reality beyond the ego. While both paths encourage personal transformation through discipline and inner reflection, I began to feel that my deep (often unconscious) craving for transcendence was more fully nourished in church than by reading ancient philosophy.

It was this combined experience of philosophical tools and theological practices that laid the groundwork for my eventual conversion to Catholicism—while still seeking to avoid any endorsement of the worst traits of Christianity, some of which I will tackle throughout this book.

Cardinal Virtues

Both Stoicism and Christianity emphasize virtue. Stoicism's cardinal virtues—wisdom, courage, justice, and moderation—find echoes in Christian moral teachings, which include faith, hope, love, humility, compassion, and forgiveness. Both Stoicism and Christianity emphasize personal growth and social responsibility. They encourage the cultivation of psychological and emotional states conducive to peace, meaning, and ethical living.[6]

Each call us to examine our thoughts and actions in the face of suffering, and to respond with resilience, courage, and compassion. While Stoicism often treats suffering as something to be endured with dignity, Christianity also sees suffering as potentially redemptive, offering a path to transformation through love, grace, and sacrifice.

The *summum bonum*—the highest good—is a shared pursuit but defined differently. For the Stoics, it is *eudaimonia*, a flourishing life achieved through living in accordance with virtue and nature. For Christians, it is union with God, realized through love and grace. Both can accommodate transcendental experiences, but from different standpoints.[7]

Looking for More...

While Stoicism was an incredibly effective philosophical partner for CBT—its techniques of reframing and self-examination are powerful tools for building resilience and mental clarity even—I reached a point where I wanted more than resilience and well-being. I was craving something deeper, though I wasn't entirely sure what that craving was—or where to find it.[8]

As I'll explain throughout this book, by the time I chose to join the Catholic Church in 2022, conversion was far less philosophically or spiritually difficult than the years of questioning that preceded it. What ultimately made the difference was the work of Father Richard Rohr, a Christian mystic whose contemplative wisdom helped me reconcile many of the intellectual and spiritual tensions I'd been grappling with.[9]

Rohr's teachings offered a sense of continuity between my background in the humanities and social sciences and the spiritual questions I couldn't ignore. He showed me that science and religion are not inherently contradictory.

Rohr's ecumenical approach to mysticism gave me a framework for understanding humanity's connection to the cosmos and the unfolding of human consciousness. Rohr's ethos extended beyond dialogue within Christian denominations: it embraced a deeper search for common ground between religious and secular worldviews, uniting believers in God with those who, regardless of faith, strive to live by moral virtue and orient their lives toward the summum bonum.

Writing in the opening pages of his book, *Immortal Diamond*, Rohr makes his intentions clear:

> I am writing this book for secular seekers and thinkers, believers and nonbelievers alike, and that huge disillusioned group in recovery from religion itself. Surprisingly, these are often more ready to see and honor Mystery than many religious people are. I can no longer wait for, or give false comfort to, the many Christians who are forever 'deepening their personal relationship' with a very tiny American Jesus—who looks an awful lot like them.[10]

Like me, Rohr was deeply influenced by Jungian psychology and recognized the metaphorical depths within myth and symbolism. His work helped me see how theology, mysticism, and psychology could be profoundly compatible—bridging a tradition I had long resisted, even as I found myself drawn to its myths, rituals, and sense of community. Rohr explicitly frames Jesus as a kind of proto-psychologist—seeing him as teaching shadow work and inner transformation long before Freud or Jung appeared on the scene.[11]

A Note of Reassurance

However, this book does not offer Christianity as the only way forward—nor as an ontological paradigm to which all readers must subscribe. Rather, it is presented as one pathway, a personal example used to illuminate universal human needs that exist both within and beyond formal faith systems, and across multiple religious traditions.

I will unapologetically have my cake and eat it. This book welcomes atheists, theists, phenomenological believers, and non-believers alike, to the same table. It unites us not through exclusionary dogma, but through our shared curiosities, our awe and wonder, our scepticism, and the existential mysteries we all face—regardless of the conclusions we draw or the paths we choose in our pursuit of transcendence (and beyond).

As I will show, Rohr's work has been profoundly influential through insights that have been pivotal for my spiritual journey and research on collective psychology. This book argues that mysticism—and the mystical futures it envisions—can help us fully realize the potential of our cosmic minds as we seek to understand our place in the universe.

Confronting "Contradictions"

Through Rohr's mystical lens, I noticed recurring patterns across various cosmological topics that resonated with the spiritual, transcendental, and psychological themes I've explored in my research and teaching. Building on those patterns, this book embarks on an unexpected journey through a tapestry of risky (but crucial) topics and phenomena. It is here that I turn my attention to the transcendental realms of collective psychology.[12]

This book applies a mystical and psychological lens to understand topics such as mystical theology, UFOs, psychedelics, near-death experiences (NDEs), and the perhaps unexpected links between them.[13] To some readers, these topics may seem tangential to transcendence, spirituality, and collective psychology. However, I will show how they are focal to the transcendental realms of modern life and popular culture in a psychological quest to understand our personal and collective place in the cosmos.

By exploring diverse, daunting, and daring topics, I show why attention to mysticism and cosmic consciousness is crucial to innovative research on collective psychology.

Science and Mysticism

Once we realize that the stories we tell about life, death, and the cosmos stem from our cosmic minds, it becomes clear that human flourishing depends on these mystical tendencies, which sit deep within the collective psyche. While these tendencies might seem out of place in a world supposedly dominated by rationality and science, this book explores how science and mysticism are two sides of the same coin. Both are essential to understanding the human experience and fostering our collective wellbeing.

Material evidence and reflective experience offer complementary approaches to making sense of our place in the world. Historically, mysticism has connected us to something greater, beyond ourselves. It is my hope that this book will help readers discover their own connections to the transcendental power of contemplative traditions within modern psychology, mysticism, science, and cosmology.

This is a book about common ground. It takes on the challenging but necessary task of showing how mystical practices and modern science align more closely than we might think. It is through our understanding of cosmic consciousness (a concept I return to later) that we can appreciate the transformative potential of transcendence in modern life—regardless of our theistic, atheistic, or agnostic beliefs.

Transcendence and Unselfing

In Chap. 2, I explore the universal human craving for transcendence—a longing that operates through the universal wiring of our collective psychology. Drawing on contemporary psychological research, I examine the science of transcendence and related concepts such as "unselfing," flow states, and the generation of ecstatic experiences.[14]

These mechanisms reveal how we regularly seek to move beyond the confines of the ego and into expanded states of consciousness. But this pursuit, while deeply human, is also fraught with complexity. Personally, and collectively, transcendence is a tricky terrain—it can liberate or mislead, heal, or harm. Whether we channel our transcendental urges toward growth or allow them to devolve into self-destructive or group-destructive behaviours often depends on how well we understand the role of transcendence in our collective psychology.

As the case studies in later chapters will show, the pursuit of transcendence is repeatedly marked by power struggles, misappropriations, and dangerous detours. From spiritual exploitation to technocratic suppression, the transcendent impulse can be manipulated or distorted if we are not attentive to its deeper functions and potentials.[15]

Grounded but Expansive

To navigate this complex terrain of transcendence—its promises and its perils—we need tools that are both psychologically grounded and spiritually expansive. This is where the work of Richard Rohr becomes vital. As a modern mystic rooted in the Christian contemplative tradition, Rohr offers not only a language for transcendence but also a practice for holding it wisely.

Rather than bypassing the ego or indulging in spiritual excess, Rohr's contemplative approach invites us to see through the ego—to unself, not by force or thrill, but by surrender and integration. In this sense, Rohr acts as a mystic mentor, grounding our transcendent impulses in practices that foster humility, compassion, and a deeper sense of belonging.

Rohr's work helps us discern when our longing for more is opening us to divine presence—and when it risks becoming an escape or a power play. As we move into the case studies that follow, Rohr's perspective will serve as a touchstone, offering both a caution and a compass for engaging the transcendental dimensions of our collective psychology.

Each case study in this book is divided into two chapters, to frame key topics more coherently while presenting the depth and breadth of data in a digestible form.[16] The opening case study focuses on the work of Richard Rohr as a Catholic priest, Franciscan friar, and Christian mystic, whose teachings offer an understanding of spirituality and transcendence to help us navigate the topics covered in the case studies that follow thereafter.

Mysticism, Trinity, and Cosmos

Chapter 3 introduces Rohr's mystical influence, contemplative practices, and non-dual approach to psychology. His work emphasizes that faith and science need not be in conflict, encouraging readers to recognise the universal dimensions of divinity and transcendence. Grounded in metaphorical truth, Rohr's theology helps individuals move beyond limiting conceptions of God and rigid religious narratives. It offers a framework for engaging with spirituality that resonates in contemporary life—whether one identifies with a particular faith tradition or approaches these questions from a secular perspective.

Chapter 4 turns to Rohr's Trinitarian theology, showing how these teachings offer a compelling lens for engaging with the present world and the future possibilities explored throughout the book. The Holy Trinity is presented not merely as a religious doctrine, but as a profound metaphor for understanding the divine, the cosmos, the nature of existence, and what might lie beyond our current materialist paradigm—including and exceeding evolutionary accounts of the universe and humanity. By embracing the possibility of non-human intelligences in the cosmos and leaning into divine mystery, Rohr invites us to approach transcendent realms with openness and curiosity—laying the groundwork for the expansive inquiries that follow.

The UFO Phenomenon

Chapter 5 explores the UFO phenomenon from psychological and theoretical perspectives, framing it as a modern encounter with the unknown that carries significant implications for our understanding of transcendence. The chapter examines key literature on UFOs and offers a progressive conceptualisation of how the phenomenon can be taken seriously within academic research and public discourse. It investigates the psychological impact of UFO sightings and considers what these encounters might reveal about humanity's evolving relationship with the cosmos.

Some suggest that UFOs may reflect both our collective consciousness and a deep yearning for transcendence. Rather than framing the phenomenon as supernatural, it is understood here as part of a broader, uncharted cosmos—one that challenges conventional assumptions about reality and the nature of intelligence in the universe.

Chapter 6 then turns to the personal experiences of UFO witnesses. These narratives show that while the specific details of sightings vary across cultures, the underlying experience of transcendence is often strikingly universal. Many experiencers describe profound psychological or spiritual transformations that reshape their worldview, frequently linking their encounters to deeper metaphysical or spiritual dimensions.

Yet such transformations are rarely without struggle. Experiencers often face ridicule, isolation, and confusion as they attempt to reconcile their expanded consciousness with the everyday world around them. As we will see, this tension is a recurring feature in the landscape of transcendence, where power dynamics frequently surface around the regulation of consciousness and the marginalisation of profound experience.

Psychedelic Experiences

Transitioning from the outer cosmos to our inner celestial realms, Chaps. 7 and 8 explore the historical and contemporary uses of psychedelics in society. This case study considers the capacity of psychedelics to alter states of consciousness in ways that often pose a challenge to established sociopolitical orders.

Chapter 7 examines psychedelics as chemical tricksters: agents that disrupt ordinary perception and provide access to transcendental realms, confronting both personal and collective ego structures. I discuss how these substances are not merely tools for introspection since they have also catalysed countercultural movements and inspired alternative ways of living and knowing. While psychedelics can be profoundly therapeutic—offering treatment for conditions such as depression—they also provoke deeper questions about the nature of reality and human consciousness.

Chapter 8 turns to the contemporary renaissance in psychedelic research, highlighting the resurgence of clinical studies and the growing recognition of psychedelics' potential for mental health and spiritual development. This chapter explores how these substances can guide individuals through ego dissolution, self-transformation, and symbolic rebirth—offering access to realms that lie beyond ordinary human experience.

Rohr's mystical theology both parallels and diverges from these psychedelic experiences. Like them, it emphasises the transcendence of ego to reach deeper layers of consciousness and divine presence. Yet Rohr's approach is less focused on esoteric journeys and more rooted in the immediacy of divine accessibility—while still allowing space for those visionary paths that point beyond materialist models of mind and self. In the spirit of non-duality, these are not opposing routes but complementary expressions within a larger tapestry of transcendental experience.

Near-Death Experiences

In Chaps. 9 and 10, the final case study explores the transformative realm of near-death experiences (NDEs).

Chapter 9 examines current research on NDEs, particularly how these experiences challenge materialist conceptions of consciousness. Medical studies increasingly suggest that consciousness may not be confined to the physical body, raising profound questions about the nature of life, death, and what might lie beyond. The chapter presents a range of scientific findings and ongoing debates, revealing the limitations of materialism when confronted with the phenomena associated with NDEs.

Chapter 10 then turns to the personal accounts of those who have undergone NDEs, illustrating how such experiences often lead to lasting shifts in one's perception of reality. While many describe their NDEs as uplifting and deeply meaningful, they also face difficulties upon returning to everyday life.

Experiencers frequently report feelings of alienation or misunderstanding as they struggle to reconcile the profound insights gained during their NDEs with the demands and expectations of ordinary material existence.

The stark contrast between the transcendent visions encountered during the experience and the return to a disenchanted world underscores both the transformative power and the challenges of integrating such encounters into everyday life.

Mystical Futures

Building on the insights of the previous chapters, Chap. 11 offers a closing reflection on what these case studies reveal about our shared humanness and the possibility of mystical futures. Rather than offering definitive answers on anomalous phenomena, this chapter makes a series of provocations—inviting readers to consider how we might move forward collectively by embracing uncertainty, ambiguity, and paradox.

I argue that mysticism, in both its spiritual and psychological forms, provides a vital counterbalance to modern life. It encourages awe, openness, and the humility to dwell in mystery—qualities that help us navigate the complexities of existence.

In an age marked by rapid change, existential unease, and technological acceleration, mysticism reminds us of the enduring power of story, symbol, and the unseen. The chapter reflects on how the arcane themes explored throughout the book—the stories of God, UFOs, psychedelics, NDEs, and more—are not distractions from reason, but expressions of a deeper human longing for meaning and connection.

Rather than framing transcendence as a solitary escape, the chapter positions it as a collective movement: one that honours difference while recognising the common threads that run through our diverse stories and arcane experiences. In this spirit, the chapter gestures toward the idea of the *superhumanities*—a space where critical reflection, symbolic imagination, and shared vulnerability might help us shape a more compassionate and curious future.

A Personal Epiphany

In the Postface, a timely example of an individual's journey through transcendent themes is presented through Ben Hendy, a YouTube creator who explores the "paranormal." His story illustrates how the convergence of mystery, material reality, and spirituality can be actively explored and shared in public discourse.

This final section underscores the importance of resilience and well-being in navigating life's challenges, while also inviting readers to consider that extraordinary—perhaps even seemingly impossible—futures may lie ahead. As Ben moves through stages of self-discovery, transcendence emerges as a vital force for human flourishing, encouraging readers to participate in a collective journey of growth and transformation.

Across the chapters outlined above, I offer analytical tools for engaging with phenomena often dismissed as fringe or implausible. Rather than calling for belief, this approach invites careful, open-minded attention—encouraging readers to take such experiences seriously, regardless of background, worldview, or belief system.

By making awe and mystery accessible to all, this perspective creates common ground between hardened cynics and romantic seekers alike. In doing so, the book opens up new possibilities for understanding life, consciousness, and the cosmos in ways that are both grounded and expansive.

Strategic Scepticism

My line of inquiry in this book applies an analytical tool that I call *strategic scepticism*. I invite readers to approach scepticism not as a tool for dismissing arcane or anomalous phenomena, but as a means of deepening our engagement with them—and with the possibilities they evoke, both within and beyond established ontological frameworks.

The key point is this: even when such phenomena are explained away in strictly materialist terms—or met with a reflexive scepticism aimed at protecting existing models of reality—they remain profoundly significant. Often, it is in the very act of reduction or denial that their psychological, cultural, and conceptual richness becomes most visible.

By treating even the most reductive explanations as serious hypotheses, strategic scepticism resists the impulse to reject. Instead, it responds with curiosity and awe. It draws attention to what is revealed through attempts to explain away the inexplicable—and to what those explanations tend to overlook. In this way, strategic scepticism becomes a method of opening rather than closing inquiry.

Pyrrhonian Logic

As medical doctor and philosopher Raymond Moody points out, when someone claims to be a sceptic yet offers a definitive dismissal, they betray the original spirit of scepticism as a philosophical discipline.[17] Rooted in the work of Pyrrho, scepticism was never about denial, but about the disciplined refusal to claim certainty in the face of inconclusive evidence.

Pyrrhonian sceptics were trained in logic and guided by intellectual humility—a recognition that strong conclusions often outstrip what the evidence can justify. Moody, a leading scholar on NDEs, reminds us that true scepticism involves asking careful, logically grounded questions rather than rushing toward closure or falling into dogma—pitfalls that can entrap both believers and non-believers. It is, at its heart, a posture of openness rather than dismissal.

Whether we are considering the power of metaphor and collective prayer, the transcendental dimensions of space travel, the visionary realms of psychedelic experience, the enduring symbolism of angels and UFOs, or the mysteries of consciousness and NDEs, each topic reveals that the pursuit of transcendence is a fundamental part of what it means to be human.

This pursuit transcends worn-out dichotomies between religion and science, or between secular and theistic worldviews. It invites us instead into a space of shared wonder—where uncertainty is not a weakness to overcome, but a fertile ground for discovery.

Navigating Complexity

As we navigate the complexities of the modern world, Rohr's theology shows how mysticism offers a pathway that is both deeply rooted in tradition and radically open to the future. It invites us to reconnect with the most profound aspects of our humanity, fostering a collective consciousness that is both integrated and expansive.

Whether through theistic or secular lenses, mysticism provides a framework that can accommodate radical paradigm shifts in our future quests for meaning, unity, and transcendence. This is where our collective psychology shapes our evolving understanding of ourselves and the universe for the benefit of human flourishing.

People of faith should be comfortable with the fact that we are all finding our way through our own paths and journey. This includes our

"Spiritual But Not Religious" (SBNR) peers who consider themselves agnostic if not atheist. As I explain in Chap. 11, author and Christian apologist Justin Brierley argues that despite the apparent decline of traditional religious affiliation, we are witnessing a resurgence of spiritual curiosity and a renewed openness to the divine. He highlights the growing number of people who identify as SBNR, suggesting this trend reflects not a rejection of transcendence, but a shift in how individuals seek and express it.

Radical Paradigms

Jeff Kripal's *Superhumanities* presents a radical challenge to the way we think about paradigms of knowledge, experience, and reality within humanities and the academy at large.[18] Kripal argues that the humanities have always been, at their core, a mystical endeavour—a space where human beings explore meaning, transcendence, and the limits of material reality.[19]

This perspective does not reject the material world or the scientific advancements that have enriched our understanding of it. Rather, it calls for a more holistic, integrative approach that embraces materialism's strengths while refusing to be confined by its limitations.[20]

This is the foundation of my own approach that I set out in the first case study on the mystical theology of Richard Rohr: an understanding of theological inquiry not as a rigid dogma, but as a way of thinking that aligns with a broader collective psychology—one that seeks to grasp the full spectrum of human experience, from the material to the mystical, and the greater unknowns of reality.

Religion, at its best, has always been an avenue for grappling with mystery, helping us orient ourselves within the vast, unknowable cosmos. Rather than dismissing early religious thought as primitive or obsolete, we should recognize its enduring power: it teaches us how to look both inward and outward, to explore our own depths while contemplating the divine architecture of existence. This is not an abstract or removed exercise but a deeply participatory and experiential one.

If the humanities are to be superhuman, as Kripal suggests, then they must have the courage to follow the human impulse toward transcendence—to let our fascinations, our most daring speculations, and our deepest yearnings take us where they will.

This book continues in that spirit, and I will return to Kripal's later. Venturing into the territories where mystery and human experience collide means we confront the liminal spaces where the unknown beckons and where the boundaries of knowledge are rewritten.

God's Place in Science

In *The God Equation*, physicist Michio Kaku explores how science and spirituality might not be fundamentally opposed, but potentially intertwined.[21] Drawing on string theory and the search for a unified theory of everything, Kaku speculates—to some extent metaphorically—about a "cosmic intelligence" embedded in the elegant mathematical laws that govern the universe. Rather than invoking a personal deity, he suggests that the fabric of reality itself may reflect a deeper order, offering a scientific lens through which the idea of a "higher power" or cosmic design becomes thinkable.

Rather than seeing science and faith as separate realms, Kaku proposes that investigating the universe's deepest mysteries through scientific inquiry can offer insights into our existence that resonate with spiritual questions. Kaku's approach highlights how the pursuit of scientific knowledge can complement a search for meaning, suggesting that science and spirituality make equally valid contributions to our understanding of the cosmos.

Likewise, Stephen Meyer, a philosopher of science, argues that intelligent design is evident in the complexity of life, particularly in the information-rich structures found in DNA.[22] In *Signature in the Cell*, Meyer presents the idea that this intricate biological information points to a purposeful designer. His subsequent book, *Darwin's Doubt*, engages critically with aspects of evolutionary theory, particularly the role of random mutations, and argues instead for a guiding intelligence behind the development of life.[23]

Nature and Purpose

Meyer's work invites reconsideration of the boundaries between science and belief, suggesting that the natural world may carry signs of intentionality and purpose. Through his exploration of intelligent design, Meyer aims to bridge scientific inquiry with the deeper philosophical and theological implications of life's complexity and origin.

John Lennox, a devout Christian and Oxford mathematician, also makes a compelling case for the compatibility of religion and science.[24] He argues that both domains offer profound insights—science into the workings of the natural world, and religion into moral, philosophical, and existential questions. For Lennox, science can deepen our sense of wonder, while faith provides the framework to grapple with purpose and meaning. He contends that, far from being in conflict, science and faith can enrich one another, offering a more complete vision of reality.

As Richard Rohr puts it: "The hope is that science gives us objective truth; religion, however, gives us personal meaning or personal truth. They should not be seen as contraries."[25] Both Lennox and Rohr promote dialogue rather than division—encouraging engagement across disciplines and beliefs to arrive at a more holistic understanding of existence.

To believe in God does not mean we must believe in a literal afterlife featuring pearly gates, white gowns in the clouds, and a Zues-like figure on a throne. As the case studies in this book show, we can contemplate other possibilities and explore deeper questions about life, souls, divinity, and consciousness.

What God Is Not

To suggest God carries a lot of conceptual and political baggage would be an understatement. Wars have been declared in the name of God, abuse has been carried out by those who claim to represent God's work, and ideological perversions of God have aggrandised a tyrannical, all-controlling, all-knowing megalomanic judge—tampering with our lives and the fate of those who do not conform to *His* way.

Such dogmas have often defined God as a being who we should fear—a master of judgement who will only grant us eternal life if we behave well and join the right tribe.

So, when I hear people assert their atheism or label belief in God as irrational or unnecessary, I often recognize definitions of God that I once shared in my own worldview. My immediate thought is, "Yes, I agree—I don't believe in that God either." These objections are often rooted in a valid critique of the absurdities found in religious dogma that many have encountered throughout their lives.

How we understand the shape of God through what Rohr calls a "mature" theological lens will become clear throughout this book—particularly in Chaps. 3 and 4. For now, let's be clear on those misconceptions of God that I seek to avoid.

For plenty of Christians (and believers in other faiths), God is not a bearded man living in the sky. God is not a tinkering tyrant. God is not a micro-manager. God is not an authoritarian surveillance practitioner. God does not offer rules to suggest hate and bigotry are acceptable in any way, shape, or form—even if they're claimed as "justified" in his name. God does not sit "upstairs" waiting for requests to be submitted via prayers for him to act upon. God is not gendered or masculine—despite the problematic (albeit metaphorical) language we use for "Him." As Rohr has repeatedly suggested, God is beyond gender.[26]

Beyond Transactional Prayer

God is not someone to whom we should appeal through begging or bargaining. This transactional view of prayer is often what leads non-believers to find faith—especially among rational individuals—perplexing. In contemplative mysticism, however, prayer is not about asking for favours or expecting replies from a distant, monarchical deity. Instead, it is a meditative, reflective, and relational practice—one that invites self-understanding, humility, and the recognition of our divine potential in communion with God. As described by the fourteenth century mystic, Julian of Norwich prayer is a movement into divine love, where the soul finds unity with God through peace and trust.[27]

Teresa of Ávila saw prayer as an intimate interior journey, a loving conversation that transforms the soul over time. Thomas Merton echoed this in his writings on contemplation, describing it as a silent encounter with God that dissolves the illusion of separation. These views resonate with Rohr's emphasis on prayer as a shift in consciousness—a spacious, unguarded presence before the divine, where we awaken to the image of God within.[28]

Many of the unhelpful, habitual, and cultural conceptions of God (and prayer) are equally objectionable to many believers and non-believers alike. Instead of reducing disturbance in the world, these God-fearing projections of a tyrannical man in the sky narrow our psychological potential for transcendental connection and transformation. For individuals and collectives, these conceptions of God provide the antithesis of spiritual growth, connection, and flourishing.

This is not to suggest that a single, definitive concept of God exists that will suddenly persuade non-believers. Rather, as discussed later, it is crucial to move away from problematic definitions that have proven toxic and counterproductive in conversations about spirituality—particularly when considering its significance for collective psychology.[29]

Avoiding Supernaturalism

As discussed in Chap. 2, studying transcendence requires attention to universal human urges—toward wonder, mystery, and meaning—that persist within and beyond the explanatory boundaries of current cultural and scientific frameworks. By attending to the symbolic, affective, and imaginative dimensions of human experience, I seek to offer a more integrated understanding of what it means to be human through the psychology of transcendence. This book invites readers to engage with forms of (un) knowing that transcend reductive paradigms, revealing deeper possibilities for how we might understand reality, consciousness, and our shared existential condition.

Rather than advocating supernaturalism, we can combine our respect for scientific rigor with the awe and mystery of human experience—accommodating our impulse toward seemingly impossible forms of sense-making within and beyond materialist paradigms. Even when grappling with the concept of God, we do not require the supernatural.

As Jeffrey Kripal points out, the term "paranormal" wasn't always problematic. French psychologists in the early twentieth century originally coined it to describe phenomena beyond the scope of normal scientific understanding—experiences that could not be readily explained by conventional science but did not invoke the supernatural.[30]

The "Paranormal" Problem

Over time, the word "paranormal" has accumulated baggage, weighed down by sensationalism and the fantastical, which often hinders serious inquiry. Despite the term's origins, Kripal contends that we must move beyond it to more productively engage with the complexities of these experiences.

Here, we can draw parallels to Thomas Kuhn's concept of scientific paradigm shifts.[31] Just as Kuhn argued that scientific progress occurs through transformative shifts in thinking, scholars like Kripal and Rohr call for a re-examination of reality through the intersection of science and spirituality. This book aims to cultivate a post-secular ethos that transcends the limitations of reductive materialism and dismissive scepticism.

Such an approach seeks to expand our framework for understanding reality by incorporating insights from both science and spirituality, taking seemingly "supernatural" and "fantastical" experiences seriously. Kripal challenges us to consider what becomes possible when we interrogate the seemingly impossible.

In *Authors of the Impossible*, Kripal argues that anomalous experiences—telepathy, UFO encounters, mystical visions—disrupt materialist paradigms and demand intellectual engagement. He examines how figures like Charles Fort, Jacques Vallée, Bertrand Méheust, and Frederic Myers treated these anomalies as cracks in the foundations of conventional knowledge.[32]

Rather than dismissing the impossible, Kripal suggests it serves as a key to unlocking latent human faculties, revealing intersections between science, mysticism, and the mythological structures that encode these insights. Expanding on this in *The Superhumanities*, Kripal calls for an academic paradigm that seriously engages with transpersonal, mystical, and anomalous dimensions of experience.[33]

Kripal argues that esoteric and paranormal discourses, long marginalized in academia, are central to understanding human consciousness and reality. As technology advances, he suggests that humanity may develop capacities once described as supernatural, requiring new methodologies that integrate subjective experience with theoretical analysis.[34]

The Radical Attorney

Joseph Maxwell was a distinguished French attorney who rose to the position of President of the Court of Appeals in Bordeaux.[35] In addition to his legal career, he was also a qualified medical doctor with expertise in amnesia and disorders of consciousness, particularly among epileptic patients. Far from being a marginal figure, Maxwell was a serious intellectual presence, engaging rigorously with the scientific and philosophical discourses of his time.

In his investigations of physical phenomena that had been documented but remained unexplained by contemporary science, Maxwell rejected supernatural explanations. He did not dismiss such occurrences as mere superstition; rather, he considered them genuine aspects of reality that science had yet to fully understand. His work was part of a broader intellectual movement seeking to frame these experiences within the category of the "supernormal"—a term originally coined by Cambridge-educated classicist and psychical researcher Frederic Myers.

For Myers, the "supernormal" referred to phenomena that exceeded the explanatory scope of existing scientific paradigms but did not necessarily defy the natural order. It was a conceptual space that allowed serious inquiry into anomalous experiences without resorting to supernatural claims. The term suggested that such phenomena might one day be comprehended through future scientific progress.

By adopting this terminology, thinkers like Myers and Maxwell created space for intellectual engagement with the unexplained—offering a way to explore anomalous experiences without falling prey to ridicule or accusations of irrationality. The category of the supernormal made room for possibilities that were material, symbolic, or psycho-spiritual in nature, treating these phenomena not as delusions or fantasies, but as potential clues to dimensions of reality still outside the grasp of current knowledge.

Bimodal Positioning

Returning to Kripal, his historical analysis of this intellectual shift towards the para/super-normal, describes this positioning as "bimodal."[36] As Kripal points out, anomalous events and experiences do not automatically lead to belief in one explanation or some spiritual conversion to religion.

Like the earliest mystics, we can sit comfortably with a non-dualist lens on mystery. This healthy mindset requires the premature conclusions of neither reductive rationalism nor magical thinking.[37] A dynamic interplay between rational comprehension and open-ended wonder underpins much of the intellectual integrity found in Maxwell's and Myers's engagements with the supernormal.

I will still avoid the language of "paranormal" due to the baggage it now carries—not merely from popular culture but from the reductive dismissiveness and cynicism of pseudo-rational progressivism. However, this historical context is important. The case studies covered in this book are explored through the spirit of Kripal and others who have maintained and rearticulated this ontological scope within the humanities.

Kripal argues that grounding such terminology dispels the literalism associated with supernatural belief while re-enchanting our understanding of what is genuinely possible. This re-enchantment, however, is not based on superstition but on an acknowledgment of the unknown—a conceptual space for phenomena that hint at new realities.

Worthy of Exploration

These realities, according to Kripal, may or may not be materially falsifiable, yet they remain worthy of intellectual and philosophical exploration. As he succinctly puts it, this does not imply that the beliefs are necessarily true, but rather that they are entirely reasonable and understandable when we seek to appreciate their meaning and the direction they guide us toward—regardless of their material verifiability.[38]

Like approaches to the study of religion, these beliefs are not merely constructions or products of cultural dogma. Instead, they arise from human capacities, patterns, and potentials of knowing and experiencing that deserve serious consideration in any holistic understanding of human consciousness. By embracing this intellectual openness, Maxwell, Myers, and their contemporaries positioned themselves at the frontier of exploring the genuinely mysterious—those elements of experience that beckon us to expand our understanding of reality.

My aim here is not to prove or disprove the data or experiences gathered in each case study, nor to declare them true or false in the conventional, material sense. Rather, it's about recognising the reasonable and meaningful ways people share these experiences. It's about understanding the stories we tell when we tell stories about the arcane, what those stories reveal about us, and why they are significant in current times.

The latter is where we arrive at key questions for inquiry. What are the stories we tell when we tell stories about the transcendental realms of arcane phenomena? And what does *this* data tell us about transcendence and the human experience?

These elements, rooted in a sense of something larger than the individual, are crucial for our collective psychology and for rebuilding the social and spiritual bonds that contribute to a more connected and resilient society. A post-secular ethos pushes us to recover these elements, not through dogma, but through a broader understanding of how humans thrive in connection with something beyond ourselves.[39]

Arcane Horizons

To speak of the arcane is to name transcendental, spiritual, and mystical experiences without invoking the problematic associations that often discourage serious inquiry. The arcane invites us to engage with such experiences thoughtfully—without immediately dismissing them as false, bizarre, or irrational.

Arcane horizons are not wrong or delusional; they are simply not yet widely understood within the collective psyche. While some phenomena once considered fringe have become more familiar or accepted, arcane horizons remain in the realm of the "unknown" or "unsolved" because their deeper nature continues to elude consensus.

In many respects, arcane phenomena belong to the natural fabric of human experience, yet they are not universally recognised or fully grasped in the way more familiar aspects of life are. A lack of explanation does not equate to a lack of reality or value.

These phenomena challenge our assumptions and remind us that reality is far more complex—and more mysterious—than we often allow. By exploring the arcane, we expand our conceptual and perceptual boundaries, making room for experiences that may one day be as accepted and intelligible as those we now consider ordinary.

Profound Mysteries

This shift calls for a more nuanced approach, one that honours both the rigor of science and the profound mysteries of existence, fostering a deeper, more expansive understanding of reality. As this book shows, we can explore transcendence rationally, through attention to seemingly "whacky" topics, without resorting to dismissive scepticism, reductive materialism, or supernatural make-belief.

This balance is crucial for advancing our understanding of collective psychology through the role of transcendence in past, present, and future generations.

So, in the spirit of Jeff Kripal and his predecessors, let's seek out new terrains in the superhumanities. Let's challenge the dominant materialist scepticism that prohibits its own line of scientific inquiry. Let's offer opportunities to expand our understanding of consciousness and reality in ways that might seem impossible at first glance but are utterly comprehendible and awe inspiring.

Whatever conclusions readers may draw from the topics explored in this book, each offers an example of a transcendental experience—a threshold for transformation. They act as portals into terrains we may not have previously considered on our spiritual and existential journeys.

Portals into the Arcane

Archetypes, as discussed throughout this book, are recurring patterns of thought and behaviour embedded in the human psyche. Carl Jung described them as universal structures within the collective unconscious—manifesting in the symbols, themes, and characters that shape both our personal experiences and the shared stories through which we interpret the world.[40]

Portals are archetypal symbols of transformation and transcendence, recurring throughout myths, religious traditions, and cultural narratives. They represent liminal spaces—gateways between metaphorical worlds—that enable movement from one state of being to another. As metaphors for crossing thresholds, portals mark transitions from life to death, ignorance to insight, or ordinary to expanded states of consciousness. Their presence in dreams, myths, and rituals underscores their universal function in facilitating profound psychological, spiritual, and existential shifts.

A portal is not just an entry point; it is a site of tension and potential. As we see throughout this book, transcendental entry points are embroiled with tension. Their potential is often considered a threat to established orders, knowledge, and world views—prompting interventions from institutions governments and groups who hold grave concern for our collective exploration of transcendental realms and what they might mean for society and social order.

Crossing through often demands trials, initiations, or a relinquishing of the old self, reflecting humanity's need for rites of passage to navigate life's transitions. Evoking both awe and anxiety, portals signify the promise and peril of change.

Cosmic Thresholds

In spiritual traditions, portals appear as the gates of Heaven in Christianity, the cosmic thresholds guarded by Yamraj in Hinduism, and the doorways to other realms encountered in shamanic rituals.[41] In NDEs, the recurring imagery of tunnels, lights, and gates aligns with archetypal depictions of transcendence, illustrating their role in navigating the unknown.

Psychedelic experiences often replicate this archetypal structure, with users describing sudden shifts in perception as crossing a threshold into a different dimension of consciousness—encountering visionary realms, entities, or profound insights that feel both alien and deeply familiar.

Similarly, the UFO phenomenon, whether approached as literal or symbolic, often functions as a portal in the psyche: abduction narratives, missing time, telepathic communication, and other contact experiences frequently involve boundary-breaking events that dissolve ordinary reality and open the experiencer to otherworldly knowledge or trauma.

Across these cases, portals serve as psychological and metaphysical thresholds—liminal crossings where the known self dissolves and something radically other, and often transformative, emerges.

Existential Questions

From a psychological perspective, thresholds and portals often symbolize moments of ego dissolution and profound shifts in consciousness, while philosophically, they confront us with existential questions. What lies beyond the threshold? Is it a continuation, a transformation, or an end? These inquiries mirror humanity's perennial quest for meaning and the anxiety tied to the unknown.

Ultimately, these phenomena challenge us to confront the liminality of existence, the spaces where boundaries blur between the known and unknown. They are the structures through which we navigate life's profound mysteries, bridging the gap between physicality and spirit, consciousness, and the infinite. Their enduring presence across time and culture reminds us that transcendence is both a deeply personal journey and a shared human experience.

The book's case studies are transcendental portals into the arcane. So, before we go any further, let's address the topic of transcendence and why it matters in modern life.

Notes

1. Kelsey (2022a).
2. The purpose of that project was not only to introduce readers to Stoicism and its benefits for personal wellbeing. It also sought to show how the

wisdom of a popular figure like Derren Brown could provide critical and progressive interventions on our collective stories in ways that impact upon our wellbeing and interpersonal relations as a society. As an archetypal magician, Brown connects with his audience through various skills, modes, transmedia platforms, and public appearances. Expanding beyond my personal story, I showed how Brown's work speaks to our collective mindset, examines our shared behaviours, and shows how significant our stories are in private and public contexts.
3. Vost (2017).
4. My conversion to Christianity involved a serious interrogation of intellectual propositions. Sunday Mass and belief in God couldn't be exclusive to my weekend or contradictory to the intellectual pursuits of my day job. On Monday mornings, my position as a social scientist and university researcher needed to accommodate this belief with a sense of reason and intellectual compatibility between science, storytelling, psychology, leadership, teaching, religion, and God. In addition to exploring collective psychology, this book reflects on my own journey of faith and the spiritual and psychological benefits I've gained from it. It demonstrates how I can pursue my research in collective psychology without experiencing cognitive dissonance. Similarly, other key figures from various academic disciplines, as discussed throughout this book, illustrate an intellectual compatibility between their personal faith and professional expertise. I reject the notion that belief in God is a deal breaker in the pursuit of common ground within our collective psychology. What's required is a paradigm shift that can accommodate both belief and non-belief in ways that foster spiritual flourishing in our collective psyche. By examining a variety of case studies and conceptual phenomena, I will argue that we are on the brink of cultural and psychological breakthroughs that will create opportunities for positive change and collective flourishing in post-religious and post-secular realms of Western society.
5. Pigliucci (2017).
6. The Stoics believed in the *Logos*, a rational and ordering principle in nature. Christianity also speaks of the *Logos*, but with a profound and expanded meaning. In the Gospel of John, the *Logos* becomes incarnate in Jesus, but for mystical theologians, like Richard Rohr, the *Christ* is not limited to Jesus alone. Rather, for the Christian mystics, Christ is the eternal Logos made manifest through all creation—a living, dynamic presence within the cosmos that unites matter and spirit, immanence and transcendence. This points not to a personal God in the human sense, but to a relational and participatory Divine Reality embedded in all things. In this sense, while Stoicism and Christianity both recognise a cosmic order, Christianity—especially in the mystical and contemplative forms offered throughout this

book—follows a more intimate and incarnational vision of that order: not as an abstract law of reason, but as a loving presence in all of creation, inviting relational transformation.

7. While both traditions reject egotistical desire, greed, and gluttony, they do so for different reasons. Stoicism discourages desire as an irrational disturbance, whereas Christianity reframes it—not as something to be eliminated, but as something to be transformed and redirected toward God.
8. Rather than self-mastery alone, Christian ethics draws on the idea that we are empowered through relationship—with others, with creation, and with God. This emphasis on relationality, love, and interdependence marks a major departure from Stoic autonomy.
9. For a quick and accessible introduction to the work of Richard Rohr, check out the website for the Center for Action and Contemplation, which Rohr established in 1987: https://cac.org/
10. Rohr (2013, p. XVII).
11. Discussing the concept of shadow work in the Gospels, Rohr (2021) states: "Jesus seems to precede Jung and modern depth psychology by two thousand years when he says, 'Why do you observe the splinter in your brother's eye and never notice the plank in your own? How dare you say to your sister or brother, 'Let me take the splinter out of your eye' when all the time there is a log in your own? Take the log out of your own eye first, and then you will see clearly enough to take the splinter out of your brother or sister's eye' (Matthew 7:4–5)." https://cac.org/daily-meditations/shadow-work-in-the-gospels-2021-11-24/
12. For the purposes of the Research Excellence Framework (REF), as with my 2022 book, all citations, datasets, methodological rationale, and the Discourse-Mythological Approach (DMA), are set out in the endnotes and bibliography. While general readers are not expected to treat the endnotes as essential to the main narrative, they serve an important function for researchers, students, and academic peers. The endnotes contain the scholarly apparatus necessary for academic review, enabling the work to meet REF standards and engage rigorously with relevant research fields.
13. It should be noted that Jung is approached with appropriate caution and care. The author's previous work (Kelsey, 2020a) has addressed some of the concerns researchers share about aspects of Jung's work, particularly concerning gender and race. However, some of Jung's insights have proven useful in a nuanced exploration of archetypes, shadow psychology, and the collective unconscious. Similarly, his work on religion, spirituality, and synchronicities are valuable when applied appropriately.
14. See Kaufman (2020); Evans (2017a).
15. Repeating and building upon the methodological framework of my 2022 book, this project employed the Discourse-Mythological Approach (DMA)

to gather and analyse the transmedia datasets for each case study. This included autoethnographic reflections and insights as part of the analysis—aligning with the recent introduction of autoethnography in DMA (see Kelsey, 2022a and below). DMA integrates tools from Critical Discourse Analysis alongside mythological and psychological concepts (see Kelsey 2016, 2017, 2018, 2020a, 2020b, 2022a; Kelsey et al., 2023). CDA's focus on social and institutional power (Fairclough, 1995; Wodak, 2015) provided a critical lens for understanding the power dynamics of transcendence—from social exclusion and public ridicule through to institutional hierarchies and negotiations of power, including but not limited to: critical reflections on ideological intersections within theological paradigms and religious institutions and teachings; governmental, political and academic power negotiations around investigations into UFOs combined with the social exclusion, isolation and ridicule suffered by experiencers and researchers; the politics of transcendence in relation to countercultures, power, state regulation, and ethical practices concerning psychedelic consumption in recreational and research contexts; the politics of researching NDEs in medical research and the necessary but often absent support for experiencers who suffer from social isolation and depression after NDEs. In terms of mythological concepts combined with and applied through discursive analysis, Jungian archetypes and persona analysis are used to explore narratives emerging in each case study—this approach being consistent with the principles of previous DMA studies (Kelsey, 2016, 2017, 2018, 2020a, 2020b, 2022a; c). For other examples of DMA applied as a dynamic framework for analysing cultural mythologies and/or public personas, see Lähdesmäki (2018), Panay (2017), Nartey (2019, 2020, 2021), and MacMillan (2020). Due to its conceptual versatility, DMA evolves (explicitly) in response to the needs of each project in which it is applied. For example, in *Storytelling and Collective Psychology* (Kelsey, 2022b), Stoicism moved beyond an object of analysis and was instead applied as a guiding philosophical practice to expand the analytical scope of DMA in relation to personal (autoethnographic) reflections as well as public discourse on a range of social and political topics. In this current project, a similar move was made with mystical theology, which became a supplementary lens for analysing psychological, experiential, and existential phenomena—bridging the spiritual and symbolic dimensions of human experience within the broader DMA framework. As before (Kelsey, 2022b), autoethnography remains a central and prominent component within DMA's dynamic structure. DMA has always been an expansive and innovative framework that has synergised new toolkits and theories throughout its development (Kelsey, 2016, 2017, 2018, 2020a, 2020b, 2022b). After early DMA studies examined storytelling in news media, digital platforms, and popular culture, autoethnography later expanded the analytical scope of DMA (Kelsey, 2022b) as a framework for self-refection and applied experiential analysis throughout my preparation of research projects on collective psychology. For eclectic and interdisciplinary examples of how autoethnographic approaches can be used in the contexts of other humanities and social science research, see Bochner (1997); Ellis et al. (2011); Bochner and Ellis (1992); Couser (1997); Denzin (1989); Evers (2006); Sikka (2021). As Ellis et al. (2011) point out: "Autoethnography is an approach to research and writing that seeks to describe and systematically analyze personal experience in order to understand cultural experience. This approach challenges canonical ways of doing research and representing others and treats research as a political, socially-just and socially conscious act. A researcher uses tenets of autobiography and ethnography to do and write autoethnography. Thus, as a method, autoethnography is both process and product." As I note elsewhere, datasets were also gathered with the practical negotiations of algorithmic curation in mind, which I explain below (see further endnotes) in relation to Robert Kozinets (2020) and his attention to the complexities of netnographic research and data gathering via online platforms.

16. The transmedia datasets gathered for each case study consist of media content across streaming services and social media platforms combined with academic and popular literature. Transmedia datasets and sources are fully referenced in each chapter. This transmedia approach allows for a layered understanding of where we are—culturally, discursively, and epistemologically—in relation to each case topic. By drawing on both scholarly knowledge and publicly shared narratives, it captures not just what is argued in academic terms, but also how these ideas are circulating, contested, and made meaningful in everyday culture and participatory media. This method reflects a commitment to mapping the evolving knowledge landscape, recognising that truth claims, collective beliefs, and experiential testimonies often coexist in complex and dynamic ways across multiple platforms. Transmedia datasets therefore include full-length documentaries, YouTube channels and interviews, audio podcasts, film and television episodes, academic articles, popular science publications. Only those sources directly analysed in the case studies were cited in the dataset for each chapter, but it should be noted that the broader consumption of materials on each topic influenced how I navigated those phenomena as a researcher—including the algorithmic curation of social media platforms (Kozinets, 2020). I engaged in reflexive, iterative sense-making—watching, noting, rewatching, and cross-referencing materials to understand the symbolic, cultural, and psychological dynamics at play in each case study. This approach recognises that meaning unfolds across multiple platforms and formats, with

audiences playing an active role in the construction of narrative and symbolic coherence—particularly independent YouTube channels that make critical interventions in the field alongside more established commentators, journalists, film makers, and content creators. As such, my analysis traces how transcendental ideas migrate and mutate across platforms—from academic texts to popular science, from long-form conversations to documentary film. The transmedia environment is not treated merely as a content delivery system but as a psychological and symbolic field through which cultural consciousness is expressed and negotiated. Many of the social media sources—particularly YouTube channels, podcasts, and public lectures—have been gathered through a combination of manual searching and algorithmic curation. On the one hand, I have actively searched for materials aligned with the topics and literature explored throughout each chapter. On the other hand, these searches have shaped the algorithmic recommendations I have received, which in turn have introduced me to additional sources. This recursive process of manual inquiry and algorithmically guided discovery has enabled a dynamic form of content curation. The decisions I have made about which materials to include have been guided by their narrative complexity and their interpretative relevance to the themes of transcendence at the heart of this book. In many cases, the expansive stories, perspectives, and discursive shifts that I analyse have emerged through this interpretative engagement with algorithmically mediated content flows. As Kozinets (2020) observes, search engines and platform algorithms are not neutral tools—they actively shape what researchers encounter. My data gathering has involved this kind of algorithmic co-discovery, where content emerges not solely through deliberate search terms but through a recursive feedback loop between my viewing behaviours and the platform's recommendation systems. This process reflects Kozinets' insight that researchers train the algorithm as much as they are guided by it, producing a dynamic interplay in which relevant narratives, discourses, and case studies surface through ongoing interaction with the platform's logic. For further literature on transmedia landscapes and participatory culture, see Jenkins (2006) and Scolari (2009). For further literature on digital ethnography, reflexivity, algorithmic curation, and platform analysis, see Hine (2015), Gillespie (2018), and Bucher (2018).

17. For a discussion of Pyrrhonian scepticism, see Moody (2024).
18. Kripal (2022).
19. See also: Kripal (2011, 2020, 2022).
20. For philosophical approaches that retain the empirical strengths of materialist science while proposing alternative ontologies, see Kastrup 2014, 2021.
21. Kaku (2022).
22. Meyer (2009, 2013).

23. For another body of literature on the compatibilities between religion and evolutionary science, see the work of John Haught (1995, 2000, 2003, 2008, 2010, 2012, 2017). Haught is a Catholic theologian and Distinguished Research Professor Emeritus at Georgetown University. Best known for his work on the dialogue between science and religion, Haught argues that the two are not adversaries but complementary ways of understanding reality. Central to his thought is an *evolutionary theology* that views cosmic and biological evolution not as a threat to faith but as the unfolding of deeper meaning. Haught offers a systematic theological framework, positioning theology as a discipline that interprets purpose and value alongside the discoveries of science. He critiques reductive materialism, challenges the "conflict model" of science and religion, and insists on a layered account of meaning that accommodates both empirical inquiry and theological reflection. Haught's work provides a rigorous academic approach to situating transcendence within evolutionary and cosmic horizons.
24. Lennox (2007, 2011, 2019, 2020).
25. Rohr (2012, p. 76).
26. As Rohr has repeatedly suggested, God is beyond gender—a point he makes throughout his work as part of a broader invitation to move beyond binary, dualistic thinking. In *The Naked Now* (2009), Rohr argues that limiting God to gendered categories distorts the mystery and unity of the divine. This theme continues in *The Divine Dance* (2016) where he critiques patriarchal depictions of God and emphasises the relational, dynamic nature of the Trinity, which defies fixed labels such as "male" or "female." Similarly, in *The Universal Christ* (2019) Rohr presents Christ as a cosmic, incarnational presence beyond any one form or identity, encouraging a mystical perception that sees God in all things, not confined to masculine imagery. Even in his reflections on spiritual development in *Falling Upward* (2011), Rohr suggests that mature faith involves letting go of rigid categories—including gender—as we grow into a deeper, more inclusive experience of the divine.
27. Julian of Norwich (1996).
28. See: Teresa of Ávila (1996); Merton (2007); Rohr (2009, 2011).
29. Throughout this book, I argue that the "God problem" can be approached with openness, without requiring either side to concede to the other. By focusing on transcendence as a shared dimension of our collective psychology, we uncover possibilities for common ground and shared experiential truths. In this light, I draw on my personal reflections, experiences of psychological growth, and encounters with religion as interpretive resources to complement my analysis of the case study data.
30. Kripal (2010).

31. Kuhn (1962).
32. Kripal (2010).
33. Kripal (2022).
34. This book extends such inquiry by considering how mysticism and arcane phenomena are significant to the shape of our collective psychology. I do this through case studies and synergies that align with my understanding of the principles and potentials of paradigm shifts and ontologies in modern life. I investigate how transcendental realms move from the seemingly mundane and every day to the surely "impossible" by reshaping the boundaries of knowledge itself.
35. See Kripal (2010) for further discussion on "authors of the impossible," including but not limited to Maxwell and Myers.
36. Kripal (2020, p. 26).
37. Kripal (2020, pp. 30–31) highlights how some cultures accommodate extraordinary or paranormal experiences without forcing them into either religious or purely secular frameworks. He uses Sweden and Denmark as examples—among the most secular societies in the world—where people still frequently report dramatic, paranormal encounters. Unlike religious communities, however, these experiences are not typically used to reinforce or construct a religious worldview; instead, they are acknowledged on their own terms. Importantly, they are not denied or dismissed as unreal, but recognised as deeply strange and meaningful aspects of human life. Kripal praises sociologist Phil Zuckerman for documenting these accounts in *Society Without God*, noting his fairness and openness as a secular scholar who treats such testimonies as genuine and significant, without reducing them to either superstition or illusion.
38. Kripal (2020, p. 28).
39. In *Storytelling and Collective Psychology*, I addressed the secular void—the existential gap arguably left by the decline of shared religious frameworks. This void reflects the absence of binding common ground for consciously understanding transcendence or spiritually reflecting on what it means to be human (Evans, 2017a; Kelsey, 2022a). I argued that while we still crave transcendence, we struggle to consciously (and, therefore, wholly and healthily) integrate it into the psyche. This absence restricts our sense of possibility, breeding a form of learned helplessness—a radical conformity to the mundane to prove how rational we are. After exploring storytelling and Stoicism in that project, the idea of the secular void continued to concern me. This book addresses that concern, engaging with stories that dwell in transcendent realms and arguing that they merit deeper consideration. Aligning with Kripal's ethos of "thinking the impossible," it pushes beyond conventional scepticism to explore what these phenomena reveal about consciousness, reality, and the future of human potential. I return

here to a premise explored in my previous book by considering how we can begin to fill the secular void—as discussed by Alex Evans in *The Myth Gap* (Evans, 2017b; Evans et al., 2018). This requires more conscious awareness of when, where, and how we find transcendence and whether we are fostering an adequate spiritual landscape for a shared psychological foundation. When Alex Evans discusses the secular void, he isn't suggesting a return to organized religion for everyone, though for some, including myself, that might be the answer. Instead, Evans calls for a conscious recognition of what we have lost since moving away from religion and a deliberate effort to reconnect with the aspects once provided by religious life: community, ritual, guidance, and the collective dynamics of shared belief.

40. Jung (1969). For more detailed discussion of Jungian archetypal theory within DMA, see Kelsey (2017, 2020b, 2022b).
41. Eliade (1964); Kinsley (1988); Turner (1969); Zaleski (1987).

Bibliography

Aurelius, M. (2006). *Meditations* (M. Hammond, Trans.). Penguin Books.

Brown, D. (2016). *Happy: Why More or Less Everything is Absolutely Fine.* Bantam Press.

Bochner, A. (1997). It's about time: Narrative and the divided self. *Qualitative Inquiry, 3*(4), 418–438.

Bochner, A., & Ellis, C. (1992). Personal narrative as a social approach to interpersonal communication. *Communication Theory, 2*(2), 165–172.

Bucher, T. (2018). *If... Then: Algorithmic Power and Politics.* Oxford University Press.

Couser, G. T. (1997). *Recovering bodies: Illness, disability, and life writing.* University of Wisconsin Press.

Denzin, N. (1989). *Interpretive biography.* Sage.

Eliade, M. (1964). *Shamanism: Archaic Techniques of Ecstasy.* Princeton University Press.

Ellis, C., Adams, T., & Bochner, A. (2011). Autoethnography: An overview. *FQS Journal, 12*, 1. https://www.qualitative-research.net/index.php/fqs/article/view/1589/3095

Evans, A. (2017a). *The Myth Gap: What Happens When Old Stories Fade and New Stories Are Needed.* Fourth Estate.

Evans, J. (2017b). *The Art of Losing Control: A Philosopher's Search for Ecstatic Experience.* Canongate.

Evans et al. (2018). *A larger us.* https://larger.us/ideas/?report

Evers, C. (2006). How to surf. *Journal of Sport & Social, 30*, 229–243.

Fairclough, N. (1995). *Language and Power* (2nd ed.). Longman.

Gillespie, T. (2018). *Custodians of the Internet: Platforms, Content Moderation, and the Hidden Decisions that Shape Social Media*. Yale University Press.
Haught, J. (1995). *Science and Religion: From Conflict to Conversation*. Paulist Press.
Haught, J. (2000). *God After Darwin: A Theology of Evolution*. Westview Press.
Haught, J. (2003). *Deeper Than Darwin: The Prospect for Religion in the Age of Evolution*. Westview Press.
Haught, J. (2008). *God and the New Atheism: A Critical Response to Dawkins, Harris, and Hitchens*. Westminster John Knox Press.
Haught, J. (2010). *Making Sense of Evolution: Darwin, God, and the Drama of Life*. Westminster John Knox Press.
Haught, J. (2012). *Science and Faith: A New Introduction*. Paulist Press.
Haught, J. (2017). *The New Cosmic Story: Inside Our Awakening Universe*. Yale University Press.
Hine, C. (2015). *Ethnography for the Internet: Embedded, Embodied and Everyday*. Bloomsbury.
Jenkins, H. (2006). *Convergence Culture: Where Old and New Media Collide*. New York University Press.
Julian of Norwich. (1996). *Revelations of Divine Love* (E. Spearing, Trans.). Penguin Books.
Kaku, M. (2022). *The God Equation: The Quest for a Theory of Everything*. London: Penguin.
Kastrup, B. (2014). *Why Materialism Is Baloney: How True Skeptics Know There is No Death and Fathom Answers to Life, the Universe, and Everything* (Illustrated ed.). Iff Books.
Kastrup, B. (2021). *Decoding Jung's Metaphysics: The Structure and Content of the World as Will and Representation*. Iff Books.
Kaufman, J. (2020). *Transcend: The New Science of Self-Actualization*. Perigee Books.
Kelsey, D. (2016). Hero Mythology and Right-Wing Populism: A Discourse-Mythological Case Study of Nigel Farage in the *Mail Online*. *Journalism Studies, 17*(8), 971–988.
Kelsey, D. (2017). *Media and Affective Mythologies: Discourse, Archetypes, and Ideology in Contemporary Politics*. Palgrave.
Kelsey, D. (2018). Affective Mythology and "The Notorious" Conor McGregor: Monomyth, Mysticism and Mixed Martial Arts. *Martial Arts Studies, 5*, 15–35.
Kelsey, D. (2020a). Archetypal Populism: The "Intellectual Dark Web" and the "Peterson Paradox". In G. Katsambekis & Y. Stavrakakis (Eds.), *Populism across Disciplines: The Return of Populists to the Political Stage* (pp. 135–157). Springer. https://doi.org/10.1007/978-3-030-55038-7_7

Kelsey, D. (2020b). Psycho-discursive Constructions of Narrative in Archetypal Storytelling: A Discourse-Mythological Approach. *Critical Discourse Studies, 18*(3), 332–348. https://doi.org/10.1080/17405904.2020.1802766

Kelsey, D. (2022a). *Murmurations Podcast: Derren Brown: Illusion, Psychology, and the Art of Influence* [Podcast]. Retrieved September 10, 2024, from https://murmurationspodcast.com/derren-brown

Kelsey, D. (2022b). *Storytelling and Collective Psychology: Ancient Wisdom, Modern Life, and the Work of Derren Brown*. Palgrave.

Kelsey, D., Yannopoulou, N., Soares, A. M., et al. (2023). The (Army) Hero with a Thousand Faces: A Discourse-Mythological Approach to Theorising Archetypal Blending in Contemporary Advertising. *Marketing Theory, 23*(1), 61–82. https://doi.org/10.1177/14705931221141732

Kinsley, D. (1988). *Hindu Goddesses: Visions of the Divine Feminine in the Hindu Religious Tradition*. University of California Press.

Kozinets, R. V. (2020). *Netnography: The Essential Guide to Qualitative Social Media Research* (3rd ed.). Sage.

Kripal, J. (2010). *Authors of the Impossible: The Paranormal and the Sacred*. University of Chicago Press.

Kripal, J. (2011). *Mutants and Mystics: Science Fiction, Superhero Comics, and the Paranormal*. University of Chicago Press.

Kripal, J. (2020). *The Flip: Who You Really Are and Why It Matters*. Penguin Books. static.fnac-static.com+3London Review Bookshop+3Blackwell's+3

Kripal, J. (2022). *Superhumanities: Historical Precedents, Moral Objections, and New Realities*. University of Chicago Press.

Kuhn, T. (1962). *The Structure of Scientific Revolutions*. University of Chicago Press.

Lennox, J. (2007). *God's Undertaker: Has Science Buried God?* Oxford: Lion Books.

Lennox, J. (2011). *Gunning for God: Why the New Atheists are Missing the Target*. Oxford: Lion Hudson.

Lennox, J. (2019). *Can Science Explain Everything?* Oxford: The Good Book Company.

Lennox, J. (2020). *Where is God in a Coronavirus World?* Oxford: The Good Book Company.

Merton, T. (2007). *New Seeds of Contemplation*. New Directions.

Meyer, S. (2009). *Signature in the Cell: DNA and the Evidence for Intelligent Design*. HarperOne.

Meyer, S. (2013). *Darwin's Doubt: The Explosive Origin of Animal Life and the Case for Intelligent Design*. HarperOne.

Moody, R. (2024). *Life After Death?* Suncoast Community. Retrieved August 20, 2025, from https://www.youtube.com/watch?v=Z_7ZijK4LzE&t=2578s

Pigliucci, M. (2017). *How to Be a Stoic: Using Ancient Philosophy to Live a Modern Life*. Basic Books.

Rohr, R. (2009). *The Naked Now: Learning to See as the Mystics See*. Crossroad Publishing.
Rohr, R. (2011). *Falling Upward: A Spirituality for the Two Halves of Life*. Jossey-Bass.
Rohr, R. (2012). *Breathing Under Water: Spirituality and the Twelve Steps*. Retrieved April 10, 2025, from https://www.youtube.com/watch?v=I8o6_IqKdy8
Rohr, R. (2013). *Immortal Diamond: The Search for Our True Self*. Jossey-Bass.
Rohr, R. (2016). *The Divine Dance: The Trinity and Your Transformation*. SPCK Publishing.
Rohr, R. (2019). *The Universal Christ: How a Forgotten Reality Can Change Everything We See, Hope For, and Believe*. SPCK Publishing.
Scolari, C. A. (2009). Transmedia Storytelling: Implicit Consumers, Narrative Worlds, and Branding in Contemporary Media Production. *International Journal of Communication, 3*, 586–606.
Sikka, T. (2021). The Neoliberalization of sleep: A discursive and materialist analysis of sleep technologies. *Journal of the Swiss Anthropological Association, 26*, 105–121.
Teresa of Ávila. (1996). *The Life of Teresa of Jesus*. Translated by E. Allison Peers. Bantam Doubleday Dell.
Turner, V. (1969). *The Ritual Process: Structure and Anti-Structure*. Aldine.
Vost, K. (2017). *Porch and the Cross: Ancient Stoic Wisdom for Modern Christian Living*. Anglico.
Wodak, R. (2015). *The Politics of Fear: What Right-Wing Populist Discourses Mean*. SAGE.
Zaleski, C. (1987). *Otherworld Journeys: Accounts of Near-Death Experience in Medieval and Modern Times*. Oxford University Press.

CHAPTER 2

Craving Transcendence

We crave transcendence. Our innate desire to connect with something greater than ourselves accommodates this deep-seated urge that has shaped human experience throughout history, influencing our beliefs, practices, and relationships.

Transcendence should not be seen as a lofty ideal or a mere spiritual buzzword; it is a fundamental psychological need that drives us as humans. Spirituality emerges as the active pursuit of transcendence; a process we often engage in unconsciously to spark those fleeting moments of connection beyond the self.

This pursuit extends beyond traditional religious practices, permeating many aspects of our lives, whether we recognize it or not. As we explore this longing for transcendence, we will uncover how it enriches our daily experiences and its essential role in fostering belonging, purpose, and meaning. This book will examine the depths of our transcendental cravings and the myriad of forms they take on in personal and public spaces.

We need to appreciate the significance of transcendence in our personal and collective lives while recognizing when and how we pursue it. The latter is what determines whether those transcendental urges are driving healthy behaviours, or not. Transcendence is not solely a religious term; it transcends the boundaries of both religious and secular traditions. It's what Aldous Huxley referred to as a universal and "deep-seated urge to self-transcendence."[1] This often creates moments of calm connection,

D. Kelsey, *Transcendence and Collective Psychology*,
https://doi.org/10.1007/978-3-032-09495-7_2

mystery, or ecstasy through our desire to connect with something greater beyond the self.

Unselfing States of Flow

In Jules Evans' work on transcendence in modern life, he discusses philosopher Iris Murdoch's notion of "unselfing."[2] Murdoch discusses the process of "unselfing" as a vital means of liberating ourselves from the anxiety that often consumes our minds. She illustrated this concept through a scenario in which she becomes trapped in negative, self-oriented thoughts, feeling disconnected from her surroundings. However, when she looks out the window and sees a kestrel, her ego-centric dwelling subsides, and suddenly, all that exists is the kestrel. This moment of connection helps her break free from her anxious thoughts and reconnect with the present.

Moments like this for Murdoch were described by psychologist Mihaly Csikszentmihalyi as a state of flow where we become so absorbed in an activity or moment that we lose track of ourselves and time.[3] In these moments, our focus narrows, and we engage deeply with that point of fascination or the task at hand, whether it's as passive as watching a kestrel from a window to playing our favourite sport or building that summer house for the grandkids. Flow states allow us to experience a sense of immersion and joy beyond the self-oriented anxieties and frustrations imposed by our egos.

Jules Evans makes the point that we all need ways to unself. He acknowledges that our egos have done a great job of enabling our survival and evolution as a species, but there are moments in modern life when we don't need to be scanning the horizon for the next threat to our lives or the opportunity to hunt down our next meal.[4]

As Evans points out, the self can be an exhausting place to be—a self-contained and isolated unit plagued with fears and desires and a sense of mortality. So, when we seek transcendence, we often immerse ourselves in activities that take us beyond a state of flow and into the realms of ecstatic experience.

Our Ecstatic Experiences

Many people take this unselfing practice to a different level—what Evans describes as a deeper form of ego-loss. This might occur through deep contemplative practices, psychedelic drugs, brushes with danger and death, or other moments of spontaneity. In the most profound moments of ego-loss, Evans explains how to develop a deep sense of connection with something greater than them—whether it's God, nature, the cosmos, or humanity.

These experiences are what mystical traditions have described as "ecstasy," coming from the Greek word *ekstasis*, which means "standing outside of the self." The topics I cover in this book are evident ways of understanding transcendence in this sense. Whether it's our cosmic gaze, religious mysticism, UFOs, psychedelics, or NDEs, these are phenomena we are collectively fascinated by as we take our communal unselfing to deeper levels of common connection beyond our egos.

What's important to remember is that transcendental experiences accommodate states of flow *and* ecstasy. As Mihaly Csikszentmihalyi explained to Jules Evans, flow is a subtle form of ecstasy, sharing some traits with the more intense experience of ecstasy itself, such as a feeling of losing oneself in something greater and a sense of time slipping away.[5]

However, flow typically occurs in everyday situations. It can arise while doing tasks like washing dishes, reading an engaging book, or having a conversation. Ultimately, as Csikszentmihalyi suggests, these experiences can lead to moments of true ecstasy. Many of these activities and experiences are pursued without a conscious reflection on the purpose they serve, yet the urge for transcendence remains regardless.

This can be a problem. As Evans points out, there are better and worse ways of transcending because transcendence can be healthy for us as individuals and societies, but it can also be unhealthy, dangerous, and destructive.

Alcohol and Addiction

Aldous Huxley used the term *downward transcendence* to explain how some individuals turn off their minds in unhealthy ways through a reliance on alcohol. Likewise, recovering alcoholic Martin Sheen described addiction as misdirected transcendence in our search for love and connection.[6]

Reflecting on his own recovery and his son Charlie's struggles, Sheen suggested that many addicts are not simply seeking escape but yearning for something greater—a transcendent experience. He emphasized that via Alcoholics Anonymous and the 12-Step programme, true healing involves surrendering to a higher power, engaging in deep interior work, and recognizing the spiritual dimensions of recovery.[7]

Richard Rohr's *Breathing Under Water: Spirituality and the Twelve Steps* (2011) offers a contemplative and theological reframing of the Alcoholics Anonymous 12-step programme. Drawing from Christian mysticism and depth psychology, Rohr argues that the 12 steps are not just a path to sobriety, but a profound journey of spiritual transformation.

Rohr highlights the parallels between recovery and the process of surrender, ego dismantling, and divine union found in Christian contemplative traditions. Rohr contends that addiction—whether to substances, power, control, behaviours, or beliefs—is a universal human struggle, and that the 12 steps can guide anyone toward healing and wholeness when approached through the lens of spiritual awakening.

I remember when I was in college and a teacher explained how a friend of his would drink a bottle of vodka every night. When asking the friend why he did this, the friend replied, "Because it gets you there." I never really knew what to make of this when I was a 17-year-old college student, but it makes sense now, and it's exactly what the likes of Huxley, Sheen, and Evans mean when considering the actions of misdirected transcendence.

This point sheds light on the journey of recovery for alcoholics: those who seek sobriety are not simply stepping into a world devoid of alcohol but are instead being introduced to a new way of transcending through spiritual practice. The Serenity Prayer exemplifies this shift in transcendental directive: *God, grant me the serenity to accept the things I cannot change, courage to change the things I can, and wisdom to know the difference.*[8] This prayer does not advocate for a specific religion or narrow conception of God but rather frames the divine as a metaphorical higher power—something greater than the self.

Moving beyond the misdirected or downward transcendence of individuals, this misdirection often occurs in collective contexts. Sport, religion, politics, and other past times that operate through tribal behaviour provide people with a sense of belonging and a purpose or cause that is shared among that group.

Flow on the Terraces

Football fandom is one example of how transcendence can be both uplifting and misdirected. When we gather behind our team, we often experience a collective flow and ecstasy. The 90-minute match flies by, and we barely notice the clock. A match-winning goal brings sheer joy, as thousands of people celebrate together in a moment of unity.

In these euphoric moments, the usual social rules dissolve: the softy nerd (me) grabs the big tough guy he's never even seen before, and they hug like long-lost friends with no threat or risk of offence. Football fans know this feeling—it's a shared sense of connection and transcendence that goes beyond the self. Other than experiencing the unconditional love and connection of parenthood, marriage, and family life, my most ecstatic experiences have occurred at football matches.

However, there's a darker side to this experience, where transcendence becomes misdirected. The same tribal energy that fuels connection and joy can turn to anger and aggression. After a tough loss or even in the heat of victory, fans can spiral into violence, seeking someone to fight. Street brawls or bar fights between rival supporters emerge as an otherwise ritualised tribalism becomes literal, physical, and destructive.

Despite the toxicity, there's still a pull toward something larger than the self, but it's a destructive form of transcendence, driven by aggression towards the other as much as unity with the tribe. This downward transcendence pulls people into harmful behaviours, illustrating how powerful these urges can be when they're not channelled appropriately.

As I have grown older and consciously appreciated what football fandom gives me as an experience, I've been able to enjoy it more. When I was younger, I craved that next goal and that next win so badly that when it didn't happen, I would be distraught for hours or even days after defeat. Now I wilfully turn off my rational mind, set the Stoicism to one side for a few hours, and completely immerse myself in the experience: singing, clapping, dancing, swearing, celebrating, hugging, booing, screaming, complaining.

It all gets bundled into one ecstatic experience. Then, when it's done, it's *done.*

Once the match is over, I stop to appreciate the day out and feel grateful that I've seen my team and had my tribal fix. We can't win every week, that's why winning is euphoric. I might sulk for a bit if we lose, but that's fine, bring on the next opportunity, and we go again.

Beyond Critical Rationality

There were many scholars I could have explored in these opening sections, but I've focused on Jules Evans because our personal and scholarly experiences align closely. When I was studying Stoicism—partly for my previous book, but also to supplement CBT for anxiety—Evans' book, *Philosophy for Life* was incredibly useful. I still use it when teaching Stoicism. However, my journey, much like Evans', led me to recognize Stoicism's limits.

As Evans explains, the Stoics had little interest in romance, intoxication, art, or ritual, elements that are essential to ecstatic experiences. They viewed human flourishing as a product of rational self-control, which worked for me during and after therapy. But, like Evans, I found that Stoicism could only take me so far.

Though grateful for the Stoic teachings that helped me build resilience, I sought something more. As Evans argues in his follow-up book, *The Art of Losing Control*, the moments where we lose control and move away from the rational self are not to be avoided. As Evans explains, he wanted to loosen up and let go through greater connection to other people, to God, or at least something beyond the parameters of ego.

When done well, the art of losing control plays a crucial role in human life. The moments of surrender in transcendental realms connect us to something greater than ourselves. It is here—beyond the calm, controlled Stoic mindset—that Evans argues we encounter the profound, transformative power of ecstasy.

This book shares some ways forward by consciously engaging with our transcendental needs for the benefit of our collective psychology. I argue that understanding how transcendence operates on personal and societal levels holds great potential for transforming public consciousness. Recognizing and integrating transcendence into our lives can help modern societies evolve in ways that promote psychological well-being and collective flourishing via awe, wonder, reflection, and exploration in spirituality and science.

The Science of Transcendence

Abraham Maslow was an influential psychologist in the early-mid twentieth century. Maslow developed the *hierarchy of needs* in the 1940s and 1950s, outlining a progression of human needs from basic physiological survival to self-actualization—the realization of one's full potential. His model identifies stages of psychological and social development that contribute to well-being and human flourishing.[9]

However, Maslow's hierarchy has been critiqued for being too individualistic, focusing heavily on personal achievement. Maslow reviewed this model later in his career when he added a final component that he deemed crucial to the complete experience of human wholeness—*self-transcendence*. But his critics were largely unaware that he was working on this idea up until his death in 1970, recognizing transcendence as the ultimate stage of human development, which goes beyond individual needs to connect with something greater, such as society, nature, or the cosmos.[10]

More recently, Scott Barry Kaufman revisited and refined Maslow's work by updating and expanding the hierarchy to incorporate transcendence with the added benefit of modern science and psychology.[11] Kaufman uses the benefits of modern psychological research to emphasize the importance of transcendence as key to human flourishing. As Kaufman shows, transcendence is not only crucial for achieving personal fulfilment but also a deep sense of connection and purpose beyond the self.

Kaufman moves beyond the traditional concept of self-actualization by showing how transcendent experiences help us find deeper, more meaningful connections with others and the wider world. For Kaufman, transcendence isn't just about achieving personal goals but about integrating our desires and ambitions with a sense of contributing to something larger than ourselves—a common good, a shared purpose, or what Alex Evans called his organization, *Larger Us*.[12]

Kaufman rejects the notion that transcendence must be rooted in religious spirituality or esoteric traditions. While such paths often emphasize hidden knowledge, spiritual initiation, or altered states of consciousness, he does not consider these necessary gateways. Nor does he confine transcendence to Eastern enlightenment or Western religious mysticism. Instead, Kaufman proposes a more inclusive, psychologically grounded model—one in which transcendence arises through everyday experiences of connection, creativity, purpose, and moral elevation.

He emphasizes that transcendence can be accessed through day-to-day, even mundane, activities. While acknowledging the power of awe and wonder, Kaufman highlights how transcendent states often emerge through personal growth, acts of kindness, meaningful relationships, and contributing to something beyond the self. His approach avoids dependence on mystical or otherworldly frameworks, instead integrating transcendence into the fabric of ordinary life—making it accessible, grounded, and psychologically meaningful for anyone—preceding the arcane topics I focus on in this book.

Mysticism and Non-duality

Given I endorse a mystical influence via the work of Richard Rohr and others, some might consider this to be otherworldly and potentially at odds with Kaufman, but this is not the case. Even the mystical figures and works I discuss in forthcoming chapters emphasize the importance of finding transcendence within the daily life and chores and quiet moments of contemplation beyond formal religious duties or ceremonies.

The likes of Richard Rohr speak to believers and non-believers alike, without requiring commitment to religion. This ethos, like Kaufman's, offers ways to experience transcendence without departing from everyday reality or relying on otherworldly interpretations. Kaufman is not dismissive of mystical traditions, but he expands the concept of transcendence beyond them, making it accessible through a wide range of psychological and everyday experiences.

My goal here is to reconnect mysticism with daily life, showing how it can help our collective states of mind, and demonstrating its relevance in modern life while maintaining the grounded approach that Kaufman advocates. Through this scope I will argue that some of the topics I cover in forthcoming chapters have been burdened by supernatural assumptions and need to be rethought and reintegrated in public discourse and our collective psychology.

Another consistency between Kaufman's work and the approach I take to transcendence is the importance of non-duality and embracing paradox. Non-duality aligns with the mystical ethos I explore through Richard Rohr's contemplative teachings—a practice Rohr advocates from a psychological and scriptural perspective to pursue the common good. Like Rohr and other mystics in the traditions I am concerned with, transcendental states help dissolve boundaries between self and others, leading to feelings of connection, purpose, and unity.[13]

As Jungian psychologist James Hollis points out, learning to live with ambiguity means accepting the true nature of life—with all its complexity, unpredictability, and unexpected turns.[14] But this can be unsettling when our dualist minds habitually offer us black and white thinking. Thinking we have all the answers through that conviction of taking one side over the other is easy and reassuring to the reactive ego, but it isn't conducive to personal growth in the longer term.

Embracing Ambiguity

As Hollis explains, the ego finds doubt deeply uncomfortable, which is why people often cling to ideologies that offer clear-cut answers. But in doing so, they shut down the very growth the soul requires. The soul thrives not on certainty, but on ongoing exploration—constantly reaching for something greater, dwelling in possibility, and moving with the ever-shifting edge of what can be known.[15] This ethos fosters personal growth and societal co-operation—especially in an increasingly polarized world where politics is so tribal and toxic that a difference of opinion seems to warrant enemy status to the other.

These real-world dynamics shape our collective psychology. We can see differences of opinion as interesting ambiguities that are worth exploring in search of some other common ground or deeper truth. We can even see political opponents as potential friends who we share more in common with than we do in our differences. As Kaufman argues, true transcendence contributes to the well-being of others, emphasizing that self-transcendence is not a solitary pursuit but one that impacts society, helping to solve problems, foster kindness, and create a more just world.

While the latter is a prevalent theme in my own work, I take this a step further by focusing on questions, challenges, and topics that are core to our collective curiosities on the nature of reality, with profound implications for human consciousness and future society. Non-duality is essential to this book and discussed in further detail in Chap. 3. It allows for multiple ways of understanding life and reality without forcing reductive, binary, and presumptuous conclusions on transcendental phenomena.

We can value the hard data of science alongside the qualitative experiences of spirituality. We can strive to be good while acknowledging our flaws. And while everyday experiences can bring a transcendental sense of purpose and belonging to routine aspects of life, we can still step into more esoteric topics like UFOs and near-death experiences (NDEs) through our general curiosities for compelling and meaningful stories, and without feeling the need to join Team Sceptic or Team Believer.

As I will show, we can take the arcane stories and experiences that people share seriously and respectfully without jumping to conclusions or claiming to have all the answers. The transcendent is where we can recognize the shared sense of awe and wonder that has resonated in the collective psyche for millennia.

We can even maintain a material understanding of reality when it's helpful, while recognizing that materialism doesn't hold all the answers to our existential questions about reality, and our place in the universe.

Cosmic Consciousness

Canadian psychiatrist Richard Maurice Bucke proposed his concept of *cosmic consciousness* long before the upheavals of the twentieth century.[16] This notion of cosmic consciousness—a deep sense of connection to the vastness of the cosmos and a heightened state of awareness—aligns with modern research on awe, flow states, and human transcendence.

In the late nineteenth and early twentieth centuries, Bucke was envisioning humanity evolving towards higher states of awareness and a sense of connection with the universe through the transcendental realms of cosmic consciousness. He believed that some individuals, like poets and mystics, had already glimpsed this heightened state, where they experienced a profound sense of unity with the cosmos and an expanded awareness of life's meaning.

Bucke documented transformative moments experienced by figures like Buddha, Jesus, Dante, Blake, and others—sudden flashes of insight, often described in nearly identical terms: a dissolution of separateness, a direct awareness of divine interconnectedness, a luminous sense of meaning. These were not private fantasies, Bucke claimed. They were previews of what the human species is becoming. He saw these mystical breakthroughs not as anomalies but as evolutionary markers—signs that consciousness itself is expanding.

Perhaps Bucke was right in this respect, but he also held an overly optimistic view of humanity's near future. He believed that as individuals evolved towards cosmic consciousness, they would naturally adopt more cooperative and harmonious ways of living. Bucke envisioned a society where conflicts over wealth and resources would be resolved through the rise of socialism, as humanity transcended ego-driven competition in favour of a more collective and enlightened state.

With the benefit of hindsight, it's clear that Bucke's expectations were premature for the turbulent century that followed.[17] Nevertheless, his vision of cosmic consciousness remained deeply intertwined with his hope that a new awareness of our place in the universe—and our connection to the cosmos—could foster a more equitable and peaceful society.

Reasons to Be Hopeful

We may have fallen short of Bucke's aspiration since his time, but that does not mean we should abandon hope. An evolving cosmic consciousness can still embrace new possibilities and pursuits with ground-breaking implications for how we understand humanity and the nature of reality. In the chapters that follow, I explore how modern science is increasingly engaging with the idea that radical paradigm shifts are required to appreciate the expansive and evolving nature of the cosmos—where consciousness may be a fundamental component of this unfolding.

The case studies in this book take the idea of cosmic consciousness into arcane realms that stretch our understanding of what it means to be human, whether we are alone in the universe, and what might happen when we die. It is through reconnecting with the awe and wonder of the cosmos that new possibilities emerge.

Bucke also deserves credit for anticipating forms of consciousness that would later be stimulated by experiences he could scarcely have imagined—such as space travel.

One powerful example is the Overview Effect: the profound cognitive shift reported by astronauts when they view Earth from space. Seeing the planet as a fragile, interconnected whole often evokes feelings of awe, unity, and a deepened sense of responsibility for humanity's future. This phenomenon offers striking support for Bucke's ideas about the transformative power of cosmic perspective.[18]

The Overview Effect is one example that supports Bucke's ideas about cosmic consciousness. This phenomenon describes the profound shift in perspective that astronauts experience when they see Earth from space. Observing our planet as a fragile, interconnected whole often evokes feelings of awe, unity, and a sense of responsibility for humanity's future.

The Case of Edgar Mitchell

In 1971, Edgar Mitchell returned from the Apollo 14 mission with his worldview transformed. As he gazed out of the spacecraft window, watching Earth suspended in the vast blackness of space, something shifted. He felt a sudden, overwhelming sense of unity—of being intimately connected to all people, all life, and the cosmos itself. Borders, ideologies, and human divisions dissolved in an instant. From that vantage point, Earth appeared fragile and borderless, and the concerns that dominate terrestrial life—competition, conflict, control—were recast as petty and absurd.[19]

Mitchell's response was to found the Institute of Noetic Sciences, convinced that something vital had occurred on that mission—something just as important as the physics and engineering that had taken him to space. The journey outward had triggered an awakening inward.

What's striking is how closely this mirrors the contours of cosmic consciousness. Though Bucke wrote long before space travel, the experience he described—an expansion of awareness, ego dissolution, moral clarity, and a felt sense of oneness—unfolds in Mitchell's account with uncanny resonance. The means may differ—mystical insight versus spacefaring revelation—but the transformation is deeply aligned.

Mitchell's journey thus becomes a modern, technologically mediated form of the same archetypal pattern. The Overview Effect might be seen as a contemporary path to cosmic consciousness: not through solitude or spiritual discipline, but through the window of a spacecraft. What Bucke framed as a rare evolutionary threshold, Mitchell encountered as a by-product of human ingenuity. Both reveal the same truth: that consciousness can be expanded, that meaning is not imposed on the universe but drawn from it, and that wonder may be one of the most reliable guides we have.

It's when we look to the stars from above or below that we stir this sense of celestial wonder.

Humanity's Cosmic Gaze

Today's cosmology, with its sophisticated telescopes, space probes, and mathematical models, takes a more mechanistic approach to the cosmos—but not without the same sense of awe and wonder. The human need for connection with the universe persists. In modern science, our gaze has shifted from mythological and spiritual frameworks to the pursuit of understanding the laws of physics and the structure of the universe.

The relationship between humans and the cosmos has long been defined by an innate, reciprocal gaze—a gaze that both reflects and shapes our understanding of the universe. For millennia, humans have looked to the stars and the heavens, constructing stories, meanings, and systems of knowledge that have helped navigate the complexities of existence. From the indigenous wisdom of celestial guidance to the technological marvels of modern cosmology, our cosmic gaze has served as both a mirror and a map, offering insight into the human psyche and its search for purpose.

Ancestral communities developed rich, interconnected systems of celestial understanding. Indigenous cultures, for example, crafted intricate maps of the night sky that served as both navigational tools and repositories of wisdom. These star maps were not merely scientific charts but living texts that connected communities to the rhythms of nature, guiding them in matters of planting, hunting, and seasonal rites.

Celestial bodies were viewed as sacred, their movements believed to hold messages or divine directions, channelling psychological projections of both collective and personal significance. The stars, in this view, were not distant, abstract objects but active participants in a web of interconnected meanings and forces.

Mythologizing the Cosmos

It's not so much that we have lost our mythological routes. They've simply evolved over time. As Joseph Campbell points out, the cosmological function of mythology is one of the fundamental purposes served by the stories and understandings of how we understand reality and the cosmos. The mythology of our times helps us make sense of the universe and our place within it, using symbols and stories that convey deeper truths about human existence.

The cosmic gaze is not a one-way phenomenon. It is reciprocal, deeply embedded in both our beliefs and our behaviours. Our view of the cosmos is shaped by how we believe it communicates with us and how, in turn, we seek to communicate with it. Whether through ritual, prayer, scientific inquiry, or the pursuit of transcendence, the gaze we cast upon the stars speaks as much about our inner world as it does about the universe beyond.

By tracing these threads from the ancient wisdom of celestial navigation to the cutting-edge discoveries of modern cosmology, our connection to the cosmos is a deeply psychological and communal endeavour. The stars, in all their mystery, continue to be a source of projection, communication, and meaning, both for the individuals who seek them and for the communities that reimagine their place within the infinite expanse.

The more we discover, the less we realize we understand about the cosmos—especially when you launch a cosmic time machine to space, and it throws back unexpected data.

The Cosmic Time Machine

Christmas day, 2021. The James Webb Space Telescope (JWST) embarks on its journey into space.[20] The world watches in collective anticipation as a technological feat, representing decades of international collaboration and human ingenuity, launches from the Guiana Space Centre.

Just as early astronomers like Copernicus and Galileo revolutionized our understanding of the universe and our place within it, the JWST represents a new chapter in this ongoing narrative. It symbolizes our collective drive to push the boundaries of knowledge, fuelled by a deep-seated curiosity and our transcendental needs being exercised through a cosmic gaze.

Washington, D.C., several months after JWST's launch, a White House representative is handed the first images from JWST. The politician turns to the scientist and asks what he should tell the president.

The scientist responds by emphasizing that the images captured by JWST are far more than just pictures of distant space: JWST is a powerful cosmic time machine, offering humans a window into the universe as it was over 13 billion years ago, providing invaluable insights into the origins and evolution of the cosmos. They reveal the conditions and events from the very beginning of the universe, helping us understand where we come from and how the universe has developed over the vast expanse of time.

JWST's ability to reveal the universe's early stages elicits deep emotional responses, echoing ancient human awe toward the cosmos. In the Netflix documentary, *Cosmic Time Machine*, we see powerful reactions of individuals as they engage with JWST ground-breaking images depicting the origins of the universe.

A White House representative reflects on how these discoveries offer profound insight into our identity and place in the cosmos, while a tearful NASA scientist highlights the significance of the moment, expressing that the magnificent images serve as a glimmer of light in dark times, showcasing what humanity can achieve when we work together.

Unfolding the Universe

These moments of emotional resonance transcend the walls of NASA or the White House. This awe unites people across diverse backgrounds in a shared experience of wonder. Under the hashtag #UnfoldTheUniverse, the mesmerizing images were broadcast onto giant screens in Times Square, igniting excitement and curiosity among onlookers.

Simultaneously, millions of social media accounts shared their own reactions, creating a global tapestry of connection centred around our cosmic gaze, illustrating how the exploration of the universe stirs the collective psyche and inspires a sense of unity among us all.

However, our cosmic gaze is not limited to those technological feats of space voyage. And this sense of cosmic awe did not begin with the likes of Galileo. It is rooted in millennia of cosmological mythology and stories that cultures around the world have used to make sense of the stars and their place within them.

Cosmic awe is intertwined with these myths and cultural practices. For thousands of years, indigenous Australian cultures, for example, have used celestial constellations like the Emu in the Sky to harvest fruits from the land, while Native American star maps connect their earthly experiences with cosmic navigation. These traditions highlight the profound, enduring relationship between humanity and the stars. It is a core feature of our collective psychology.

Modern space exploration endeavours, including those by SpaceX and Virgin Galactic, represent contemporary extensions of these celestial connections, like those early astronomers who transformed our understanding of the universe. The likes of Elon Musk launching a Tesla into space stimulate a multitude of passionate responses and critique in public discourse: from criticism of cynical publicity stunts by tech billionaires through to praise for inspiring a sense of new possibilities for human futures beyond Earth.

Symbolic Projections

The intersection of space exploration and psychological projections reveals much about the human need for transcendence and connection. Our drive to explore the cosmos is not simply motivated by a quest for knowledge or scientific discovery, but by a deep, intrinsic desire to communicate with something beyond ourselves. This longing for cosmic communication is rooted in our collective psychology, shaping the way we approach space exploration and how we interpret the signals we send into the universe, as well as the signals we believe are sent back to us.

From the moment we launched our first satellites and probes into space, we began sending messages into the cosmos, hoping to make contact with other forms of life and intelligence. These efforts, such as the famous "Golden Record" aboard the Voyager spacecraft, are as much about our desire to reach out and make a connection as they are about understanding the universe.

But the human tendency to project meaning onto the unknown goes beyond the scientific and into the symbolic. Our scientific endeavours often morph into myths—our stories that transcend the literal and venture into the realm of the speculative, the mysterious, and the profound. We are fundamentally mystical creatures, and we thrive when we exercise our mystical tendencies.

Extraterrestrial Codes

Take crop circles, for example. These intricate patterns that appear mysteriously in fields have been widely interpreted as potential messages from extraterrestrial civilizations. While many scientists attribute crop circles to human hoaxes or natural phenomena, a significant portion of the public has embraced the idea that these designs represent an intergalactic code or communication from otherworldly beings. The phenomenon taps into our psychological need for cosmic dialogue, offering a tangible symbol of our collective longing for connection with intelligent life beyond Earth.

These interpretations of crop circles—and other similar phenomena—further reveal how our curiosity about space is often mythologized. What starts as a scientific endeavour to understand the cosmos becomes transformed into a story of cosmic communication, where the boundary between science and myth blurs. This mythologizing reflects our deep-seated psychological need to believe that we are not alone in the universe and that there are other intelligences with whom we might one day connect—catering once again for our transcendental cravings.

In this way, space exploration and its associated phenomena become more than just scientific quests; they become cultural narratives, imbued with psychological projections about our place in the cosmos. The search for extraterrestrial life is not only about finding biological organisms but also about finding a mirror to reflect our own desires, fears, and hopes.

These stories of cosmic communication give meaning to our exploration of space, transforming it from a technical pursuit into a symbolic journey towards connection and transcendence.

Projection and Reception

In our pursuit of a connection with the cosmos, we engage in a deeply psychological process that involves both projective and receptive dynamics. These dynamics reflect the emotions, angsts, and curiosities embedded within the collective psyche.

As we look to the stars, we project our desires, fears, and aspirations onto the vast expanse of space. The cosmos, in turn, becomes a mirror, reflecting our inner landscapes and offering us a framework through which we can explore not only the universe but also ourselves. The act of looking outward to the heavens is, in many ways, a metaphorical act of looking inward.

The vastness of space, coupled with the knowledge that we are peering into the earliest moments of the universe, brings with it a humbling reminder of our shared origins. It reminds us of our fragile existence within the broader cosmic timeline. As we contemplate the birth of galaxies and the unfolding of time, we are also reminded of our own small yet significant place in this grand narrative.

This shared perspective has the potential to transcend the boundaries that divide us—national, cultural, and ideological—and foster a sense of unity. In this sense, space exploration becomes more than a scientific endeavour; it becomes a means of cultivating a collective identity, one that links us not only to the past but also to a common future.

This universal perspective, however, is not limited to the stars. It has profound implications for how we view ourselves and each other. As we expand our understanding of the universe, we begin to consider the future of humanity as a collective species. Will we become a multiplanetary civilization? What will this mean for our collective psychology?

As we venture into space and deepen our understanding of the cosmos, we are inevitably confronted with questions about our role in the grander scheme of existence. Space exploration, with its promise of new frontiers and greater knowledge, offers an opportunity to challenge and enrich our collective psyche. It holds the potential to reshape our intercultural identities, offering new ways of thinking about our place in the universe and our connection to one another.

Meaning in the Cosmos

Our sense of connection with the cosmos has continued to grow through the developments of modern science. As the physicist Brian Greene explains, he does physics because it helps him to understand how the world works, and this gives him a feeling of "deep communion with the cosmos."[21]

Likewise, when physicist Brian Cox was given one minute to say anything he wanted to world leaders on climate change at a COP summit in 2021, he said:

> As far as we can tell, this planet is the only island of meaning in an ocean of 400 billion suns. So, what is meaning? Whatever it is, it's surely a property of living things. We know it exists because the universe means something to us. ... We've made the only island of meaning in an ocean of 400 billion suns, and therefore, if we destroy this, we may eliminate meaning in a galaxy of 400 billion stars, potentially forever.

Meaning is real. The most resonant meanings we pursue are transcendental because they take us beyond ourselves into something greater "out there" in the universe.[22]

In terms of our collective psychology, the crucial point here is that regardless of our spiritual or intellectual beliefs, our pursuit for transcendence gives us meaning—from the biggest questions about life and the universe to our personal pursuits for purpose in daily life. The realness of meaning provides the collective desire to wonder about the cosmos and value the sacredness of our planet.

Although Cox and Greene are atheists, they don't advocate for antagonistic debates over the existence of a higher power. Instead, they promote thoughtful explorations of human existence and our place in the cosmos. Both scientists highlight how grappling with the universe's mysteries can evoke deep feelings of awe and wonder, allowing individuals to experience a profound sense of belonging within the vastness of existence. Their perspectives emphasize curiosity and contemplation over conflict, encouraging a more open and reflective dialogue about life's biggest questions.

Science is not a monolithic field of atheism. Other scientists, who are equally respected in their fields, take an alternative view to God and religion. As Kaufman's non-dualist ethos would suggest, we can be comfortable with these differences.

Our opening case study draws on the wisdom of a mystic mentor to show us how and why this is absolutely fine.

Notes

1. Huxley (1945). See also: Evans (2017) for more on Huxley, Maslow, and Csikszentmihalyi's thoughts on transcendence, flow, and states of mind.
2. Evans (2017).
3. Ibid.
4. Ibid.
5. Ibid.
6. Moring (2011).
7. See Alcoholics Anonymous World Services, 2001.
8. Ibid.
9. Maslow (1943, 1954).
10. See Maslow (1968). For a discussion of this journey in Maslow's work, see Slusarczyk (2020).
11. Scott Barry Kaufman's *Transcend: The New Science of Self-Actualization* (2020) does not simply update Maslow's hierarchy in its traditional pyramid form. Instead, Kaufman critiques the rigidity of the pyramid model and offers a dynamic alternative: the sailboat metaphor. This model emphasizes psychological growth as a fluid and adaptive process, responsive to both internal and external conditions, rather than a fixed sequence of needs.
12. Larger Us website can be found here: https://larger.us/
13. For some examples of works by other mystics, see Eckhart (1994, 2009). John of the Cross (2010). Teresa of Ávila (1964); Merton (2003); Julian of Norwich (1996).
14. Hollis (2009).
15. Hollis (2005).
16. Bucke (1901).
17. Bucke also made significant mistakes in his social and behavioural observations across cultures. His views on race and gender have not withstood the test of time, as they reflect the colonial and patriarchal biases of his era. Even within the framework of his own theory, Bucke overlooked rich traditions that embody precisely the kind of cosmic consciousness he sought to define. For example, the extraordinary celestial pedagogies of Aboriginal cultures integrate the stars into systems of land navigation, seasonal cycles, and spiritual storytelling, with elders transmitting cosmic knowledge for survival and meaning. Such traditions reveal sophisticated connections between cosmos, self, pedagogy, and community. Stripping away Bucke's outdated assumptions, we can still recognize a core idea that pulses with potential: human consciousness is dynamic. It moves toward wholeness—

not only at the individual level, but also in relation to the cosmos itself. Mystical experience may thus be understood as an indicator of this trajectory, a sign that inner evolution mirrors the unfolding of the universe. See Kelsey (2017, pp. 6–7) for more on the cosmological functions of mythology and specific examples of Aboriginal cultures as discussed above.

18. See, for example, extended discussions of these developments, in the work of philosopher Philip Goff (2019) on panpsychism and consciousness as a fundamental feature of the universe; Armen Azarian's *The Romance of Reality* (2022), which draws on evolutionary theory and complexity science to address the explanatory gap and frame consciousness as an emergent reality; and Ervin Laszlo's systems-theoretical model of a self-actualizing cosmos grounded in the Akasha paradigm (Laszlo 2020). These scholars represent a growing interdisciplinary movement that challenges reductive materialism by integrating consciousness into the structure of physical reality.
19. Astronaut Frank White suggested that politicians should experience the Overview Effect (OE) before running for office—creating the capacity for more co-operative and compassionate decision making. White argued that seeing Earth from space can profoundly change one's perspective, fostering a greater sense of responsibility toward humanity and the planet. This idea emphasizes the transformative potential of space travel in shaping leaders' understanding of global interconnectedness and the importance of cooperative solutions to pressing challenges: "White … defines the OE as a cognitive shift in worldview experienced by astronauts when they view the Earth from space and in space. He further catalogues the experience as seeing the Earth as a tiny, fragile ball of life, eliciting a profound feeling of awe, an understanding of the interconnection of all life, and a renewed sense of responsibility for taking care of the planet. The OE can be considered an atypical method of engaging with the natural environment, yet it is one that offers demonstrable and perhaps enhanced benefits in terms of promoting self-transcendence, eudaimonic well-being and feelings of connectedness with nature. This chapter presents the case for self-transcendent interventions in mental health, inclusive of psychedelic-assisted psychotherapy, nature-based interventions, and the OE. It concludes with an analysis of how the OE can be understood, studied, and applied within the therapeutic context to promote individual, societal and planetary well-being" (Nezami et al., 2021).
20. See Gal (2023).
21. Greene (2003).
22. Cox & Cohen (2021).

Bibliography

Alcoholics Anonymous World Services (Ed.). (2001). *Alcoholics Anonymous: The Big Book* (4th ed.). Alcoholics Anonymous World Services.

Azarian, A. (2022). *The Romance of Reality: How the Universe Organizes Itself to Create Life, Consciousness, and Cosmic Complexity.* BenBella Books.

Bucke, R. M. (1901). *Cosmic Consciousness: A Study in the Evolution of the Human Mind.* Macmillan.

Cox, B., & Cohen, A. (2021). *Universe: Exploring the Astronomical World.* William Collins.

Eckhart, M. (1994). *Selected Writings* (O. Davies, Trans. and intro.). Penguin Classics.

Eckhart, M. (2009). *The Complete Mystical Works of Meister Eckhart* (M.O'C. Walshe, Ed. and Trans.). Crossroad Publishing Company.

Evans, J. (2017). *The Art of Losing Control: A Philosopher's Search for Ecstatic Experience.* Canongate.

Gal, S. (2023). *Uknown: Cosmic Time Machine* [Documentary episode]. Netflix.

Goff, P. (2019). *Galileo's Error: Foundations for a New Science of Consciousness.* Rider.

Greene, B. (2003). *The Elegant Universe: Superstrings, Hidden Dimensions, and the Quest for the Ultimate Theory.* W.W. Norton & Company.

Hollis, J. (2005). *Finding Meaning in the Second Half of Life: How to Finally, Really Grow Up.* Gotham Books.

Hollis, J. (2009). *What Matters Most: Living a More Considered Life.* Gotham Books.

Huxley, A. (1945). *The Perennial Philosophy.* Harper & Brothers.

John of the Cross. (2010). *Dark Night of the Soul* (E. A. Peers, Trans.). Dover Publications.

Julian of Norwich. (1996). *Revelations of Divine Love* (E. Spearing, Trans.). Penguin Books.

Kaufman, J. (2020). *Transcend: The New Science of Self-Actualization.* Perigee Books.

Kelsey, D. (2017). *Media and Affective Mythologies: Discourse, Archetypes, and Ideology in Contemporary Politics.* Palgrave.

Laszlo, E. (2020). *Reconnecting to the Source: The New Science of Spiritual Experience, How It Can Change You, and How It Can Transform the World.* St. Martin's Essentials.

Maslow, A. H. (1943). A Theory of Human Motivation. *Psychological Review, 50*(4), 370–396.

Maslow, A. H. (1954). *Motivation and Personality.* Harper & Row.

Maslow, A. H. (1968). *Toward a Psychology of Being* (2nd ed.). Van Nostrand Reinhold.

Moring, M. (2011). Interview: Martin Sheen Finds Transcendence. *Christianity Today.* [Online] 4 October. Retrieved July 25, 2025, from https://www.christianitytoday.com/ct/2011/october/fatherbecomesson.html

Nezami, A., Persaud, L. M., & White, F. (2021). The Overview Effect and Well-Being. In C. Impey, A. Spitz, & W. Stoeger (Eds.), *Expanding Worldviews: Astrobiology, Big History and Cosmic Perspectives* (pp. 163–177). Springer. Retrieved August 20, 2025, from https://ui.adsabs.harvard.edu/abs/2021ASSP...58..163N/abstract

Rohr, R. (2011). *Falling Upward: A Spirituality for the Two Halves of Life*. Jossey-Bass.

Slusarczyk, R. (2020). #06: Public Relations in Times of Global Crisis—With Ramona Slusarczyk. *Murmurations*. YouTube. Retrieved August 20, 2025, from https://www.youtube.com/watch?v=uPzBxkO-sx0

CHAPTER 3

The Mystic Mentor

Do you have wise elders in your life? Not just elderly people, but true mentors—individuals who have gained deep life wisdom and are eager to share it for the benefit of others. These mentors reach a point where they are less focused on themselves and more motivated to guide others, helping them find their path, and providing something back to the community. Wise elders aren't present to flaunt superior knowledge; they embody a distinct *archetypal* role that is crucial to our psychological development and the growth of those around us.[1]

Archetypes emerge from recurring patterns of thought and behaviour in our humanness. They manifest between individuals and collectives, shaped by the dynamics of change, personal development, and collective growth.[2] As we move into the second half of life, Jung suggested our focus often shifts dramatically. During the first half, we're typically busy establishing ourselves in the world, making our mark, serving our egoic drives, and "slaying dragons" to achieve personal goals and ambitions that define our sense of identity and orientation for life, work, family, and purpose.

However, as Jung observed, once we've found our place in the world, we become less motivated by the dragon slaying and individual triumphs. Instead, a deeper, more collective purpose emerges: to give back and support others to instigate their own flourishing.[3] This involves sharing our accumulated skills, wisdom, and knowledge for the benefit of others and for causes that extend beyond our own self-interest.[4] This is where mentors and wise elders emerge.

D. Kelsey, *Transcendence and Collective Psychology*,
https://doi.org/10.1007/978-3-032-09495-7_3

By understanding Richard Rohr's role in this context, we can better understand his work as a spiritual guide who offers the wisdom of transformational theology as a pathway to transcendence. Rohr has expressed his concern for the lack of wise elders in modern life. He suggests we risk losing touch with this tradition of collective growth and transition—healthy cyclical patterns for ourselves as much as the communities and generations we have a duty to serve and guide.

By Rohr's admission, clergy are often increasingly unrelatable to those who feel betrayed and disillusioned by the church's spiritual immaturity—leaving them bewildered and spiritually impoverished in their sense of belonging. Rohr's work has spent decades addressing this context.

Action and Contemplation

In 1987, Rohr established the Center for Action and Contemplation (CAC) in Albuquerque, New Mexico, to create a space where contemplative spirituality and social engagement could be explored together. Rohr envisioned the CAC as a hub for individuals interested in both inner transformation and a commitment to compassion and justice in the world. The CAC offers resources, teachings, and retreats, emphasizing a balanced approach to spirituality that includes both personal growth and social responsibility.

Thomas Merton, the Trappist monk, mystic, and writer, was a central influence on Rohr's approach to integrating contemplation with action. Merton advocated for a spirituality rooted in silence, self-reflection, and prayer, and he believed this inner work was essential for understanding oneself and one's role in the world.[5] For Merton, contemplation wasn't an escape from reality but a grounding practice that could help people engage more thoughtfully and compassionately with the world around them. Rohr was deeply influenced by this perspective, which helped shape the CAC's mission to encourage spiritual development that has an outward, positive impact on society.

Merton's teachings offered Rohr a framework for linking personal authenticity with a broader sense of social responsibility. In Merton's view, the journey of contemplation involves going beyond the ego—its desires for control and affirmation—and accessing a more profound sense of connection with others and with the divine. Rohr, inspired by Merton's emphasis on inner transformation, structured the CAC's programs around this idea that genuine spiritual growth involves a dismantling of the ego to create space for a deeper, more compassionate engagement with others.

Merton's writings on topics like personal integrity, social justice, and nonviolence reinforced Rohr's belief that a contemplative approach to life could help address the challenges of addiction, self-centeredness, and a society often oriented around competition and tribalism. Through his work at the CAC, Rohr carries forward Merton's legacy, blending personal transformation with a commitment to compassionate action. The CAC encourages individuals to cultivate a contemplative mindset that supports social responsibility, creating a path for those seeking a spirituality that is both inwardly focused and outwardly engaged.

In his understanding of prayer, Rohr again draws on Merton's influence, framing it as a practice that moves beyond simple requests or affirmations towards a quiet openness to the divine. This contemplative approach to prayer fosters a sense of inner peace and humility, qualities that the CAC aims to nurture in its participants as they engage with social issues through scripture *and* psychology.

Ancient Wisdom in Modern Life

It's remarkable how often we find ourselves returning to ancient wisdom for modern guidance—not because we're completely lost or broken, but because that's how the collective psyche works.

Like individuals, we often *know* without consciously knowing. For example, when I'm anxious and need to talk to someone, I often turn to friends who truly get it. My mate Kieran always says, *"Remember, you already know the answer."* And he's right. The wisdom is there—it just needs a nudge to resurface. This rhythm of knowing and forgetting plays out not only in our personal lives but in the collective story of humanity. We discover, learn, forget, unlearn, relearn. Again and again. The knowledge isn't gone—it's just buried sometimes.

Our task is to help each other remember. Rohr's work offered me a pathway to God and spiritual growth through an ancient theological tradition—one that, intriguingly, echoed my earlier attraction to an ancient school of philosophy.[6]

In *Storytelling and Collective Psychology*, a chapter on street philosophy and the Stoics showed how Stoicism, as taught in the marketplaces of ancient Athens, provided a practical and grounded alternative to unhelpful messages we receive from the self-help industry.[7] The focus in this book shifts from *street philosophy* to *street theology*—away from elites and intellectual hierarchies and into the everyday spaces where we connect with divinity beyond authority.

Rohr provides a critical intervention here. He responds to the unhelpful messages that we are often fed by religious and secular voices that compromise our sense of collective wellbeing and spiritual nourishment. Just as the Stoics brought philosophy out of elite academies and into daily life, Rohr's mystical theology is not confined to the dogma of authoritarian clergy or theological elitism—it is lived, embodied, and accessible.

Street Theology

Rohr defines Franciscan mysticism as an experiential encounter with the divine rather than an intellectual belief system. Rather than relying on external or institutional authority, mysticism is rooted in direct, undeniable experience. Rohr asserts that mystics do not merely believe; they *know* from a certainty that emerges from their lived encounter with God's presence. This certainty, however, is tempered by humility, recognizing that divine truth can be expressed and perceived in multiple ways.

Rohr traces this shift from traditional, monastic mysticism to a more embodied, accessible form through St. Francis of Assisi.[8] In early Christianity, mysticism was largely confined to the desert ascetics and later to monastic traditions, where it became increasingly academic and structured. Francis, however, radically transformed this model by bringing mysticism into the streets. His way was not about retreating from the world but engaging with it—becoming a communal friar rather than a cloistered monk, living among people rather than separating from them. This shift represents what Rohr calls an "alternative orthodoxy," one that prioritizes lived experience over abstract doctrine.

St. Francis was less concerned with theological debate than embodying divine presence in daily life.[9] His famous Canticle of Brother Sun reflects this incarnational theology, where grace is not something distant or bestowed from above but something inherent in creation itself. Rather than looking upward for divine revelation, St. Francis directed attention downward—toward the earth, nature, the elements, and the physical world as the very dwelling places of God.[10] This marks a profound transformation in how we understand grace: it is not external but inherent in our being.

This "street theology" makes the transcendent accessible within everyday existence—from the familiarities of daily life through to the greatest mysteries of the cosmos. From washing the dishes to flying saucers. From the school run to NDEs. From mowing the lawn to psychedelic journeys. From an octopus's garden to a yellow submarine. This ethos challenges the assumption that divine connection requires exclusive withdrawal from the world and instead reveals that *the sacred is embedded in all life*—through nature, relationships, and embodiment. Our wondrous cosmic mysteries are an extension of life and being rather than allusive destinations beyond the reach of many.

By reclaiming this grounded mysticism, Franciscan spirituality offers a path to faith that is both deeply personal and universally available. This foundational perspective hosts Rohr's broader theological vision. From this starting point—where mysticism replaces dogma and grace becomes a lived reality—he moves into his teachings on contemplation. Contemplation, as the next step, deepens this experiential faith by fostering awareness, presence, and non-dual thinking.

The Contemplative Way

The human mind is naturally wired to divide reality into either/or categories—good vs. bad, male vs. female, black vs. white, right vs. wrong. This binary way of thinking, Rohr argues, is the root of much of society's anger and division.[11] When people become trapped in dualism, they must choose one side and defend it against the other, which leads to conflict, ego-driven identity, and the inability to perceive deeper truth. Rohr argues that much of American society's current polarization is a direct result of this mental framework, where people define themselves by opposition to others rather than by participation in a larger, unifying reality.

Contemplative prayer offers an alternative—a way of seeing beyond dualistic divisions and entering a deeper state of awareness. Rohr explores the lost art of contemplation, how Christianity's understanding of prayer has been diminished, and why recovering a non-dualistic mind is essential for both spiritual depth and societal transformation. He traces the historical decline of contemplative practice, critiques modern religion's fixation on dualistic thinking, and offers a vision of faith that integrates mysticism, presence, and surrender to divine flow.

The contemplative path invites us to turn inward—to use presence as a doorway into deeper connection. This is why collective rituals of prayer can serve us so powerfully when they offer a contemplative pathway. They're not about gathering to confess our collective naughtiness to a Zeus figure in the sky. They are about reconnecting with a sense of wholeness—something both incarnate and divine. When we commune together in this way, we are reminded that transcendence is not elsewhere, but here, flowing through us and between us.

Clinical and Collective Healing

Lisa Miller's research in clinical psychology has provided empirical grounding for a contemplative pathway to healing. Despite early scepticism in the scientific community, her studies have shown that group prayer can significantly improve outcomes for patients with clinical depression. Neuroimaging has even revealed physical changes in the brain linked to spiritual practices—offering powerful evidence that collective prayer does more than soothe the soul—it can literally rewire the mind.[12]

Miller's findings suggest that group prayer not only alleviated symptoms of depression but also fostered a deeper sense of connection, belonging, and existential purpose among participants—elements often missing from conventional clinical interventions. Her work supports the notion that contemplative traditions and the communal rituals of religion hold valuable insights for our personal and collective psychology. Miller's findings underscore the need for equilibrium, recognizing that cutting-edge science and spiritual practices both contribute to a holistic understanding of human well-being.

My Shift in Perception

While valuing my time in church and exploring theology, consciousness, and spirituality in my research, my stubborn atheism began to waver. But prayer still baffled me. I recognized the value of church in our community, and I valued the meanings I took from the rituals and stories at Mass, but I just couldn't get my head around prayer.

I often wondered, *Who were they actually talking to? Did they really think someone was listening? Does this really work or make any difference to what happens in the world? What happens when rival football fans both pray for their team to win against the other—could that be why we have draws?*

Of course, I raise the last question in jest, but it reflects the scepticism I held about prayer, which many people share to this day. This transactional view of God and prayer is what many of us were taught when we were young, and it is why so many people fail to take religion seriously. Contemplative prayer fundamentally challenges this perspective. Rather than a practice of asking and receiving, it is about dwelling in divine presence, fostering a state of being rather than bargaining for outcomes.

A History of Distortion

Rohr notes that the concept of prayer was already trivialized within two centuries of Christianity's emergence. Instead of contemplative state of divine union, prayer took on that functional, transactional act—telling God what we need and asking for interventions. This shift was exacerbated when Christianity became the official religion of the Roman Empire in 313 AD, turning faith into a cultural identity and authority rather than a transformative pathway.

In response, sincere spiritual seekers withdrew from the mainstream church to form the desert monastic movement in Egypt, Palestine, Syria, and Cappadocia, which marked the birth of monasticism. These early contemplatives sought to reclaim Jesus' deeper spiritual teachings, emphasizing a form of prayer that was not about reciting words but about dwelling in continuous union with the divine. They suggested prayer was less about asking for things from a distant deity, and more about entering the healing rhythm of a transcendental flow—less about personal petitions to God, and more about participation in something greater.

As Rohr explains, the word "contemplation" emerged to describe this deeper prayer where we are present in a state of unitive consciousness with God and all creation. He highlights Paul's instruction to "pray always" as an indicator that prayer cannot simply mean verbal requests—it must mean a state of always being in communion with divine presence. This is the contemplative way.

For Rohr, the Reformation and denominational splits in Christianity further eroded the contemplative tradition, as Christians increasingly turned towards intellectual debates, doctrinal purity, and competition between religious factions rather than mystical union with God. Rohr credits Thomas Merton for reintroducing contemplation into modern Christian discourse, calling attention to how the Western church had largely abandoned non-dual thinking in favour of rigid theological conflicts.[13]

According to Merton and Rohr, once Christianity became obsessed with *being right* rather than *being present*, it lost touch with its mystical core.

Transformational Theology

In the spirit of the mystics, Rohr's theology centres on transformation, emphasizing a faith that leads beyond rules and institutional obedience into genuine personal and communal growth. Throughout his work, Rohr critiques how institutionalized forms of religion, including Catholicism, often fail to inspire transformative faith, instead promoting adherence to rules that lack spiritual depth.

Rohr refers to this stagnant form as "baby Christianity," where faith is reduced to strict dogma and a fear-based obedience to a "tyrannical God."[14] According to Rohr, those forms of religion that have become so unappealing to so many spiritual souls in modern life remain deeply appealing to those who can comfortably identify as Christian yet still harbour bigotry or mean-spirited judgements of others. Such faith becomes more about upholding cultural norms or establishing order—within their own psyche as much as the communities in which they hold influence—rather than experiencing authentic inner change or, heaven forbid, sitting comfortably with paradox.

Father Nicholas Buxton is an Anglican priest in the UK. Buxton acknowledges that many people have rightly rejected a "childish form of religion," even while still believing in God.[15] However, he warns that the secular tendency to dismiss religion and abandon church attendance altogether offers another kind of literalism beyond immature theology. This alternative rigidness in secular orthodoxy, he suggests, has lost touch with the language and imagination of faith. For Buxton, our culture has weakened its ability to draw deeper meaning from scripture and to engage with the symbolic relationship to reality that these traditions once helped to illuminate.

Missing the Meaning

Buxton observes that many turn to what they consider "rational" alternatives to religion, but these are often no less simplistic. As a result, we are left with both religious and secular fundamentalisms—worldviews that, in their reductivity, mirror the left-hemisphere-dominated psychology that Iain McGilchrist critiques.

This leads to a tragic shortfall in our imaginative engagement with reality and possibility. As Buxton points out, our spiritual needs, like our physical ones, have remained constant throughout human history. Though the ways we attend to those needs may have evolved, many spiritually attuned people—and even believers in God—find themselves yearning for a religion they can no longer locate.

I know this to be true because I was there myself: the God-shaped hole in my soul was vast, dwelling in my simmering unconscious mind, and spiritually impoverished to the point of unnecessary suffering. While Buxton fully acknowledges the culpability of religious institutions in contributing to our collective spiritual disillusionment and fragmentation, he highlights how the problem also reflects the naïve certainties of secular presuppositions.

We should take note of Rohr and Buxton here, because this is what the ego does on a collective scale: across those religious and secular contexts, the ego craves that sense of reductive clarity that we all share and should try to resist. For Rohr, when the ego clings to religion to *provide all-encompassing answers with definitive authority and control over reality*, it actively resists the necessary ambiguity, mystery, and wonder crucial for authentic spiritual growth. This resistance, in turn, hinders one's ability to understand the profound experiential significance of other arcane phenomena and the mysteries of our shared reality, as explored in this book.

Shielding Without Healing

One of the traps Rohr identifies is the tendency to mask personal insecurities or unresolved issues behind religious adherence, using faith as a kind of shield rather than a source of healing. He argues that spiritual transformation should help us confront these insecurities, guiding us beyond them and cultivating compassion, humility, and empathy. A faith limited to rules can create a culture of judgment and exclusion, where people become *addicted* to their own ways of seeing the world, stuck in cycles of self-righteousness or critical assessments of others.[16]

Rohr also points to the issue of addiction itself, noting how people often move from one extreme to another—like a rigid sobriety that may avoid drinking but fails to address the root causes of dependency.[17] Real transformation, according to Rohr, goes beyond simply stopping harmful behaviours; it involves a shift in consciousness that enables individuals to develop a new way of being. This is what he considers the essence of spiritual transformation: a process that doesn't just stop at outward conformity but changes our entire way of relating to the world, fostering a kinder, more open-hearted perspective.

For Rohr, the ultimate goal is not simply to be "religious" but to become deeply human in ways that radiate compassion and love. This is why I focus on transcendence within *and beyond* the religious pathway I've taken in my personal journey; not to convert anyone reading this book, but to share the diverse, meaningful, and mysterious ways in which we can pursue a healthy transcendence in modern life.

Rohr's theology invites us to seek a spirituality that not only challenges our ego but opens us to an experience of divinity that is *life-giving, inclusive, and always evolving.*

Pathways to Presence

For Rohr, contemplation is the key to breaking free from the egoic need to win arguments, dominate others, or assert superiority. Contemplation allows for a "long, loving look at the Real," a phrase Rohr uses to describe the practice of perceiving reality as it truly is without judgment, projection, or self-interest.

This involves three standout ways of being present: seeing others and events around us without immediately categorizing, judging, or analysing; consciously recognizing the divine in the ordinary moments of life and daily business; surrendering control rather than forcing personal agendas onto reality or placing demands on the universe to meet our needs and desires.

This is reflected in the Serenity Prayer that has been so widely advocated across religious and secular spiritualities—including its commonly recognized use for participants in 12-step recovery programmes such as Alcoholics Anonymous:

> *God, grant me the serenity to accept the things I cannot change, courage to change the things I can, and wisdom to know the difference.*[18]

The term "God" in this prayer is not meant to be an exclusive theological definition. Rather, it invites an acceptance of a Logos or higher power—a force or principle beyond our individual control or mastery—that guides the very distinctions the prayer seeks.

I used this prayer when I was practising Stoicism in a secular context. My brother used it in rehab for recovery from drug and alcohol addiction. And I now use it in moments of prayer whether I am in church, on the bus, or getting ready on a morning before a challenging day ahead. We can be at peace with ourselves when we surrender to what lies beyond our control while reserving action for those pursuits where we can make serve the common good through the pursuit of courage and wisdom.

Towards Divine Union

Rohr describes contemplation as being so simple that it is hard to teach because it requires unlearning the mind's constant need to label, control, and evaluate. True contemplation is looking at something—a leaf, a person, a moment—with such presence and openness that one naturally moves into love, acceptance, and reverence for what is. This is the gateway to union with God and is what allows a person to begin to pray authentically.

This is where contemplative prayer becomes a practice for fostering adoration, gratitude, and participation in divine flow. Prayer, in its deepest form, is not just something we do, but something that happens through us when we are in alignment with divine reality.[19] Rohr notes that a contemplative mind enables effective agency for change because it doesn't come from a place of ego, anger, or attachment to being right. The principle of action and contemplation pursues justice, but without needing to control all arguments and outcomes. Rohr sees the secret to wisdom, prayer, and effective action is to stay in the flow of divine presence.

When people remain in this flow, their words and actions come naturally and spontaneously, without the strain of overthinking or proving themselves. By Rohr's admission, some of his most resonant teachings and sermons arose not from careful preparation but from the flow of divine presence.

Resting with God

Cynthia Bourgeault is a CAC teacher and writer on contemplative practices. Her approach to Centering Prayer has gained significant attention in contemporary Christian circles.[20] Centering Prayer, at its core, is about silent prayer that invites a person to rest in God's presence, allowing one to let go of distractions and thoughts to become more attuned to divine love.

The practice involves choosing a sacred word, such as "God," "love," or "peace," that represents one's consent to God's presence and action. Practitioners sit quietly, eyes closed, gently focusing on their breath or sacred word, returning to it each time their mind wanders, eventually letting go of thoughts, attachments, desires, and opinions. This surrender to God's will and openness to silence is a means of receiving divine guidance. For Bourgeault, Centering Prayer is not confined to the time spent in silence; rather, it's about integrating this contemplative approach into one's everyday life, which ultimately transforms how one interacts with the world.

Through this ongoing practice, individuals become more receptive to divine love, and the fruits of that openness flow into every aspect of life—attending to our *inner condition* and *external responsibilities.* Practitioners attend to everyday tasks not as distractions from our spiritual life but as integral parts of it—leaning into that ever-present urge for transcendence.

The Emergence of Meaning

For Rohr, real meaning emerges when stories resonate with us, aligning with the deepest (even unconscious) longings of our lived experience and translating into something coherent within our own theological journeys. A problem for secularism lies as much in our linguistic presuppositions towards scripture as much as our perceptions of reality and our place in the cosmos.

According to Rohr, once we literalized our metaphors from scripture into the "rational" world, society began equating what could be rationally proven with what is real. In response to the rise of rationalism and scientism, religion attempted to become more "rational" itself to defend its relevance. Ultimately, this caused it to lose its alternative consciousness, and this is where mystics like Merton, Bourgeault, and Rohr have called for a return to *contemplation* within in a non-dualist framework.

Rohr suggests that this "rational" shift has seen us trying to confront mystery using the wrong tools, or "software." By focusing on so-called rationalism, religion lost access to higher levels of consciousness, including the transrational, transpersonal, and transcendent required to explore the case studies in this book. For Rohr these are the greatest challenges facing religion today, and for future generations.[21] His generation, he notes, took religious symbols (metaphors) literally, while the current generation has discarded them as irrelevant. But as Rohr points out, when we literalize a metaphor, we miss the literal meaning.[22]

Metaphors We Pray By

In *Metaphors We Live By*, Lakoff and Johnson argue that metaphors are not just linguistic flourishes but fundamental to how we structure thought, shape experience, and understand reality.[23] The metaphors we use define the way we perceive and engage with the world, often in ways we are unaware of. This insight is crucial when considering the metaphors we pray by as religious language is inherently metaphorical, shaping not only our concept of God but our relationship to the divine, the self, and the cosmos.

Rohr's work reveals how many dominant religious metaphors—especially those tied to transaction, judgment, and separation—have limited our spiritual imagination, turning prayer into a mechanical request rather than a mystical participation in divine reality. Scripture is not meant to be read like a legal document; it is a sacred text woven with metaphor, symbolism, and mystery—designed not just to be understood but to be felt. Hence Rohr's point that those who literalize metaphors miss their literal meaning.[24] This paradox might seem counterintuitive at first, but it is at the heart of how we approach scripture, prayer, and even our own lives.

As Rohr argues, religion relies on metaphor because it's the most truthful way to express the unknowable nature of Mystery. For much of its history, religion understood the power of metaphor and symbol, using them to convey deeper truths of the human experience. However, in the last few centuries, particularly during the Enlightenment of the seventeenth and eighteenth centuries, this *experiential* understanding was overshadowed.

Like Rohr, my approach in this book responds to the need for radical paradigm shifts that accommodate religion and science. I aim to show how both fields need to collectively rethink their place in public and intellectual discourse.

Even science relies upon metaphor to communicate some the deepest truths of its findings. Our experiential reflections and meanings are equally valid and reliant on metaphors as the communicative portals to truth. To test these provocations, let's consider some of the questions I had during my journey of faith, and how this understanding of metaphorical symbolism resonated in my sense-making of scripture via Rohr.

How can I be expected to believe in a supernatural event like the Virgin Birth?

Rohr invites us to approach the Virgin Birth as a profound spiritual metaphor.[25] He prioritizes the symbolic significance of the story, seeing Mary's virginity as a representation of radical receptivity—an openness to divine presence that is not achieved through human effort but received through surrender. In this light, the Virgin Birth becomes less about biological claims and more about the nature of divine wisdom as a gift rather than an attainment.

Rohr reads the story as a poetic way of expressing that Jesus embodied a divine consciousness—not rooted in ego or domination, but in vulnerability, love, and unity. Just as Mary gives birth to Christ without conventional means, so too does true spiritual awakening emerge not from personal striving, but from allowing grace to work through us.

This approach aligns with Rohr's broader theology, particularly in *The Universal Christ*, where he presents Christ not as a surname of Jesus, but as the eternal pattern of divine presence woven into the fabric of the cosmos. Christ is always present, waiting to be recognized and birthed within each of us.[26]

In a collective sense, the Virgin Birth mirrors how transcendent wisdom and transformation arise—not from control or mastery, but from yielding to a deeper, ever-present reality. Mystical traditions across cultures—from contemplative Christianity to Buddhist enlightenment—speak to this same paradox: that the greatest awakenings come not through effort, but through release.

How might I understand Jesus as the Son of God if I struggle with other beliefs about the supernatural?

Rohr presents the Christ not primarily as a miracle-worker or distant supernatural figure, but as the archetype of what it means to become fully human. In *Immortal Diamond*, he writes: "The Risen Christ is the standing icon of humanity in its final and full destiny. He is the pledge and guarantee of what God will do with all of our crucifixions. At last, we can meaningfully live with hope. It is no longer an absurd or tragic universe. Our hurts now become the home for our greatest hopes."[27]

In this framing, Jesus as the "Son of God" reveals the divine potential within each of us. He embodies a pattern of death and resurrection that reflects our own cycles of suffering, transformation, and renewal. Rohr invites us to see Jesus not just as a historical figure but as the clearest expression of a universal mystery—that the divine is fully at home in the human, and that union with God is not the exception but the destiny of all creation. The "Son of God" is not merely a metaphysical title; it's a relational and existential truth. It points to Jesus' profound intimacy with the divine, and to the possibility that we too are invited into that same relationship. For Rohr, we are invited not to place Jesus on a pedestal, but to follow him on the path he revealed: one of transformation, belonging, and awakening to the Christ within and around us.

Rohr recognizes "Christ" as the name of a cosmic reality. In *The Universal Christ*, he describes Christ as the eternal pattern—the divine blueprint—through which God is present in all things, uniting heaven and earth. Jesus, then, is the embodiment of that Christ mystery: a living, historical manifestation of our inherent union with God, with nature, and with one another.[28]

Rohr's approach opens space for meaning-making that can speak to both religious and non-religious seekers. Jesus becomes a model for living in alignment with what Rohr calls the "Great Pattern"—a flow of grace, love, and surrender embedded in reality itself. The divine is not "out there," but revealed in the ordinary, the broken, and the beautiful. As Rohr suggests, Christ is not Jesus' last name, but the name of the universal presence through which God is revealed in all things. As Rohr often says, quoting Paula D'Arcy: "God comes to us disguised as our life."[29]

How can the death and resurrection of Jesus be understood in a way that speaks to human experience without a belief in the supernatural?

For Rohr, the resurrection is not a one-time miracle that happened to Jesus, but an ever-unfolding reality woven into the fabric of existence. He sees it as the archetypal pattern of transformation—what he calls "necessary suffering"—where the death of the old self gives rise to something entirely new.[30] This cyclical rhythm of death and renewal is present in nature, myth, and psychological development.

In *The Naked Now*, Rohr expands on how non-dual awareness allows us to recognize that resurrection is not about the one-time resuscitation of a body, but about a transformation in perception—a new way of seeing that emerges through surrender, letting go, and trust.[31] It's a reorientation of consciousness, where we move beyond the ego's need for control and open ourselves to deeper truths.

From a collective perspective, resurrection speaks to the human longing for meaning, renewal, and transcendence—whether through personal crises, historical shifts, or spiritual awakenings. As depth psychology has long understood, true transformation requires a descent before ascent; in myth and mysticism, death is always the precursor to rebirth. The resurrection story, then, is not only central Christian doctrine, but also an existential map of human experience.

Jesus' death on the cross is framed by Rohr as a universal pattern of transformation—not merely a historical execution, but the symbolic and real enactment of divine love's willingness to enter human suffering. In *The Divine Dance*, Rohr explains that the crucifixion represents the necessary suffering that precedes resurrection. This is not suffering for its own sake but suffering as a portal—a breaking down of the small self so that a greater wholeness can emerge.[32]

Mythologically, this resonates with the monomyth (hero's journey), where descent into darkness is necessary for ascent into wisdom. Psychologically, the cross represents the painful yet transformative process of ego death—the surrender of control so that a deeper truth can rise. Jesus' crucifixion, then, is more than a one-time event; it becomes an archetype for the human experience of surrender, transformation, and rebirth.

This view doesn't negate the sacrificial love Jesus embodied—it deepens it, showing how his surrender mirrors the universal cycle of death and renewal that shapes every spiritual life. It's a way of understanding our own inclusion in this cycle—through the many psychological deaths and rebirths we endure, and through the natural cycle we contribute to in death itself.

For Rohr, to call Jesus the "Son of God" is not to isolate him as a supernatural exception to humanity, but to reveal him as the clearest expression of what is true for all of us: that divinity and humanity are not opposites, but united in deep and mysterious ways.[33] Jesus, Rohr argues, fully embodied the eternal Christ—a divine presence that has existed from the beginning of time and is present in all things. He did not merely *possess* divine qualities; he *lived out* the fullness of union with God, becoming a true and lived archetype of awakened, embodied love.

This framing does not diminish Jesus'. Rohr is careful to affirm Jesus as the decisive and particular manifestation of the Christ mystery in history. But rather than limiting that revelation to one figure, he sees it as an invitation—a model of what it means to become fully human by becoming fully united with the divine. Jesus reveals the pattern: surrender, love, self-emptying, death of the false self, and resurrection into deeper life.

In this light, "Son of God" points to Jesus' profound intimacy with the divine and to the possibility that we too are invited into that same relationship—not by achieving greatness, but by consenting to grace. Rohr draws on contemplative traditions and echoes the Eastern Christian concept of *theosis*—union with God—as a shared human destiny.

To see Jesus as the Son of God is to affirm both his uniqueness and our inclusion in the same divine flow. It invites us not to place Jesus on a pedestal, but to follow him on the path he revealed: one of transformation, belonging, and awakening to the Christ within and around us. In Rohr's words, Christ is not Jesus' last name, but the name of the universal presence through which God is revealed in all things.

Why does so much religious language around original sin, repentance, and salvation often come across as harsh or guilt-ridden?

Rather than focusing on inherited guilt, Rohr enables us to understand original sin through the condition of separation from divine love.[34] In *Falling Upward*, he suggests that much of human dysfunction arises from the illusion of disconnection from God, which gives rise to cycles of fear, control, and violence.[35]

The story of Adam and Eve, in this view, is not primarily about a legal transgression, but about a fall into dualistic thinking—the mistaken perception that we are separate from God, from one another, and from the deeper unity of all things. This interpretation resonates with both mystical theology and depth psychology, where the spiritual task is to see through the illusions of the ego and return to a more integrated and unified awareness. If original sin is the misperception of separation, then salvation is the unlearning of that illusion—a return to what has always been true at the deepest level.

This process of awakening is what true repentance (*metanoia*) means—not self-condemnation, but a radical shift in consciousness.[36] Rohr emphasizes that repenting is not about shame or punishment, but about learning to see differently: turning away from the small, divided self toward the expansive reality of divine love. In this way, repentance is not about earning forgiveness, but awakening to a love that was never withdrawn—only forgotten or obscured.

For Rohr, salvation is not about escaping damnation but about waking up to the divine presence that already surrounds and sustains us. In *Everything Belongs*, he insists that salvation is not a transactional process but an unveiling—an opening of the heart and mind to what has always been true. Like the biblical teaching that the Kingdom of God is already within us, Rohr draws on this tradition to show that salvation is not something we achieve, but something we recognize and receive.

This view aligns with contemplative traditions that speak of enlightenment not as achievement but as remembrance. Psychologically, salvation resembles self-realization—the moment when one sees through the ego's limited perceptions and awakens to the deeper Self. Spiritually, it is an encounter with the indwelling Christ—a recognition that the divine is not distant, but alive in the ordinary, the broken, and the present.

Theologically, this involves a movement from dualistic thinking to participatory being—a shift from seeking salvation outside ourselves to embodying divine presence in daily life. It is an incarnational awakening to the sacredness of all things, including ourselves.

If there is only one God as the source of all creation and being, how can this oneness also include three persons in the Holy Trinity?

Rohr views the Trinity not as a static doctrine but as a dynamic flow of love—an eternal movement of divine relationship that reflects the structure of reality itself. In *The Divine Dance*, he describes the Trinity as participation rather than hierarchy, movement rather than stasis. The Father, Son, and Spirit are not separate entities bound in a fixed framework, but a relational unfolding of divine presence—an invitation into God's life rather than a distant theological abstraction.

For Rohr, the relational nature of the Trinity is not just a truth about God, but a deep truth about the nature of being itself. This understanding resonates with the vision of panentheism—the idea that God is in all things and all things are in God, while still transcending creation. Unlike classical theism, which often pictures God as a separate, external ruler, panentheism sees divinity as the very ground of being: the source, sustainer, and relational field in which all life unfolds.

Rohr suggests that God is not an object to be observed but the very medium of existence. Just as the Trinity expresses divine relationship, creation itself is a dance of interdependence—everything existing through connection, participation, and flow. This perspective dissolves rigid boundaries between the sacred and the secular, the spiritual and the material.

This relational vision of reality finds echoes in modern science. In quantum physics and systems theory, reality is increasingly understood in terms of interconnectedness. Subatomic particles behave not as isolated entities but as part of relational fields. Likewise, biology and ecology reveal that life flourishes through dynamic systems of cooperation and mutuality. While theology and science might speak somewhat different languages, both suggest that the fabric of reality is more unified, relational, and fluid than once imagined.

Rohr's interpretation of the Trinity as a living pattern—rather than merely a doctrinal formula—offers a bridge between mystical theology and contemporary science. It encourages a spirituality that is not about earning divine favour but awakening to the divine flow already present. In this view, we are not separate from God, striving to reach a distant deity, but already included in the great field of divine life.

This Great Mystery—that God is both beyond us and yet intimately woven into reality—is a central theme of the next chapter. There, we will explore how early Christian thought, especially in its mystical and incarnational strands, anticipates patterns of consciousness and relationality that resonate with emerging insights from neuroscience, cosmology, and quantum theory.

Rohr's vision of the Trinity—as dynamic, relational, and participatory—suggests that mysticism and science are not enemies, but complementary ways of understanding the sacred interconnectedness of all things. This book's exploration of cosmic consciousness builds upon that foundation, seeking to bridge ancient theological insight with contemporary understanding in a way that expands our vision of what it means to live within the divine flow.

Are Heaven and Hell really meant to be literal places we go after we die?

Rohr sees heaven and hell not as distant locations awaiting us after death, but as states of consciousness that shape our experience of reality in the present moment. In *The Naked Now*, he describes hell as the radical experience of separation from love—a self-imposed condition of isolation, fear, and alienation. Heaven, by contrast, is the fullness of divine union: a deep attunement to the love that underlies all of existence.

This theological metaphor reflects a psychological insight: the inner world we cultivate profoundly influences the world we perceive. Rohr's view aligns with the idea that perception shapes experience. A life dominated by fear, control, and egoic self-preservation tends to produce suffering, anxiety, and disconnection—a kind of living hell. Conversely, a life rooted in trust, openness, and self-giving love fosters a sense of joy, peace, and unity—a foretaste of heaven.

This reframing challenges the transactional logic of religious fundamentalism, where heaven and hell are imagined as rewards or punishments assigned as eternal destinations after death. Instead, Rohr suggests that we are already, moment by moment, shaping our participation in divine reality—or resisting it. Heaven and hell, in this view, are not destinations imposed upon us, but lived realities we begin to enter through the choices we make, the consciousness we nurture, and the love we embody.

This understanding carries profound implications for our exploration of near-death experiences (NDEs) in later chapters. Many NDEs describe a "life review" in which individuals re-experience their actions—not just from their own perspective, but from the perspective of those they affected. If dying involves an encounter with the truth of our lives, then how we live now may shape what we experience in the process of dying. This raises the possibility that consciousness itself carries forward the states of love or separation we cultivate in life, reinforcing Rohr's claim that heaven and hell are realities we help co-create.

This intersects with Rohr's wider reflections on ego, surrender, and transformation. He often speaks of the need to "die before we die"—to begin the inner process of letting go of illusion, separation, and control so that we are prepared for the deeper letting go that death demands. Spiritual growth in this life becomes, in a very real sense, a preparation for what lies beyond. The more we cultivate a heavenly consciousness (grounded in connection, love, and humility while still alive), the less traumatic the process of dying may be.

In this way, Rohr's theology integrates mysticism, psychology, and the testimonies of those who have undergone NDEs. Rather than invoking a fear-based notion of judgment, it suggests that the life we live now is the foundation for whatever reality awaits. Death is not framed as an interruption, but as a continuation—a transition into the deeper truth that has always been present but is so often resisted.

In future chapters, we will explore how modern research into NDEs reveals intriguing patterns that resonate with this psychological and spiritual framework. While these findings remain open to interpretation, they may in fact affirm the insights of ancient mystical traditions: that life is a process of transformation, consciousness continues beyond death, and divine participation begins long before our final breath.

If God is love, how do we make sense of the evil and suffering in the world—and what role does the devil play in that story?

Evil and the devil, in Rohr's theology, are not external forces waging war against God, but profound symbols of the collective shadow—the repressed and unintegrated aspects of human consciousness. Drawing from both mystical theology and depth psychology, Rohr understands evil not as an independent power but as a distortion of good, born of fear, illusion, and separation.

In *Falling Upward*, he suggests that much of what we call evil arises from unconscious wounds, egoic attachments, and fear-based power structures—the very dynamics that entrench suffering and alienation. The devil, in this framework, is best understood not as a literal being but as a personification of our resistance to love, integration, and transformation. It embodies the part of the psyche that clings to dualism, control, and the need for enemies—what Jung would call the unexamined shadow self.

When individuals and societies refuse to confront their own darkness, they tend to project it outward—onto scapegoats, ideologies, or imagined embodiments of evil. Rohr's perspective shifts the focus away from externalizing evil and toward recognizing that our participation in suffering is not merely passive but often complicit. Evil is not simply something done to us; it is something we are capable of co-creating when we live from fear and disconnection.

This psychological and spiritual understanding of evil is essential as we transition into the book's case studies. The human search for transcendence—whether through mysticism, psychedelics, or near-death experiences—is never free from the unconscious material we carry. As discussed in Chap. 2, the impulse to transcend the self can be both a longing for union with the divine and a temptation to escape the difficult work of integration.

Transcendence, if not consciously grounded, can devolve into fanaticism, spiritual bypassing, or even the misuse of power. This is what Rohr means when he warns that unexamined spiritual experience may reinforce the very shadow it seeks to escape. Recognizing the shadow is not a detour from the spiritual path—it is often the first and most necessary step.

Rohr's theology calls us into a lifelong practice of "dying before we die"—a surrendering of the illusions of control, superiority, and separateness. The devil, in this sense, is not something we defeat but something we learn to name and integrate. The more we become aware of the parts of ourselves we would rather reject, the more we create space for genuine transformation.

Seen this way, evil is not simply the opposite of good, but the refusal to participate in the divine flow of love and reality. And the devil is not a supernatural entity, but the symbolic face of our resistance to that participation. This understanding lays the groundwork for the chapters that follow, where we will continue exploring how transcendence must pass through the crucible of the shadow if it is to be real, enduring, and transformative.[37]

Literalizing the Metaphor

Metaphors are often misunderstood—literalized by religious fundamentalists and dismissed by secular cynics alike. Both extremes seek to dismiss intelligible meaning in metaphors. However, literalist dogma is fragile and encourages a vulnerable psychology that grips onto a false sense of order in the psyche. Such rigid and doctrinal "authority" is easily threatened by science, history, or personal doubt—with the latter often torturing the soul deep within those shadow realms of self-denial.

A faith that understands metaphor, on the other hand, is resilient. As Rohr reassures us, it can evolve, expand, and integrate new knowledge without losing its core truth. Instead of being limited to the question *"Did this really happen?"*, scriptural symbolism moves towards the deeper inquiry: *"What does this mean for my life?"*

By recovering contemplative metaphors, we move towards a symbolic truth that is not opposed to literal reality but one that makes it intelligible sense of the human experience and Mystery. Just as Lakoff and Johnson revealed how deeply metaphors structure our everyday lives, Rohr's theology shows that the metaphors we use in prayer shape not only how we talk to God but how we experience and embody the divine presence in our lives.

It is through this contemplative scope that we are offered pathways to a deeper understanding within—one that integrates psychology and spirituality rather than setting them at odds. Another metaphor Rohr draws on is the Immortal Diamond—through which he observes the tensions between our True Self and False Self.

As Jung observed, we spend our lives adopting masks and personas to meet the demands of our cultures and the roles we are expected to adopt within them. But there is more beneath the surface, and we are more than blank slates for manipulation.

Immortal Diamond

Rohr distinguishes the False Self (the constructed ego, shaped by societal expectations and personal conditioning) from the True Self (the soul's deepest identity, rooted in divine reality). The Immortal Diamond is a symbol of an unbreakable, hidden essence—the part of us that is already whole, already connected to God, and waiting to be uncovered.[38]

For Rohr, the True Self is discovered beneath those layers of ego, conditioning, and false identity we accumulate over time—those personas we adopt and adapt to across a myriad of personal, societal, and professional performances and contextual personalities that are expected of us in daily life. These metaphors are not meant to diminish faith but to deepen it, offering a contemplative lens through which faith becomes an ongoing process of unveiling, rather than a rigid set of external beliefs.

Rohr highlights the paradox of this realization. On the one hand, it is humbling to recognize that we have no control over its origin or ultimate existence. On the other hand, it is profoundly liberating, as it reveals an unshakable foundation of being that cannot be lost or destroyed. The task, then, is not to construct the True Self but to uncover it, allowing its radiance to shine through. Like a diamond formed under immense pressure, this eternal essence is refined through life's trials, emerging with clarity and brilliance when we surrender to its presence within us.

Rohr is clear that the False Self is not inherently bad, it is necessary for survival—it includes our roles, our personas, our coping mechanisms. The False Self is built through social conditioning, family expectations, and the need for security. It is who we think we must be in order to be accepted, loved, and safe. But beneath all of that is the True Self—the unconditioned, God-given essence of who we are. It is not something we need to achieve or construct since it is already there, waiting to be uncovered.

Rohr often points to Jesus' words, "You must lose your life to find it," as the key to this transformation. We do not need to create the True Self;

we need to strip away everything that is not it—the personas, the defences, the metaphorical demons who whisper that we are unworthy.

Within the church, Rohr suggests even some clergy may not yet grasp the crucial distinction between authentic spiritual transformation and religious performance. He notes that some enter religious vocations for reasons unrelated to deep personal encounter—perhaps for stability, identity, or the cultural status it provides. As a result, institutional religion can sometimes reinforce the ego or False Self, particularly when it offers external rewards like public respect, titles, financial stability, or the appearance of holiness.[39]

Connection to our Immortal Diamond is not a one-time revelation but a recurring search of the soul. It is why we continually return to prayer, silence, and contemplation. The goal is less about self-improvement than self-remembrance—to recall who we were before the world told us who to be. This isn't exclusive to Christian teaching, but relevant to the psychological dynamics of multiple religions and secular traditions.

Rohr's Ecumenical Ethos

Rohr's teaching focuses on the universal traits of human experience and psychology—the dialogue between faiths is more important than one faith winning over the rest. Rohr shows that different traditions, whether Christian, Buddhist, or 12-Step spirituality, are all pointing towards the same deep truth. We are all looking for a pathway back to God, Logos, or the True Self—whatever we call it—and while the routes may vary, the destination remains the same.

Despite the deeper meanings that I have cultivated in my conversion to Catholicism, the ethos behind it can sit comfortably with other religious and secular perspectives.[40] There is a common ground here that can accommodate difference in ways that are conducive to a shared journey into the arcane horizons I explore under Rohr's guidance.

Rohr's theology was the key that unlocked so many pathways in my spiritual and intellectual journey and associated curiosities. I had often felt torn between faith and reason, between the mystical and the rational—as if they truly were opposites, and as if the material atheism I clung to, despite its reductive and restrictive possibilities, was the only rational and reasoned truth.

But Rohr and the mystics showed me that I didn't have to choose one or the other in either case. I could have my cake and eat it. I could embrace the mystery, the paradox, the deep unknowing, and it would only make my faith stronger, not weaker, and my scientific explorations would expand, not reduce.

Once those doors were open, it wasn't just theology that I saw differently. It was everything.

If transcendence was real, if mystery was woven into the fabric of reality, then why should we dismiss the "bonkers" topics that have fascinated humanity for centuries? This requires an ontological paradigm shift—one that can be enabled through the collective evolution of hemispherical psychology within and beyond public, religious, and scientific institutions.

Hemispherical Happenings

According to Iain McGilchrist, the dominance of left-hemispheric thinking in Western culture has shaped our intellectual and spiritual landscapes in ways that limit our capacity for deeper, transcendent experiences. His research offers compelling scientific insight into how this overemphasis on linear, analytical, and control-oriented thinking has reduced our ability to engage with the more holistic and relational forms of consciousness.[41]

McGilchrist's work demonstrates that the left hemisphere tends to prioritize categorization, analysis, and a desire for control, all of which have led to an increasingly fragmented and reductionist view of the world. This approach is fundamentally at odds with the mystical experiences that emphasize interconnectedness, unity, and transcendence.

Rohr's call for non-dual consciousness—where the individual transcends binary, dualistic thinking—echoes McGilchrist's advocacy for greater integration and less neglect of right-hemispheric psychology. The right hemisphere, according to McGilchrist, is more attuned to the broader, more expansive, and relational awareness necessary for mystical experience and spiritual growth. This hemispheric shift isn't just a theoretical or mystical proposition but has real, biological and psychological underpinnings that support it.

Like Rohr, McGilchrist emphasizes the importance of contemplative practices that nurture the right hemisphere. Practices such as meditation, silence, and prayer allow individuals to engage with a reality that is more fluid, holistic, and connected to the divine. When we move away from rigid, left-hemispheric thinking and open ourselves to the right hemisphere's capacity for creative, expansive thinking, we become more open to experiences of transcendence and deep spiritual connection.

This shift is essential not only for individual spiritual growth but for fostering a more integrated, holistic understanding of reality that transcends the fragmented, control-oriented worldviews.

Integrating "Opposites"

The left and right hemispheres of the brain are not opposites to be pitted against each other—neither is inherently better nor worse. Rather, they are complementary, and both play crucial roles in our experience of the world. The left hemisphere supports logic, analysis, structure, and control—essential for everyday tasks and practical decision-making. The right hemisphere, on the other hand, facilitates creativity, intuition, and our ability to experience deeper connections and transcendence.

The goal isn't to abandon one hemisphere for the other, but to integrate both in a healthy balance. This integration allows us to move beyond dualistic thinking and embrace a more holistic, expansive, and integral view of reality.[42]

Spiritual growth, as Rohr suggests, is about moving towards this non-dual consciousness, where we don't reject the ego-driven, logical aspects of ourselves, but rather find a way to harmonize them with the broader, more intuitive understanding that the right hemisphere offers. Through hemispherical equilibrium, we open ourselves to richer experiences and can better connect with the divine, each other, and the world around us.

McGilchrist's research supports this by showing how an overemphasis on left-hemispheric thinking has shaped modern culture in ways that diminish our capacity for deeper, relational awareness. Rather than seeing the left hemisphere's current dominance as entirely negative, the challenge is to find the right balance—one where both hemispheres contribute to a more integrated, complete sense of self and a fuller, more awakened experience of life.

Integrating the Arcane

In *Everything Belongs*, Rohr deepens his vision of spirituality by insisting that nothing—no emotion, experience, or strange phenomenon—is outside the reach of the divine. For Rohr, the spiritual path doesn't begin with purity or perfection, but with raw honesty and imperfection. We grow not by getting everything right, but by stumbling, falling, and learning through those very missteps. Even failure has its place: the fall and the recovery are expressions of divine mercy.

This radically inclusive vision affirms that every part of life belongs, no matter how messy or marginal. Transformation, for Rohr, is not sparked by abstract belief, but by lived experience—by allowing life itself to shape our thinking. True freedom emerges when we rest in God and make peace with who we are: in all our contradictions, limitations, and potential. The present moment, in this light, becomes sacred—not something to escape, but a sacrament to awaken to.

Rohr encourages spiritual growth that embraces the full spectrum of human experience. Instead of dismissing moments of confusion, pain, or other transcendental states that might seem abstract or irrational, he invites us to view these as valuable teachers. The point is not to shy away from or judge these experiences, but to engage with them through openness and curiosity.

Evolving Paradigms

As consciousness shifts and intellectual paradigms evolve, we may encounter moments that challenge our most certain understanding of reality. These moments, however strange or elusive, are opportunities for deepening our connection with the divine. Rohr's message in this context aligns with the notion that transcendence is not linear nor limited to elevated states of consciousness. Transcendence is about learning to see the sacred in every corner of existence, whether or not it fits neatly into our intellectual frameworks.

By paying attention to all experiential phenomena, we expand our understanding of the divine and invite a more holistic, inclusive approach to spirituality. In this way, Rohr teaches that everything belongs within the larger tapestry of spiritual reality. In *The Naked Now*, Rohr emphasizes that transcendence is not about escaping the material world but about perceiving the sacred that underlies it. Rohr invites readers into a transformative way of seeing—one grounded in presence, humility, and surrender.[43]

As Rohr points out, personal growth often requires a process of letting go—releasing former ways of thinking and passing through a period of uncertainty or disorientation before arriving at a deeper level of awareness or new understanding.[44] This urges us to release the ego's grip and embrace the mystery of spiritual growth.

For Rohr, contemplative living means shifting from the need to be right or to control others: when you no longer feel the need to prove you're right, and when you can let go of the urge to judge, shame, or mentally retaliate against those who have wronged you. Ultimately, as Rohr explains, the path to healing and transformation begins within—by cultivating in ourselves the very qualities we long for in the world around us.

What we perceive is shaped by our inner readiness, our expectations, and our desires. In this mystical framework, there is a deep connection between the inner state of the seeker and the nature of what is revealed; we find only what we are prepared to recognize.

Accessible Realms

As we shall see in later case studies, this means we can collectively oscillate between transcendental realms that are part of the here and now and instantly accessible to us all. Meanwhile, we can recognize that some transcendental toolkits and phenomena take us into entirely unique realms beyond our current understanding of material reality. And we can sit comfortably with the possibility that current materialist paradigms may even limit our understanding of reality.

Having said that, Rohr also challenges the modern tendency to separate spirituality from the mundane aspects of life, urging readers to embrace the present moment and adopt a non-dualistic perspective. Transcendence occurs, Rohr asserts, when individuals move beyond their ego-centred perspective, cultivating a deeper awareness of how interconnected all things are.

This shift in consciousness helps individuals to see the world as a web of interdependent experiences, where each person and event contributes to the collective whole. But as I will show, the collective incentive to make this transition throws a whole new set of challenges at us when institutional powers become concerned with the impact of mass transcendental awakenings.

Towards Collective Growth

Rohr highlights the connection between individual growth and collective psychology. He argues that human consciousness is not merely an isolated experience but is inherently collective. Our personal spiritual evolution, he argues, is intertwined with the collective consciousness of humanity.

By transcending ego-driven thought, individuals can contribute to the spiritual development of the whole, fostering a more unified and harmonious world. This ethos is crucial to those topics covered in my case studies: this is about understanding the significance human experience while escaping those addictive presuppositions and patronizing dismissals we typically apply to the arcane—whether that's scriptural, cosmic, or otherworldly altogether.

But such radical departures from our habitual perceptions require us to collectively rethink how precious we are about our historical, social, and personal paradigms of science and religion.

Rohr suggests that true growth occurs when we move beyond the limited perspective of the ego and open ourselves to a more expansive, humble understanding of life. In *Falling Upward*, Rohr emphasizes this shift as being essential for spiritual maturity, and that we can only fully experience the richness of life by moving through this transition. He encourages readers to embrace the second half of life, as discussed at the start of this chapter, as an opportunity for deeper connection, collective purpose, and spiritual awakening.

This principle is not just about individuals but entire communities, institutions, and nations. It's about evolution of consciousness for humanity. Humanity has entered a time where we must transcend our adolescent identities—the narrow, self-centred ways of thinking that have historically held us back.

We are poised at the threshold of a new kind of awakening, one where the collective ego must dissolve for the True Collective Self to emerge. This is where the second half of life begins: a deeper understanding of our place within a vast, interconnected cosmos.

Uncomfortable Awakenings

This awakening is not a comfortable one. Contemplating the seemingly impossible requires our acceptance that the collective reality we are familiar with is not the complete story of reality itself. Beyond the limitations we currently know, there exists a greater, expansive consciousness waiting to be discovered—one that transcends the boundaries of our current intellectual and spiritual paradigms.

As we "fall upward" into this new understanding, we awaken to the possibility of guiding future generations into realms of consciousness that, for now, seem unimaginable. It is in this journey that we begin to mature, to step into our role as wise elders, preparing to lead humanity through the evolutionary stages ahead.

The path forward requires us to embrace uncertainty, discomfort, and the dissolution of familiar structures and conceptions of the universe and ourselves. However uncomfortable this might feel, we will grow into a more expansive, enlightened state of being—a state of cosmic consciousness that allows us to tap into the True Collective Self—those deepest realms or divinity and reality that await our discovery.

When we seek to understand where we sit in the creation of the universe, whether we are religious or not, science and spirituality can provide a coherent lens for understanding some of the deepest cosmic mysteries of all. In Chap. 4, I'll show how Rohr does this through the Great Mystery of the Holy Trinity.

Notes

1. Swiss psychologist Carl Jung (1969) identified archetypes as recurring patterns of thought and behaviour inherent in the human psyche. Partly shaped by their cultural influences, these universal symbols and themes often manifest as distinct character types and traits in the stories we tell, reflecting what Jung called the collective unconscious of humanity. Archetypes, such as the Hero, the Mentor, the Trickster, the Shadow, and many more shape our understanding of ourselves and our cultural narratives, influencing both individual psychology and societal behaviour (see also Kelsey, 2017, 2022a).
2. Mentors and magicians are typically wise elders: archetypal figures that frequently appear in stories, serving crucial roles in guiding the hero on their journey (Kelsey, 2022b). They often intersect with the hero early in the narrative, offering wisdom, guidance, or special powers that assist in overcoming challenges. In fiction, we see this archetype exemplified by characters such as Gandalf in J.R.R. Tolkien's *The Lord of the Rings*. Gandalf provides guidance and support to Frodo and his companions as they embark on their quest to destroy the One Ring. His vast knowledge and magical abilities help the heroes navigate perilous situations. Yoda in *Star Wars* acts as a mentor to Luke Skywalker, imparting wisdom and training that enable Luke to discover his potential as a Jedi. Yoda's teachings emphasize the importance of patience, mindfulness, and understanding the Force. Dumbledore in J.K. Rowling's *Harry Potter* series further illustrates this archetype as a powerful wizard and mentor to Harry. Dumbledore's guidance and insight are critical throughout Harry's journey as he confronts the dark forces threatening the wizarding world.
3. Jung (1959); Campbell (1949); Kelsey (2022a).
4. In my previous book (Kelsey, 2022b), I showed how the psychological illusionist Derren Brown could be understood as an archetypal magician in

personal and collective contexts. As a performer and writer, Brown uses his craft not just to entertain but to inspire reflection and transformation. His performances invite participants to explore the boundaries of perception and reality, creating spaces where they can gain insight into their own lives. Brown's writing also engages with philosophy as practical wisdom on how to live well in modern life. Brown's real-world performances reveal how the archetypal magician sparks personal growth and collective transformation, prompting audiences to question their assumptions and find the extraordinary within the ordinary. Although he doesn't believe in God, Brown points out that despite its flaws and failings, the historical purpose of religion was to help people find transcendence. My focus on Rohr in a role similar to Brown's is to argue that removing institutional corruptions, divisive tribalism, and reductive dogmas can help people reconnect with our healthier pursuits for transcendence. These traditions were originally designed to help us find meaning and common ground in our quest to understand our place in the cosmos. My research shares how both Brown and Rohr have served as mentors in my life and the lives of others. In this book, I highlight how Rohr engages with audiences to provide wisdom that facilitates transformation both within and beyond religious frameworks. His theology integrates psychology and modern science, creating a mystical pathway that embraces diverse lines of inquiry. As this book focuses on another influential figure who employs wisdom for collective transformation, it becomes crucial to explore what our wise elders teach us about personal growth throughout life's journey. To appreciate the psychological significance of magicians, mentors, and wise elders, Jung's concept of the two halves of life provides us with a deeper developmental insight—a healthy ego recognizes when it's time to give back, using hard-won knowledge and experience to guide the next generation.

5. Merton (1948, 1961, 1968).
6. For a personal account, further resources, and a quick read, see Kelsey (2025).
7. Derren Brown's critique of self-help culture exposed its blind faith in individualism, often at the expense of wisdom and realism.
8. Rohr (2014).
9. Rohr (2014, 2019a).
10. This is why I enjoyed the reflections of Ben Hendy in the Postface chapter to this book. Even from a secular perspective, it reflected this deep dwelling for connection with nature.
11. Rohr (2018, 1999).
12. Lisa Miller's *The Awakened Brain* (2021) also explores Jung's concept of synchronicity in depth, applying it to lived experience alongside her work in neuroscience. She presents synchronicities as meaningful, non-random events that can serve as markers of spiritual attunement and guidance when

we learn to notice and take them seriously. Rather than dismissing them as mere coincidences, Miller frames synchronicities as openings into a deeper awareness of the connection between inner life and the external world. More recently, neuroscientist Tara Swart has taken this rationale further and argued that recognising such "signs" can also function as a mode of communication with deceased loved ones (2025a, 2025b).

13. Rohr (2022c).
14. This is a recurring point throughout Rohr's work. Rohr suggests that the first two millennia of Christianity may ultimately be seen as its infancy, with the real depth of the revelation only now starting to emerge. From the perspective of geological time, the Bible itself has existed only for a fleeting moment, and widespread access to it has been possible for just a few centuries. Because individual verses can be selected to justify almost any position—many even standing in direct contradiction—scripture cannot be reduced to simplistic readings. This is especially evident in Jesus' parables, which are intentionally layered and resist a single, definitive interpretation.
15. Buxton (2009).
16. Rohr (2011).
17. Rohr (2016a).
18. Rohr (2012).
19. Rohr (1999, 2009).
20. Bourgeault (2016, 2017).
21. Rohr (2009).
22. Rohr (2023).
23. Lakoff and Johnson (1980).
24. Rohr (2022b).
25. See Rohr (2019b, 2009).
26. Rohr (2019a, 2019c).
27. Rohr (2013, p. 84).
28. Rohr (2019a).
29. Rohr (2011, p. 66).
30. Rohr (2016c).
31. Rohr (2009).
32. Rohr (2016a, 2016b).
33. See Rohr (2019a, 2019c).
34. Rohr (2011).
35. Rohr (2011).
36. In a conversation with Brene Brown, Rohr expressed his concern with the translation of scripture into the language of repentance that fails to capture the true essence of meaning here (Rohr & Brown, 2021).
37. Rohr reframes evil not as a cosmic battle between opposing forces, but as the shadow side of human consciousness—our resistance to love, truth,

and integration. Psychologically, he sees the devil not as a literal being, but as a powerful archetype: the personification of ego, fear, and projection. When we repress the shadow—our unconscious wounds, rage, and insecurities—we tend to project it outward onto scapegoats, enemies, ideologies, and entire communities. This fuels cycles of exclusion, violence, and division. Rohr reminds us that evil is not only something we endure—it is something we enact when we live from fear, separation, and unawareness. See Rohr (2022a) and Kelsey (2025).

38. Rohr (2013).
39. Rohr (1999, 2011, 2013).
40. For insights on other mystical traditions, see Hanh (1991) on Buddhist mindfulness as a path to divine presence in everyday life; Rumi (2004), Fadiman and Frager (1999), Muedini (2020) and Vaughan-Lee (1995) for Sufi reflections on divine love and union; Coomaraswamy (1946) for the metaphysical underpinnings shared across Hindu, Buddhist, and Christian mysticism; and Armstrong (2009), who explores how compassion and mystery form the basis of many spiritual traditions beyond dogmatic belief; and Donlin-Smith & Shafiq (2023) for further discussion of mystical traditions and peaceful coexistence.
41. McGilchrist (2009, 2019).
42. Rohr shares common ground with Ken Wilber who covers several overlapping themes here in his work on integral psychology (see, for example, Wilber, 2000).
43. Rohr (2009).
44. Rohr (2011).

Bibliography

Armstrong, K. (2009). *The Case for God*. The Bodley Head.

Bourgeault, C. (2016). *The Heart of Centering Prayer: Nondual Christianity in Theory and Practice*. Shambhala Publications.

Bourgeault, C. (2017). Christian Centering Prayer | Rev. Cynthia Bourgeault | 2017 Festival of Faiths. Retrieved April 10, 2025, from https://www.youtube.com/watch?v=1aQmQu4lufo

Buxton, N. (2009). *Tantalus and the Pelican: Exploring Monastic Spirituality Today*. Bloomsbury.

Campbell, J. (1949). *The Hero with a Thousand Faces*. Princeton University Press.

Coomaraswamy, A. K. (1946). *The Transformation of Nature in Art*. Harvard University Press.

Donlin-Smith, T., & Shafiq, M. (Eds.). (2023). *Mystical Traditions: Approaches to Peaceful Coexistence*. Palgrave Macmillan.

Fadiman, C., & Frager, R. (1999). *Essential Sufism*. HarperOne.

Hanh, T. N. (1991). *Peace Is Every Step: The Path of Mindfulness in Everyday Life*. Bantam.

Jung, C. G. (1959). *Four Archetypes: Mother, Rebirth, Spirit, Trickster*. Princeton University Press.

Jung, C. G. (1969). *The Archetypes and the Collective Unconscious (Vol. 9, part 1 of the Collected Works of C.G. Jung)*. Princeton University Press.

Kelsey, D. (2017). *Media and Affective Mythologies: Discourse, Archetypes, and Ideology in Contemporary Politics*. Palgrave.

Kelsey, D. (2022a). *Murmurations Podcast: Derren Brown: Illusion, Psychology, and the Art of Influence* [Podcast]. Retrieved September 10, 2024, from https://murmurationspodcast.com/derren-brown

Kelsey, D. (2022b). *Storytelling and Collective Psychology: Ancient Wisdom, Modern Life, and the Work of Derren Brown*. Palgrave.

Kelsey, D. (2025). FR RICHARD ROHR: THE MYSTIC MENTOR. *Arcane Horizons* [Substack]. Retrieved June 30, 2025, from https://dkelsey.substack.com/p/fr-richard-rohr-the-mystic-mentor

Lakoff, G., & Johnson, M. (1980). *Metaphors We Live By*. University of Chicago Press.

McGilchrist, I. (2009). *The Master and His Emissary: The Divided Brain and the Making of the Western World*. Yale University Press.

McGilchrist, I. (2019). *The Matter with Things: Our Brains, Our Delusions, and the Unmaking of the World*. Perspectiva Press.

Merton, T. (1948). *The Seven Storey Mountain*. Harcourt, Brace and Company.

Merton, T. (1961). *New Seeds of Contemplation*. New Directions Publishing Corporation.

Merton, T. (1968). *Zen and the Birds of Appetite*. New Directions.

Miller, L. (2021). *The Awakened Brain: The New Science of Spirituality and Our Quest for an Inspired Life*. Random House.

Muedini, F. (2020). *Sponsoring Sufism: How Governments Promote "Mystical Islam" in Their Domestic and Foreign Policies*. I.B. Tauris.

Rohr, R. (1999). *Everything Belongs: The Gift of Contemplative Prayer*. Crossroad Publishing.

Rohr, R. (2009). *The Naked Now: Learning to See as the Mystics See*. Crossroad Publishing.

Rohr, R. (2011). *Falling Upward: A Spirituality for the Two Halves of Life*. Jossey-Bass.

Rohr, R. (2012). *Breathing Under Water: Spirituality and the Twelve Steps*. Retrieved April 10, 2025, from https://www.youtube.com/watch?v=I8o6_IqKdy8

Rohr, R. (2013). *Immortal Diamond: The Search for Our True Self*. Jossey-Bass.

Rohr, R. (2014). *Eager to Love: The Alternative Way of Francis of Assisi*. Franciscan Media.

Rohr, R. (2016a). *The Divine Dance: The Trinity and Your Transformation*. SPCK Publishing.

Rohr, R. (2016b). *Divine Dance: The Trinity and Your Transformation | Richard Rohr | Talks at Google*. Retrieved April 10, 2025, from https://www.youtube.com/watch?v=U1rA_gOgcjs

Rohr, R. (2016c). Resurrection: Not a One-Time Miracle. *All Saints Church Pasadena*. YouTube. Retrieved August 20, 2025, from https://www.youtube.com/watch?v=XU5f72VVvsg&t=186s

Rohr, R. (2018). *What is Contemplative Prayer and Why is it so Needed?* [Video online]. Retrieved April 10, 2025, from https://www.youtube.com/watch?v=b0o5J0-8OA0

Rohr, R. (2019a). *Richard Rohr on THE UNIVERSAL CHRIST*. Retrieved April 10, 2025, from https://www.youtube.com/watch?v=KD7B3wr3xeY

Rohr, R. (2019b). *What Do We Mean by Dualistic Thinking*. Contemplative Interbeing. Retrieved April 10, 2025, from https://www.youtube.com/watch?v=5Oc7qF_msMw

Rohr, R. (2019c). *The Universal Christ: How a Forgotten Reality Can Change Everything We See, Hope For, and Believe*. SPCK Publishing.

Rohr, R. (2022a). *Jesus' Alternative Plan: The Sermon on the Mount*. Franciscan Media.

Rohr, R. (2022b). *The World, the Flesh, and the Devil: What Do We Do with Evil?* Franciscan Media.

Rohr, R. (2022c). Interview with Richard Rohr: On Thomas Merton. *nuncenter*. YouTube. Retrieved August 20, 2025, from https://www.youtube.com/watch?v=cEhnmikd15Q

Rohr, R. (2023). The Resurrection of All Things. *Center for Action and Contemplation*, 10 April. Retrieved April 10, 2025, from https://cac.org/daily-meditations/the-resurrection-of-all-things-2023-04-10/

Rohr, R., & Brown, B. (2021). The Two Halves of Life with Brené Brown. [Podcast] *Center for Action and Contemplation*, 17 March. Retrieved April 10, 2025, from https://cac.org/podcasts/the-two-halves-of-life-with-brene-brown/

Rumi, J. (2004). *The Essential Rumi* (C. Barks, Trans.). HarperOne.

Swart, T. (2025a). *The Signs: The New Science of How to Trust Your Instincts*. Transworld Publishers.

Swart, T. (2025b). Neuroscientist (Dr. Tara Swart): Evidence We Can Communicate After Death! *The Diary of a CEO* podcast, 14 August. YouTube. Retrieved August 20, 2025, from https://www.youtube.com/watch?v=yfEQRqFo2bI

Vaughan-Lee, L. (1995). *Sufism, the Transformation of the Heart*. The Golden Sufi Center.

Wilber, K. (2000). *Integral Psychology: Consciousness, Spirit, Psychology, Therapy*. Shambhala.

CHAPTER 4

Dancing and Flowing

For Richard Rohr, what is fundamental to the shape of God is our welcomed participation in the relational flow of the Holy Trinity—we are part of a "divine dance," as he calls it. We are welcome at God's table. To express this vision of inclusion, a Russian iconographer painted what Rohr considers the most complete and profound example of religious art ever created.[1]

Andrei Rublev's *Icon of the Trinity* uses three main colours to represent different aspects of the Holy Trinity through three angelic figures seated around a table. Rohr explains how Gold represents the Father, symbolizing wholeness, perfection, and the ultimate source of all. Blue represents the Son, Christ, connecting with the sea and sky as it reflects God taking on humanity and uniting spirit and matter through Christ. Green symbolizes the Holy Spirit, the divine force of growth, much like photosynthesis, transforming light into life and guiding human growth as part of creation.[2]

The three angelic figures share a common bowl, symbolizing unity and communion. An empty fourth seat at the table invites the viewer's presence. Below the table, a small rectangle—believed to have once held a mirror—was likely intended to reflect the viewer's image, symbolically including them in the divine relationship.

This design reflects the early Church Fathers' idea of *perichoresis*—meaning "dance" or "choreography"—which describes the dynamic, inclusive flow of divine love and communion. Rublev's table is not reserved

D. Kelsey, *Transcendence and Collective Psychology*,
https://doi.org/10.1007/978-3-032-09495-7_4

for just three; it is open to all, offering an invitation to join in the divine flow. This eternal fullness, from which Christ came, calls us to participate in the divine banquet—God's everlasting dance of love and unity.

Like Rohr, I have a copy of Rublev's *Icon of the Trinity* hanging in my office. It has become the centrepiece of my personal space, surrounded by green painted walls, gold (plated, of course) accessories, and occasional hints of blue décor. As I write this chapter, I keep glancing up at the icon, still in awe of the deep meanings and contemplative wisdom Rublev conveyed through his art.

For Rohr, the problem Christianity faces is the restrained tendency for cultural and institutional change. Like so many major fields of knowledge and hierarchy, the church requires its own relational shift in how it understands the shape of God and the centrality of a contemplative foundation that brings the Trinity to the centre of spiritual practice. This requires a paradigm shift, and this is not a problem exclusive to the church, it's a recurring problem in our collective psychology.

Weaving Machines

At the end of *Storytelling and Collective Psychology*, I explained how humans are collective weaving machines.[3] We weave stories and meanings through our personal and collective lives to make sense of who we are and our place in the world. This chapter expands the scope of that principle to show how Rohr's mystical theology helps us to consider how religion and the story of Christ can provide us with a framework for understanding the deepest patterns of reality—patterns that extend beyond the human realm into the cosmos itself.

This weaving is not confined to human storytelling. It is apparent in the fabric of the cosmos itself—in the grand interconnectedness of the universe and the ways in which we continually seek to understand the seemingly impossible mysteries of nature and reality. As Rohr states, "mystery isn't something that you cannot understand – it is something that you can endlessly understand!"[4] This idea resonates not just with religious experience but also with modern scientific inquiry and the expanding frontiers of consciousness studies.

Mystery is not a barrier to knowledge but an invitation to deeper and deeper engagement. As we learned in the previous chapter, Rohr's emphasis on experiential contact with divinity and the power of true meaning through metaphor allows us to engage with religious mystery without falling into the trap of rigid literalism.

This chapter focuses specifically on Rohr's *The Divine Dance* and *The Universal Christ*, both of which provide a cosmic vision of spirituality that moves beyond individual belief systems into an expansive, interconnected reality.[5] Rohr's theology opens doorways to a wider sense of consciousness—one that embraces modern science, mystical traditions, and the most arcane horizons of reality.

Divine Relationship

Rohr's Trinitarian theology takes us further into the mystical journey of this book. The Great Mystery of the Trinity is an awe-inspiring case of the arcane that prepares us to engage with realities that seem impossible through conventional thinking but profoundly real in both scientific and spiritual terms. Rather than a rigid doctrine, the Trinity in Rohr's vision is a living, dynamic flow of love—a cosmic dance of divine relationship woven into the very fabric of existence.

This divine cosmic weaving is not merely a metaphor but a mystical and scientific reality, one that anticipates the interconnected nature of the universe as understood in modern physics, consciousness studies, and deep ecology. As discussed in the previous chapter, Rohr's approach aligns with panentheism—the idea that God is in all things, and all things are in God—bridging early theological insights with contemporary scientific exploration.

Just as quantum mechanics reveals an invisible web of connection between all particles, Rohr's vision of the divine suggests that everything participates in the flow of God's presence, whether we recognize it or not. This participatory understanding of the divine dissolves the artificial boundaries between spirituality and science, matter and mysticism, self and cosmos.

As this book moves into explorations of UFO phenomena, psychedelics, and near-death experiences (NDEs), Rohr's theology helps us grasp how these subjects—so often dismissed as fringe or supernatural—may in fact be expressions of a deeper reality that science and mysticism are both beginning to recognize as interwoven into the very nature of existence.

In every tradition of meaning-making—whether rooted in religion, science, or spirituality—there exists a yearning to understand the threads that weave together the fabric of existence. Creation is not merely a one-time act, but an ongoing story, written and rewritten in the interplay of forces that shape the universe and our lives.

The Archetypal Weaver

I apply the archetypal role of the divine weaver here because it conceptually integrates the metaphors and knowledge of religion and science—offering a unified lens to explore creation, interconnection, and continual renewal. At the heart of this archetype is the Creator: the source of all being, the origin of life, order from chaos and negotiations between life-forms (not a being, not a man, not a tyrant, not a monarch, a *source* we cannot currently comprehend).

For Rohr, in the Christian tradition, the Trinity embodies this relational creativity—a divine dance between Father, Son, and Holy Spirit that not only initiates existence but sustains and resurrects it in every moment. This vision portrays creation as inherently relational, dynamic, and interdependent. As Rohr acknowledges, science offers us a vision of interconnectedness, where the cosmos operates as an intricate web of forces, from the quantum entanglement that binds particles across vast distances to the ecosystems that thrive through collaboration and balance.

In this sense, science mirrors archetypal creation mythology, illuminating the continuous weaving of life and energy across time and space. In religion, this divine weaving articulates the sacred interrelationship of all things. In science, it is seen in the delicate synchrony of the universe. Both disciplines remind us that creation is ongoing—each discovery, act of imagination, or moment of transcendence participates in this continual unfolding. Rohr's Trinitarian theology bridges the tangible and intangible, harmonizing the spiritual and material worlds.

From my perspective, this is an important task for researchers in the humanities to take on.

Integrating Materialism

As discussed earlier, Jeff Kripal highlights the humanities as a fundamentally mystical pursuit—a space for exploring meaning, transcendence, and reality's limits. This approach doesn't reject materialism but seeks a broader, more integrative perspective that values science while reaching beyond its constraints.

Theological inquiry need not resort to rigid dogma but offer a way of thinking that aligns with collective psychology, bridging the material and the mystical. At its best, religion helps us navigate mystery, offering orientation within an unknowable cosmos. Instead of discarding early religious thought, Rohr's work is showing us how we can recognize its lasting power—guiding us to look both inward and outward, to explore ourselves while engaging with the divine patterns of existence.

This is not an abstract exercise, but a lived and participatory experience. Jeff Kripal's key concept in *The Flip* is helpful here: the moment when an individual undergoes a radical shift in perception, breaking free from conventional epistemologies and beginning to take seriously that which once seemed impossible.[6] For Kripal, this transformation opens a *cosmic comparative* scope of perspective. This perspective, Kripal suggests, "reorients us within an immeasurably larger vision of who we are as a species of the cosmos and what we might yet become. The future of knowledge, it turns out, is also the future of us."[7]

The humanities, if they are to be truly bold, must embrace these moments of rupture—those encounters with the unknown that force us to reimagine what human consciousness is capable of. This is where Rohr's work has taken me—enabling my exploration of topics and lines of inquiry I would previously have avoided when grappling with the existential matters arising in modern myths.

Embracing the Big Flip

Following Kripal's premise, we should be willing to engage with taboo topics and extraordinary experiences not as fringe curiosities but as vital clues to the nature of reality itself. This is precisely what Rohr's work enables us to do with theology, God, the cosmos, and more. His mysticism provides a language for understanding transcendence—not as an escape from reality, but as a deeper engagement with it.

Rohr's reading of biblical storytelling reveals a cosmos woven with divine mystery, one in which we are actively enmeshed. In this sense, we are not merely observers of the sacred but participants in an unfolding, interwoven reality that is at once material and more-than-material. We are mystical beings, not in an abstract sense, but in the way we navigate the lived realities of existence—experiencing awe, seeking meaning, and being transformed by encounters with mystery.[8]

The mysterious and arcane topics covered in this book are not standalone or abstract; they are facets of a unified whole and interconnected in ways we are able to explore and comprehend. By understanding the *actions* of this divine weaving, we can see ourselves as participants in this eternal process of creation and resurrection. Whether we engage with the natural world through scientific inquiry or contemplate the mysteries of the divine cosmos, we are part of a story that is forever renewing itself. Every act of creativity, every attempt to understand the universe, and every moment of connection with others is a thread in this cosmic tapestry.

The previous chapter showed how Rohr guided me through those questions and doubts I had about the relevance of religious texts in modern life and whether they can help us find transcendence. Now, by further exploring Rohr's Trinitarian theology, this chapter explores our cosmic consciousness through the interconnectedness of science and spirituality, while recognizing our role as co-creators in this great dance of existence.

The Forgotten Trinity

Karl Rahner, a twentieth-century Catholic theologian, noted that the Trinity has often been neglected in Christian teaching and practice.[9] He famously suggested that if references to the Trinity were removed from Scripture, many Christians might not even notice. Rahner argued that instead of being central to the spiritual lives of believers, the Trinity has been sidelined, overshadowed by rigid doctrines focused more on structure and certainty than on the living, relational reality of the divine.[10]

From Rahner's perspective, this sidelining of the Trinity exemplifies Ian McGilchrist's concerns regarding the hemispherical tensions and tendencies discussed earlier. The hemispherical bias in our culture typically struggles with the metaphors of divine flow and unfolding Mystery that we shall explore here.

For Rohr, when religion is adamant on depicting God more as a distant monarch or figure of judgement and authority, then we lose that sense of an active and loving presence. The relational and dynamic nature of the Trinity is then overshadowed, with fewer opportunities for Christians to experience a God who is more than authority through presence, unity, compassion, vulnerability, and mutuality. Rohr emphasizes the Trinity with profound humility via a contemplative ethos we can apply in further case studies throughout this book.

Rather than offering certainty, the Trinity invites believers to embrace its ineffable nature, fostering a deep and sometimes unsettling reverence for the unfathomable complexities of divine reality. This exercises our right-hemispherical psychology with gentle ease and expansion—comfortably sitting with paradox and possibility. Through non-dual thinking, we can contemplate this paradox, allowing it to guide us into unknown realms and less familiar aspects of reality—dimensions that offer meaning and experience beyond our typical reliance on rational certainty and the material world.

Goodbye Santa Claus

Rohr engages with cosmology, modern physics, and psychology to make sense of our place in the cosmos and in relation to God. He suggests we need to let go of the Santa Claus figure many of us have been taught to believe in: the bearded white man on a throne keeping an eye on us, checking whether we are naughty or nice, and tinkering with our fate accordingly.[11]

It is no coincidence then, as Rohr reminds us, that the Latin word for God is Deus, which sounds like Zeus because it is the same concept. It's what Rohr calls the monarchical God who is more like a lone substance and always omnipotent—to the point where over half the prayers in the Catholic sacramentary begin with "Almighty God."

Instead, Rohr suggests we'd be better off opening the other half of our prayers with "All vulnerable God," acknowledging not the Eternal Threatener, but God as the "Ultimate Participant – in everything – both the good and the painful."[12] We are intimately involved here, with all our flaws, failings, and lessons to learn. This is where Trinitarian theology takes us—to a place of participation with God where we are still responsible for our actions, but closer to God than mere fear and judgement would otherwise suggest. For Rohr, we are a part of the Trinity—The Father, The Son, and the Holy Spirit—where God is not that lone monarch.[13]

Vulnerable God

Rohr argues that genuine love cannot easily flourish in the presence of dominance, perfection, or grandeur—such qualities tend to inspire fear or dependence rather than true intimacy. Instead, love becomes possible when there is mutuality, when both parties meet as equals. This, he suggests, is why vulnerability is essential: it softens power and invites connection. In the Christian tradition, Rohr affirms this through the radical idea that God chose to enter human experience not through majesty, but through the fragile and humble figure of Jesus—an act that reveals divine love by embracing equality and vulnerability.[14]

I say "traditional" deliberately here, given the criticism Rohr's teachings have often faced from self-proclaimed "traditionalists."[15] While such complaints fail to be upheld, Rohr was once reported to Church authorities when he referred to God as She rather than Him.

Rohr was making the point that our dualistic conception of an imperial, monarchical God has pulled us away from a Trinitarian contemplation in which we realize God is beyond human labels and gender categories. Here, instead of a participatory God within the flow of Trinity, we end up with the authoritative patriarch who rules over us.

When it comes to Jesus, Rohr suggests we've made the mistake of pulling him out of the Trinity and putting him on a throne with the monarchical God who must be a man. When we do this, we lose the shape of God.

Knowing the Shape of God

This is not to suggest that nobody cares about the Trinity. Neither is it the case that all Christians avoid its meaning. But its contemplative nature doesn't fit comfortably with a dualist theology that has become so commonplace in Christianity and Western culture. The contemplative nature of the Trinity can feel at odds with such dualistic theology. Rohr believes that, as we work to build bridges across Christian denominations, we need a foundational theology that can support renewal from the ground up. For Rohr, the Trinity is central to this process.

A mystical approach to the Trinity—one that reconnects with its early contemplative roots—holds appeal not only for believers but even for those hardened by scientific scepticism. While this doesn't mean atheists will suddenly embrace Christianity, this approach respects science, and the human need to explore our place in the universe.

The Trinity is, therefore, about the "shape" of God. As Rohr says, if we have the wrong foundational understanding of God, then everything built upon it becomes unstable. According to Rohr, it's this instability that has troubled Christianity for centuries. This shakiness is why so many Catholics and other Christians are leaving the church, while non-believers often look on in bewilderment at the church's ways.

Yet Rohr is quick to point out that many of these people are not spiritually disconnected—in fact, many of them are deeply searching, perhaps more earnestly than regular churchgoers. For Rohr, it's Christianity's rigidity, not a lack of spirituality, that makes it unattractive to seekers.

Radical Relatedness

As Rohr explains, God is not merely the dancer, God is the dance itself—the dynamic flow at the heart of all being.[16] Here we see that God's flow is a radical relatedness through perfect communion between Three. Returning to my earlier point, we are reliant on metaphor in this respect. Rohr describes how we constantly look for similes, analogies, and metaphors because theological vocabulary is a tentative expression of Holy awe.

In other words, we can only speak of God through the language of approximate feelings and similarities that resonate with us, but we cannot definitively say what God *definitely is* because the realms of transcendence and mystery exist beyond the limitations of language and metaphor. Hence, Rohr suggests we maintain a fundamental humility towards the Great Mystery.

Saint Bonaventure offers a profound metaphor for understanding the Trinitarian nature of God: he described God as relationship itself, like a water wheel with three buckets that continually empty out, knowing they will always be refilled. For Rohr, this dynamic of self-emptying and refilling captures the essence of Christian love.[17]

Without this balance, we lose a truly Christian conception of love. In modern culture, this wisdom of self-emptying is often overshadowed by a fixation on self-filling, as we lack the faith that self-emptying will indeed lead to being filled again. Even within religious circles, there is a drift toward viewing God's love as conditional—a "finite God" who loves only if one is "good." In contrast, Bonaventure's vision is of an "infinite God" whose love flows unconditionally through the relationship among all things.

Author William Young suggests that bad theology is like pornography: it imagines a relationship without the risk of one. Stripped of vulnerability, it becomes transactional—concerned with statements and certainties rather than with mystery and encounter. Such an imaginary relationship removes the need for trust or genuine care, reducing faith to self-gratification. In the process, it dehumanizes both the individual and the community by sidestepping the hard but essential work of humility and trust.[18]

Young suggests poor theology is harmful because it dehumanizes God. This reduces the awe and complex mystery of a close relationship into something to be exploited or discarded.

The Trinitarian Verb

Young argues that the solution to this crisis lies in rediscovering mystical traditions—wisdom that he believes is beginning to re-emerge in both religious and public life. He views figures like Rohr as part of a larger invitation to transform how we live and what we open ourselves to by participating consciously in a divine rhythm of mutual love. This mystical path, according to Young, disrupts systems of domination and affirms connection instead. It reframes God not as a fixed entity, but as an active, living process—more verb than noun.

The imperial authority is not a static ruler, but a relationship between three: Father, Son, and Holy Spirit. Young prays that we might sense the life of Jesus flowing through us—using our hands to heal, embrace, and honour our shared humanity—and celebrate the sacredness of everyday life through our participation in the Trinity. He envisions spiritual vitality as something lived through action and connection, not detached belief, inviting us into a deeply embodied, relational faith.

What's important to note here is that, as Rohr repeatedly clarifies, this is not some new trendy or faddy New Age theology or pop psychology.

This is early Christian teaching.

A Threefold Tradition

Despite accusations of heresy, Rohr's theology is, as he claims, about as traditional as you can get. In the third century, Tertullian, often referred to as the founder of Western Christian theology, used the term *Trinity*—derived from the Latin *trinitas* (meaning "triad") or *trinus* (meaning "threefold"). As Rohr points out, this term isn't found in the Bible because it emerged as early Christians sought language to capture the complex, dynamic nature of the relationship between Father, Son, and Holy Spirit.[19]

Similar to Rohr, Brother Elias Marechal[20] described the Trinity as an eternal "Round Dance" that transcends human conceptions of time. A

Trappist monk in Georgia, Marechal drew from the early Greek Fathers, portraying the Three not as static beings, but as a continuous, dynamic flow of love and unity. This dance of divine relationship has always existed, long before the concept of time was known to humans, and continues endlessly, symbolizing a boundless, circular exchange of love within the Trinity.

Even if non-believers are unconvinced by Rohr's offering of an accessible spirituality to all, the requirements for a paradigm shift in how we understand the universe should still provide a sense of common ground in our motivations to explore subsequent case studies in this book. This is a shared incentive required across religious and scientific fields.

Protective Paradigms

Rohr refers to the scientist Thomas Kuhn who coined the term "paradigm shift." Kuhn made the point that even in science a paradigm shift is the same as what religion refers to as "major conversion" and it is equally rare in science as it is in religion.[21] Rohr makes the point that this is a common problem in both fields because we are dealing with the ego—humans tend to hold on to their beliefs that have become some embroiled and tightly woven with their opinions and worldview.

Professional and organizational coach, Andrew Scott makes the point that people are highly protective of their stories.[22] Science and religion rely on compelling stories about their respective fields and what they offer to human knowledge and experience. People's sense of identity is deeply tied to their view of the world and their place in it, shaped by the stories they tell themselves about their role and the roles of those around them.

As Scott shows, when these narratives are challenged with hard facts or compelling evidence, people often respond by clinging even more tightly to their stories and associated beliefs. This behaviour isn't limited to everyday disagreements or workplace conflicts—it extends to entire fields of knowledge, where it can hinder paradigm shifts that are essential for human progress and the advancement of understanding.

Kuhn makes the case that scientists who claim to only be interested in facts and evidence are prone to this behaviour as much as anyone else. For new scientific progress to occur, Kuhn observed that a generation often dies off before new knowledge can flourish. Likewise, as Rohr suggests, the same happens with Christianity when it departs from the contemplative mind and becomes entrenched in the appealing sense of order that the dualistic mind offers instead—it becomes increasingly difficult to claw back the teachings that get left behind and the spiritual practice that it advocated.

Cultural Impulses

For Rohr, dualistic thinking is so commonplace in Western culture partly because the Church has not been doing its job. As Rohr points out, his Franciscan routes deter him from dividing everything into the dualistic categories that seemingly force us to remain in permanent states of tribalism. Rohr encourages us to leave the field open and accept that what is, is. Without the early Church's original framework for thoughtful contemplation, Rohr argues, the Church bears some responsibility for today's divided, opinion-driven culture.

A culture's impulse to constantly approve or condemn runs contrary to the essence of faith. Rohr argues that the enlightenment also pulled us away from the contemplative mind—encouraging a supposedly rational and ordered thinking typically attributed to left-hemispherical psychology. From what Rohr is saying, we can see where the expansive, creative, and experiential traits of right-hemispherical psychology are suffocated by the dominance of dualistic thinking.

Since the arrival of social media and digital technology, Rohr points to research that has shown millennials, on average, seek stimulation every two and a half minutes—checking phones, messages, notifications, and so on. The culture wants to be kept "whirling," as Rohr says, not with Trinitarian love and connection, but with distraction, disconnection, and tribal confirmation.[23]

This stimulation is the waypoint into a faceless world of reductive opinions that has grown colossally in recent decades. For this reason, Rohr sees the contemplative mind as a crucial alternative form of thinking that is more valuable than ever and readily available in the Trinity.

But what does this radical paradigm shift look like when we consider a contemplative pathway that aligns with modern science, physics, cosmology, and psychology? This is where the Trinity proves helpful in moving beyond our participation in divine flow to consider how we got here and what this means for Christian theology.

From the Big Bang to Now

In *The Universal Christ* Rohr sees divinity as being present in all things, seamlessly connecting with the Trinitarian theology he advocates. He suggests that God the Father, the ultimate source, was revealed for the first time through the Big Bang—Christ's first material appearance in the world, according to current cosmology and physics. Over time, through cosmic and biological evolution, human consciousness develops, and Jesus, the Son, joins us. From Him, we learn that we are part of the divine communion, sharing in the Holy Spirit.[24]

As Jeffrey Kripal argues, we can understand the cosmic-human story without abandoning our scientific and medical knowledge of the material world and the human body.[25] The current materialistic framework of science is not wrong, but it is incomplete. While the human mind can be seen as rooted in matter, Kripal emphasizes that matter itself is also "minded."

Like Rohr and the mystics, Kripal advocates for the view that consciousness is fundamental to the cosmos, rather than being a random or accidental property of matter. For both Rohr and Kripal, it is not a leap to recognize that matter could be an expression of a cosmic mind, manifesting through the intricate structures of mathematics, physics, and quantum realms.[26]

Rohr maintains that if Christian theology had remained centrally focused on the Trinity, Christians would have been at the front of the line when it came to understanding and agreeing with evolution. In his view, God has planted this universal tendency towards growth and multiplication and cycles of renewed everywhere in life.

As discussed earlier, resurrection is not something that happened once in one person; it is the fundamental nature of the universe. In this view Christ becomes that stand in for all life—humanity and divinity was not unique to Christ as some would insist. Rather, Christ appeared to take us with Him, to follow Him, and to know that we can do what he did.

Through this cosmic theology, Rohr outlines a *panentheistic* view of the Trinity, defining God as both *immanent within and transcendent beyond the physical universe.*

Don't be confused here. The Trinity might be the Great Mystery and full of wonder. But panentheism is simply the idea that God is in and beyond all things. God is not equal to all things as *pantheism* suggests. Pan*enth*eism sees God in all things because God is within *and beyond* material nature—all matter, therefore, contains the DNA of its Creator.

This perspective offers a theological framework that is expansive and inclusive, integrating the divine presence within all of creation. Using a psychological and metaphorical paradigm, Rohr presents a theological approach that aligns with modern physics and cosmology. This approach helps us appreciate the complexity and interconnectedness of the cosmos, while expanding our understanding beyond materiality.[27]

Emphasizing the relational and dynamic nature of divinity, Rohr's view aligns closely with emerging philosophical and scientific paradigms that consider consciousness as a fundamental aspect of reality. In this way, panentheism offers a coherent pathway to philosophies of mind that move beyond the confines of reductive materialism.

Panentheism and Panpsychism

While the Christian mystics might have been historically marginalized within the Church, the Trinitarian theology Rohr offers here is not out on an intellectual limb in the academy. Panpsychism is a philosophy increasingly embraced by both theists and atheists, as well as by philosophers and physicists, to explain consciousness. This growing interest reflects a shift towards viewing consciousness as inherent in the fabric of the universe, aligning with the panentheistic idea of a divine presence that is both immanent in, and transcendent of, nature.

Panpsychism holds that consciousness, and "minded" properties, are fundamental and pervasive throughout the universe, present in everything from the smallest particles to complex beings. It suggests that all matter possesses an intrinsic experiential quality—though not necessarily "mind" or "intelligence" as humans typically understand it, but rather a basic form of consciousness underlying the material workings of the universe.[28]

From here, philosopher Philip Goff proposes pan-agentalism.[29] This is Goff's attempt to move beyond traditional panpsychism by suggesting that not just consciousness, but agency—the capacity to act—is fundamental and ubiquitous. While panpsychism claims that all matter has some form of consciousness or experience, pan-agentalism claims that all matter has some form of agency, even at the smallest levels of reality.

The intersections of Rohr's theological panentheism and Goff's philosophical panpsychism open the possibility that divine presence is not only all-encompassing but also intimately intertwined with the consciousness that permeates the universe. Together, these perspectives offer a profound understanding of both God and consciousness, revealing the divine as both immanent and transcendent—within and beyond our material immersion in the universe.

Shared Understandings

The compatibility between panentheism and panpsychism lies in their shared understanding of the relationship between consciousness, the divine, and the cosmos. Both frameworks assert that consciousness is a fundamental aspect of reality, but while panentheism views the divine as encompassing and interpenetrating the universe, panpsychism posits that consciousness exists in all things, even at the most basic levels of matter.

In this sense, panpsychism lends itself naturally to theistic frameworks like panentheism. If consciousness is a ubiquitous feature of reality, as panpsychism suggests, then the idea of a divine, conscious presence that permeates the universe—something central to panentheism—becomes both plausible and coherent. In a theistic view of panentheism, God is not merely transcendent but also immanent, and active within creation, suggesting that divine consciousness could be an ever-present, underlying reality that works through the consciousness inherent in all things.

This view allows for a more relational, intimate understanding of the divine, where God is both beyond and within creation, intimately connected with the world while not confined by it. However, even with a panpsychist view of reality, and its seeming compatibility with incarnational theology, some of the most cutting-edge minds in philosophy can still hesitate in their commitment to knowing the shape of God.

The Case of Philip Goff

Philip Goff's move from not believing in God to becoming a Christian reflects the kind of questions and struggles many people face—especially within the academic world. Despite his influential work on panpsychism, which made a significant impact on analytical philosophy, Goff resisted any commitment to or recognition of a divine mind behind the cosmos.

More recently, Goff made that leap of faith.[30] In a meeting with a local Anglican priest in Durham, I was sharing some of the ideas I had for this book when Goff's work came up in conversation. Having read and enjoyed Goff's work on panpsychism, the priest said he found it perplexing how Goff made such a compelling case for panpsychism but still resisted belief in God. I explained that just days earlier I had seen Goff speaking at an event where he declared this integration of theistic logic into his philosophical worldview. This made complete sense to the pair of us.

Goff's journey reflects the tension between feeling drawn to belief in God and remaining critical of traditional religious structures and dogmas. I could relate here. This conflict between faith and scepticism, between seeking divine meaning and rejecting institutional rigidity, mirrors a broader intellectual journey that many thinkers and seekers, including myself, share.

Like Goff, my journey of faith was not straightforward. It was marked by a deep intellectual struggle with questions of faith, meaning, and the challenge of reconciling belief with reason. When I listened to Goff's reflections, I found a kindred spirit in his willingness to embrace mystery, reject rigid orthodoxy, and seek a conception of God that more comfortably (and ethically) aligns with contemporary thought.

Anticipating Heresy

Like myself, Rohr, and other mystics, Goff anticipates accusations of heresy because his belief in God is rooted in a mystical understanding that goes beyond the confines of traditional religious dogma and institutional authority. Goff has publicly declared his awareness that accusations of heresy will inevitably come his way from many other Christians.[31]

But, as Rohr would point out, Goff's mystical framing of God reflects a long tradition of questioning, refining, and expanding religious thought. Trinitarian theology, from a mystical standpoint, bridges intellectual rigor with spiritual openness that is robust in the face of such accusations. Although Rohr still faces accusations of heresy, he does a compelling job of exposing flaws in those accusations, and by his own admission, the Franciscan community have shown great resilience and loyalty in protecting him against ideologues and pseudo-traditionalists over the years.

So, I reached out to Goff. I wanted to share my view that his perspective is far from heretical. I explained how my own journey of faith was influenced by Rohr's panentheistic view of God—the divine cosmos offers a compelling model for those navigating serious philosophical inquiry and a deeper spirituality. For me, all Goff was doing was distancing himself from the same God that the mystics have dispelled—that authoritarian, distant figure being replaced with cosmic agency and incarnational presence in the universe.

Another Pathway

As that Anglican priest in Durham suggested, Christianity is a pathway and is far more accessible and less daunting when seen as a pathway in this sense. Goff's approach to panpsychism provides an intellectual pathway to God—in his personal case, in tandem with Christianity and Western culture.

If consciousness is inherent in all things, the universe itself can be seen as infused with divine awareness, aligning closely with Trinitarian panentheism and philosophical panpsychism. The divine, both immanent and transcendent, becomes not a distant entity but an intimate, ever-present force at the heart of creation. This perspective does not alienate modern seekers; instead, it expands our understanding of a divine cosmos.

Ultimately, Goff's journey shows that the real barrier to faith for many is not the concept of God, but rather the rigid dogmas associated with religion and the monarchical God who upholds those rules and judgements. The intellectual resistance to theism in academia tends to reflect an equally narrow conception of divinity. Far from being heretical, the common ground between panentheism and panpsychism reflects a rich tradition of intellectual and theological exploration—bridging ancient wisdom and modern science.

Goff's journey is part of a larger movement that seeks to reconcile the mysteries of the divine with the insights of modern science and philosophy. In this way, he stands as part of a tradition that continues to evolve and enrich religious thought. Core to this understanding of God is the idea of relational flow—again, with God as a verb as much as a noun.

The Language of Mind

If consciousness is fundamental to life and the universe—preceding even matter itself—how can we meaningfully distinguish our own conscious experience and human agency from the more diffuse forms of consciousness suggested by panpsychism? Likewise, how do we differentiate between our personal sense of sacredness or spiritual connection and the broader, more encompassing vision of divine immanence proposed by panentheism?

The challenge in reconciling panpsychism and panentheism is not only metaphysical—it's linguistic. The terms we use to describe consciousness, intelligence, mind, and even "God" are especially problematic when we attempt to speak about forms of awareness or agency that predate, exceed, or differ from the kind of self-modelling consciousness we associate with human minds.

Neuroscientist, Bobby Azarian sees integrated information theory (IIT) as a bridge in neuroscience that has enabled mystical influences in the philosophy of mind to be taken more seriously. According to IIT, even atoms might possess negligible amounts of consciousness, in the sense that they integrate information and self-organize. But, for Azarian, this doesn't imply self-*reflective* agency.[32] The kind of consciousness that emerges through brains is qualitatively different—it models the world, builds a self-model, and creates a first-person perspective. Without this recursive modelling, there is no "observer" in the sense we typically mean as humans. I am not suggesting that the likes of Rohr, Goff and Azarian have offered a shared or consistent definition of consciousness—there are complexities to unpack beyond the scope of this chapter—but the mystical influence that often points us to a conscious agency in the universe is apparent.

Self-modelling Organisms

Atoms might possess only negligible amounts of consciousness, but when these micro-level components assemble into increasingly complex systems of self-reflection and self-modelling, something profound begins to happen. This is where the language of consciousness in a human sense occurs. For Azarian, through self-modelling organisms—particularly those with brains capable of encoding and reflecting on the consequences of their actions—consciousness becomes rich, reflexive, and transformative.

In this view, the universe is a fertile matrix that contains the potential for consciousness as we experience it—through the reflective awareness of human minds, the sensory intelligence of animals, and the subtler, more diffuse forms of responsiveness found in plants, trees, and grasses. Each operates with its own mode of consciousness, shaped by the complexity and structure of its being.

Azarian suggests that through evolutionary processes, as life emerges and complexifies, the universe begins to *wake up*. Consciousness, in this sense, is not evenly distributed or uniformly present like a human mind from the start, but gradually crystallizes through the recursive feedback loops of living minds themselves. It is in these loops—this capacity to reflect, to feel, to act with awareness—that consciousness becomes meaningful and experiential to us, and agency takes shape.

The Proof Paradox

Azarian makes the argument that, paradoxically, we keep *proving* what could be called the "God hypothesis." Yet, with each scientific breakthrough that meets the criteria historically associated with divine action, we convince ourselves we've *disproved* it. He points to three key developments: first, the Big Bang theory, which posits a moment of cosmic creation; second, the fine-tuning of universal constants, which suggests an improbable precision; and third, the teleological narrative that sees evolution moving in a purposeful direction towards increasing complexity and consciousness.

Azarian posits that if we were to ask a rationalist from the Newtonian era what signs might confirm the existence of a Creator, these would likely be among them. And yet, when such signs appear—supported by scientific models rather than religious doctrine—we simply absorb them into a self-contained, mechanistic story. The very moment something like "magic" becomes explainable, we no longer call it magic.

What's the Problem Here?

In Azarian's view, the problem lies in how we define God: as something *outside* nature, something fundamentally unprovable. And so, every time science gets close to what would have once counted as evidence of the divine—a created universe, apparent design, directional evolution—we dismiss it, precisely because it is now part of the natural order. We keep discovering what we used to call God, and then explaining it away.

But panentheism doesn't have this problem, and neither do mystics such as Rohr. By seeing God as present both within observable forms of reality and beyond those current sensory capabilities we can sit comfortably with the paradox between possible knowledge and seemingly impossible mystery.

Like Rohr and the mystics, what I am proposing here is *not* a "God of the gaps" argument. We are not locating God in the unexplained leftovers of science, nor are we defending belief by appealing to mystery as a last resort. On the contrary, our understanding of God does not shrink in response to scientific discovery—it expands. Scientific insight does not threaten the sacred, it deepens it. As we come to understand more about the universe, we also come closer to the divine mystery that permeates it.[33]

Matter Is Minded

As Jeffrey Kripal points out, the materialist frameworks of modern science are not wrong—they're just half right. Yes, mind is mattered. But as we see from the likes of Azarian and others—and throughout the case studies in this book—*matter is also minded.*[34] This realization takes us back to Kripal's concept of *the flip*: a reversal in perspective that doesn't discard science but reframes it. Rather than viewing consciousness as a latecomer in a dead, mechanical universe, this flip in perspective invites us to see mind as fundamental, threaded through the fabric of reality from the very start.

This resonates with the likes of Azarian, Goff, Rohr, Jung, and others *across* academic disciplines. If even the smallest units of matter exhibit tendencies—preferences, responsiveness, a kind of proto-intentionality—then perhaps agency is not something that emerges *from* complexity, but something that expresses *through* it. In this light, consciousness is not an illusion generated by the brain, but a deep pattern of the cosmos, made visible in us.

For Rohr, the divine is not separate from the world but expressed through it: matter itself is the hiding place of Spirit. The flip here, in Rohr's terms, is a contemplative re-seeing of the cosmos—not as dead or inert, but as infused with presence, agency, and relationship. Christ becomes a name for this universal pattern of coherence, not a doctrinal boundary but a mystical lens through which everything can be seen as sacred, interconnected, and alive.

Jung arrives at a similar truth from the direction of depth psychology. His concept of the *psychoid* refers to a foundational layer of reality that is neither purely psychic nor purely physical, but a kind of hybrid domain in which both mind and matter emerge from a common source.[35] At this level, archetypes are not just symbolic patterns of thought—they are psychoid structures, shaping both inner experience and outer reality.[36] For Jung, the psyche was not confined to the brain but deeply embedded in the fabric of reality. His concept of the Self—representing total psychic wholeness—was not merely an individual goal but a transpersonal mystery, reflecting a collective and potentially cosmic dimension of the human condition.

What we see here is that the flip Kripal calls for is not just theoretical, it's experiential. It invites us to live differently—to engage with the world not as a collection of objects, but as a communion of subjects. The cosmos is not mute, but mysteriously communicative, echoing with agency, meaning, and invitation.

Flowing Relationality

For the mystics, God is not an external puppet-master but the flowing relationality at the heart of being—a dance that invites participation, evolution, and even vulnerability. The self-reflective consciousness made possible through human minds carries a particular responsibility because it has the capacity to recognize and align with divine intention in ways that other agents might not.

In this view, evil becomes a distortion of agency—a point I touched up in those metaphors in the previous chapter. Diseases, cancers—agents of destruction—are not conscious in the self-reflective sense, but they are still part of the whole. As such, we don't exclude them from our model of reality, but we begin to understand their distorted agency and we try to intervene to counteract them in whatever ways we discover to be possible via critical, interventionist agents.

The intelligence in the cosmos may not be centralized like a monarch on a throne—it may be distributed, emerging, even struggling towards coherence. But that doesn't make it any less sacred. It makes it more fragile, more relational, and more responsive to the ways in which we—tiny fragments of that cosmic intelligence—learn to love, to think, to imagine.

Religion and the Cosmos

G.K. Chesterton once wrote that your religion isn't defined by the church you attend, but by the cosmos you inhabit. In other words, faith is not limited to institutional boundaries but is shaped by the vast, interconnected reality of creation. It is in recognizing the divine presence throughout the cosmos that one truly experiences a sense of belonging and sacredness in the world.[37]

Rohr makes the point that the universe's true energy doesn't lie in individual objects like planets or particles, but in the relationships that connect them.[38] This theology offers a framework that is more beneficial to collective psychology and common ground in our view of the cosmos, moving beyond traditional dogmas and fostering a more fluid and relational understanding of the divine.

The term *Catholic* comes from the Greek *katholikos*, meaning "universal" or "according to the whole." In this light, Rohr critiques the rejection of universalism, including the idea of universal salvation, as heresy. He notes that many Christians today resist universal concepts altogether, sometimes even opposing global organizations such as the United Nations. Some religious communities, he observes, define belonging through ethnic or cultural boundaries, dividing people into insiders and outsiders. For Rohr, such exclusions contradict Christianity's core claim that one God created all things.[39]

For Rohr, once we realize that the entire physical world—everything around us in its cosmic entirety—is both a hiding place and a revelation of God, the world transforms into an enchanted home, offering grace to those who look deeply.

Mature Theology

For Rohr, this is the contemplative mind doing what it does best. It takes us beyond the limits of dualistic thinking for the sake of mature theology that makes God accessible and creation all-inclusive. Rohr believes that only mature Christians see Christ in everything and everyone else, making the point that this definition can never fail us, while always demanding more of us, and gives us no reasons to be exclusionary or rejecting towards anyone.

Rohr points out that God didn't begin communicating only with the arrival of the Bible, the Church, or the prophets. It's unreasonable to believe that the Divine was silent for 13.7 billion years, only speaking up in the final instant of cosmic time. Truth and meaning weren't absent before sacred texts emerged. For Rohr, the light of Divine Presence has been shining and unfolding since the dawn of time—long before any human was here to witness it.[40]

Rohr argues that love is the universal force drawing all things towards connection—a fundamental energy that transcends language, culture, and belief. Though difficult to define, love is instantly recognizable in action. For Rohr, true love is not confined to any religion, denomination, identity, or label. Acts of compassion, faithfulness, and hope are not the property of any one group—they reflect a shared human and divine reality. We instinctively recognize when love is present—when it flows freely—and when it is withheld. Everything else, he suggests, is secondary to that deeper, unifying truth.[41]

The contemplative mind encourages us to release control, surrender to mystery, and embrace the love of faith, while resisting the ego's urge to dominate.

(De)colonizing God

In the same way that Jeff Kripal suggests we need to decolonize reality—a point I return to in the conclusion of this book—we must also decolonize God. This challenge is two-fold: first, to liberate God from the domineering authorities who have exploited a pseudo-unity with divinity to control people; and second, to free conceptions of God from atheists who reduce divinity to the same absurd tyranny for the sake of their own ontological control.

Rohr notes that controlling people project their need for control onto God, while true love requires surrender. Instead of reshaping God in our own image, faith invites us to be reshaped by the divine.[42]

Rohr challenges us to be open to new possibilities, including the potential discovery of life on other planets. Far from being a source of fear or existential threat to religion, Rohr suggests that such discoveries should be seen as further evidence of the vastness and inclusivity of the divine dance, reinforcing the idea that the cosmos is teeming with divine life and energy.

By presenting God as a dynamic, relational force *within and beyond* the cosmos, panentheism provides common ground for understanding the interconnectedness of all life while setting the scene for deeper explorations of collective psychology, transcendence, and spirituality in the chapters to come. Only through this expansive and mystical view of God can we really open people's minds to radical cosmic possibilities.

Rohr argues that creation exists primarily for its own sake, second to reveal God's goodness, diversity, and generosity, and third for humans to use responsibly. He believes our narrow, scarcity-based worldview is a significant distortion, contributing to the rise of atheism and the "practical atheism" that dominates many Western societies today.

Rohr suggests that the image of God presented to people has often been too limited and unwelcoming, making it difficult for open-hearted individuals to trust or love such a God. But what happens when we challenge this wrong turn in Christian teaching? And what does it look like when someone tries to place a depiction of this Trinity in popular culture—that reflects a mystical theology with appeal to multiple audiences within and beyond Christianity?

Let's consider what a friend of Rohr's came up with through his dramatization of the Trinity in a story that became a bestselling book and critically acclaimed film.

The Case of William Young

In *The Shack*, William Young presents a story of grief, faith, and forgiveness that explores the Trinity in an unconventional, yet profoundly symbolic, way.[43] The main character, Mackenzie ("Mack"), suffers the tragic loss of his daughter, Missy, who is abducted and murdered. This trauma drives him into deep anger and a crisis of faith, distancing him from his family and his understanding of God.

Mack later receives a mysterious invitation to revisit the shack where his daughter was killed. He goes, though he remains sceptical. Upon arriving, he falls unconscious, slipping into what seems like a vivid dream state. In this state, he encounters the Trinity in forms that challenge his preconceptions and personal biases.

God the Father, referred to as "Papa," appears to Mack as a large African American woman who embodies warmth, motherly care, and familiarity—qualities of love and reassurance. This choice is especially significant for Mack, as this figure was a nurturing presence he recalls from his childhood—a woman who provided comfort during a time when he faced a harsh, authoritarian father.

Struggling to view God as loving due to his upbringing, Mack's encounter with "Papa" in this familiar, compassionate form allows him to move beyond his association of God with strict authority. This opens him to experience divine love in a profoundly personal way.

Jesus appears as a Middle Eastern man, highlighting the historical and earthly dimension of Christ. He embodies a humble, approachable presence, emphasizing Jesus' humanity and the idea of God walking alongside humanity in shared experience. Finally, the Holy Spirit appears as Sarayu, an ethereal, Asian woman symbolizing wisdom, mystery, and the omnipresent nature of divine inspiration and guidance.

Sarayu embodies the role Rohr attributes to the Holy Spirit—one who brings about both diversity and unity. Like a creative wind, the Spirit animates the world with endless variety, yet also draws all things into harmony. This echoes Augustine's vision of "one Christ, loving Himself," where all creation is united in divine love.

These representations of the Trinity guide Mack through a journey of emotional healing, helping him confront his anger, pain, and guilt. They teach him that forgiveness is not about excusing wrongs but about freeing himself from the corrosive grip of resentment. Through these encounters, Mack learns to forgive both himself and others, opening the way for him to reconnect with love and trust.

Young's portrayal reflects other aspects of Trinitarian theology, such as *diversity within unity*, the interconnectedness of love, and the distinct roles of each person of the Trinity. Papa, Jesus, and Sarayu help Mack experience God's love and healing presence even amid suffering.

The story emphasizes themes of relationality and community, mirroring how the Trinity exists in constant relationship and love. The point about diversity within unity is important because it accounts for a recurring ethos in this book's subsequent case studies—differences can still point to common ground and common ground can accommodate a variety of interpersonal complexity.

By the end of his journey, Mack wakes up with a transformed perspective on God and life. This shift reflects a new understanding of how the Trinity's love and forgiveness can reshape personal pain and restore one's relationships with the divine and others, resonating with the Trinitarian ethos of God's boundless compassion and active engagement in human suffering and reconciliation.

Accusations of Heresy

Perhaps predictably, Young's work ignited intense criticism, especially among conservative Christians, due to its unconventional portrayal of the Trinity. Critics argue that the depiction of God as an African American woman ("Papa") risks anthropomorphizing God in a way that softens or misrepresents divine attributes. For some, representing God in human form, especially as a maternal figure, undermines the traditional, transcendent image of God the Father.

In defence of Young, this is another example of a theological metaphor, which, to return to Rohr's earlier point, means that those literalizing the metaphor risk missing the literal meaning. In this case, the metaphorical figure of Papa is there to help Mack—and readers—grasp the intimacy and depth of God's love, reminding us that scripture itself occasionally uses motherly metaphors to express God's nurturing qualities.

A common criticism of *The Shack* is that it promotes universalism, implying that all people will be reconciled to God regardless of belief or repentance. Detractors see this as undermining the central Christian claim of salvation through Christ—understood narrowly as possession of Jesus rather than the cosmic wholeness of Christ. Supporters, however, argue that Young's work highlights God's limitless love and mercy. Rather than dismissing repentance, the narrative stresses personal transformation and invites readers to encounter God's grace in the universal Christ.

Translating Repentance

Another counterpoint here considers Rohr's own critique of translations and conceptions of repentance in doctrinal teaching. In a conversation with Brené Brown, Rohr critiques the way many Christians approach faith, especially the focus on innocence and righteousness over personal growth. He suggests that for many, being Christian is about proving they're right, holy, or innocent. This mindset, Rohr explains, can prevent the genuine inner transformation that Jesus taught.[44]

Rohr points to the word "repent" as a misinterpretation of what Jesus truly intended. The Greek term, "metanoia," is often translated as "repent" but more accurately means "to change" or "to shift one's mindset." Yet, for Rohr, the word "repent" has taken on connotations of guilt and a moral impurity, missing the original emphasis on openness and personal transformation.

Rohr argues that this emphasis on innocence can lead to a kind of scapegoating where people project blame onto others—on other groups, races, or religions—deflecting attention from their own flaws to maintain a sense of self-righteousness. This need to assign blame to others, Rohr notes, is deeply divisive and undermines the personal change Jesus sought to inspire in his followers.

For Rohr, this restrictive approach to faith is a "tragic place" that inhibits true spiritual growth and the compassionate understanding that lies at the heart of Jesus' teachings.

Redemption and Justice

Some Christians also feel that the book downplays divine justice, replacing God's righteous anger towards sin with an emphasis on forgiveness. Critics argue that this could excuse wrongdoing, misrepresenting God's character. But as Rohr points out, God already knows us: God did not take human form to change His mind about humanity, but to change our understanding of God.[45]

Advocates of *The Shack* argue that Young does not dismiss the importance of justice, but instead invites readers to trust in God's redemptive and relational approach to it. Rohr makes a similar point in his critique of rigid moralism, noting that Jesus rarely focused his harshest criticism on obvious moral failings. Rather, he challenged those who believed themselves to be without fault—those blind to their own inner darkness and unaware of how they participated in systems of power and exclusion.

During a public talk, Rohr recalled with wry amusement how some conservative Catholics once recorded him speaking at an Episcopalian church and reported him to local bishops. His response drew laughter from the audience, as he proclaimed, *if Jesus can eat with prostitutes and drunkards and tax collectors, the least he could do is stretch himself to eat with Episcopalians.*[46]

As Rohr has stated on several occasions, "baby Christianity," as he calls it, excludes and shrinks its scope for love and acceptance. The tribal mindset of immature religion that cannot accommodate other Christians or belief systems offers us little hope for the exploration of arcane phenomena in this book. We must let go and look for unity among diversity within and beyond Christianity—including other religions and secular world views.

Returning to *The Shack*, Mack is taught to let go of vengeance, leaving judgement to God, aligning with Biblical calls to forgive, and to recognize our place within that Trinitarian flow of Father, Son, and Holy Spirit. *The Shack* has remained theologically divisive, with some dismissing it as heretical while others find it a powerful exploration of God's love, forgiveness, and the Trinity's relational nature. For many readers, it serves as a tool to explore faith, forgiveness, and divine empathy in a way that resonates deeply with the gospel, albeit through unorthodox representations and symbology.

Enthusiasm and Caution

Rohr was struck by the public's enthusiasm when he joined Protestant priest Cynthia Bourgeault along with William Young for a discussion on the Trinity.[47] The venue was packed with a public audience striving for a deeper, mystical understanding of the Trinity. For Rohr, this enthusiasm seemed to reflect a desire for a teaching that emphasizes graceful change, personal growth, and divine love—qualities that many find missing in more exclusionary theological views.

However, Rohr stresses the importance of approaching this with caution. The mystical path does not call us to judge or condemn those with more conservative interpretations of faith. These perspectives, while sometimes appearing overly rigid, restrictive, or even mean spirited, often come from a desire (or perceived necessity) to find order and stability, especially in the face of inner struggles or uncertainties. Recognizing the limitations of a human institution like the Church, Rohr suggests that we must work to balance different perspectives within faith and non-faith communities.

Rohr reminds us that scripture is always written by humans from a human perspective. While we call it the "word of God," the only Word of God the Bible clearly affirms is Jesus, the eternal Logos. According to Rohr, the mystical tradition of Trinitarian theology has become almost entirely absent from our dominant ways of knowing. He suggests that the conflicts of the Reformation and the rationalism of the Enlightenment intensified earlier tendencies in the Church (rather than departing from them), giving rise to new articulations of fundamentalism on the Right and to atheism or agnosticism on the Left.[48]

Even those who may seem disconnected from Jesus' original message have the potential to change and grow. Engaging with the Trinity as a living flow between Father, Son, and Holy Spirit offers a reminder that no one is beyond the reach of divine love and redemption. Embracing this inclusive, transformative view of the Trinity can create a space where all are welcomed into a kingdom grounded in love and acceptance.

Exploring the Arcane

Rohr argues that unless we recognize the shared meaning of all creation we will keep retreating into our own small, isolated worlds in search of personal safety and peace of mind. He believes that privatized salvation can't lead to collective transformation because it primarily attracts individualists from the start. But this is not only relevant to individuals: this is a collective message that should resonate with how we understand humanity in relation to the cosmos.

The latter is essential for the case studies in the subsequent chapters. Whether we are thinking about the potentials for extraterrestrial life, the vastness of the cosmos and our place within it, altered states of consciousness beyond our usual window on reality, or the potential for non-material realms of consciousness beyond our physical selves, we need to move beyond the isolated worlds we've created for our own sense-making purposes. We must be open to the transcendent realms of arcane horizons to enable collective transformation.

This also means we need to be open to believers and non-believers having a sense of shared connection with the universe—even if their pathways to connection differ. The mystical way provides a container for unity in difference and diversity in content belonging.

Believers and Non-believers

Rohr speaks to non-believers as much as believers because he is speaking to a universal ethos of non-discriminatory spirituality that seeks connection with the greatest and deepest truths of what it means to be human, and to *live in this cosmos.*

It is fine to accept that some people find this communion through different religions, they're not wrong, and they just have a different pathway to God. Likewise, atheists aren't incapable of developing a deep sense of oneness with the cosmos, nor do they struggle to connect with others through a spirituality that makes sense to them and accommodates the rational facts of science. But believers and non-believers alike know that there is much to discover about the universe, and whether we are theists, atheists, or agnostics, we all crave transcendence.

Contemplative thinking, Rohr suggests, goes beyond the need to prove or disprove; it's more about embracing unknowing through knowing, which fosters transformation through continual flow and change. Contemplative spirituality and non-dualistic thinking open mystical pathways to consider what the arcane realms of life mean to us, and what we might learn about them for the sake of positive change and transformation in the future.

The case studies in subsequent chapters will take believers and non-believers alike through the stories and possibilities that arise from arcane phenomena. Through the mystical grounding Rohr has provided, we can view the cosmos as that hiding place and revelation place for God or whatever source of all life or higher power makes sense to us.

Whether it's the Great Mystery of the Trinity, the possibility of non-human intelligences linked to the psyche and the cosmos, or questions about the afterlife, our consciousness can grow and flourish when we accommodate and integrate paradox.

Paradoxical Experiences

The 1989 film, *Communion*, based on author Whitley Strieber's alleged alien encounters, explores themes of memory, trauma, transcendence, and the ambiguous nature of reality.[49] While the film centres on UFOs and alien abductions, it primarily focuses on Strieber's internal journey as he grapples with encounters that defy categorization as either purely psychological or physical. His experiences push him into a non-dualist space where fear and awe coexist, prompting deep existential questions.

The film intentionally blurs the line between reality and imagination, reflecting Strieber's psychological turmoil and raising questions that remain unsolved. This ambiguity is central to the non-dualist ethos, where mystery is not seen as an obstacle to truth but as an invitation to greater understanding.

In this framework, the pursuit of certainty is set aside in favour of embracing the unknown. Strieber's journey becomes one of accepting mystery without needing it to be definitively explained—an essential aspect of mysticism. Mysticism, as a way of engaging with awe inspiring knowledge *and* the wonders of unknown, encourages individuals to be content with unresolved experiences, recognizing that some aspects of life and existence might always elude complete comprehension.

Strieber's marital struggles provide an emotional anchor for the film. His wife is unable to fully relate to his alien abduction dreams, which often seem traumatizing and destabilizing. This tension highlights the difficulty of integrating deeply personal, unexplainable experiences into relationships and daily life.

Integrating the Arcane

In the final scene, however, their conversation—captured by a circling camera not dissimilar to the Rohr's dance and Rublev's table—reveals a mutual *integration* of each other's perspectives. Strieber's wife, although sceptical of the details of his encounters, sees them as expressions of divine mystery, something she calls "God." For her, it doesn't matter what he saw. It's his experience that matters.

Strieber, in turn, acknowledges that his encounters may serve as catalysts for evolution, recognizing that such experiences are part of a larger journey of personal and human growth. This moment of communion transcends their views on alien encounters, symbolizing the broader integration of lived experiences into the collective psyche. The film suggests that we can hold space for paradoxical and mystical experiences without reducing them to simplistic beliefs or dismissing them as mere fantasy.

This integration is key to the non-dualist approach to life and the unknown, where both rational understanding and acceptance of the unknown coexist. *Communion* demonstrates how embracing the mystery of life can lead to deeper connections with others, as well as a more profound understanding of self and reality. The film's refusal to offer a clear answer to the question of whether the alien encounters are "real" or not speaks to the wisdom of accepting mystery, rather than forcing closure.

Communion ultimately embodies the non-dualist ethos, where embracing unsolved mystery via contemplative practice and shadow integration is an essential part of both personal growth and collective understanding.

Mysticism helps us live more comfortably with paradox and uncertainty while fostering an openness and humility towards humanity's biggest questions.

Pathways to Transformation

This mystical approach provides a profound framework for navigating the mysteries of consciousness, human experience, and the cosmos. A contemplative ethos invites us to grapple with the arcane horizons of reality—those mysteries that often seem beyond our grasp. Rohr serves as a modern guide for mystical wisdom, offering tools for transformation, new possibilities, and an integration of opposites—two seemingly contradictory forces that, when reconciled, bring us closer to a deeper understanding of the human experience.

Rohr's teachings show us how to approach the unknown with humility and reverence, regardless of faith or belief, while acknowledging that transformation often arises from paradox and the merging of opposites. This sets us on a path where we no longer seek simple answers but instead allows us to hold complexity and mystery with grace, awe, and wonder.

Those transcendental realms I explore in the rest of this book begin with the question of whether we are alone in the universe. As Rohr points out, this question is not to cause alarm for people of faith: the Catholic church and other religious institutions have accepted that the likelihood of other life existing in the cosmos is high, and in principle would be part of God's creation like the rest of us, and they might even have their own Jesus figure that they worship.[50]

My point here? If the Catholic Church can be at ease with the topic of my next case study (in Chaps. 5 and 6), then so can we. So, let's relax, enjoy the journey, and catapult ourselves into the transcendental realms of cosmic consciousness—embracing the seemingly "impossible" capacities of arcane horizons.

Notes

1. Ibid: 29–32.
2. See Rohr (2016a). While this analysis and those descriptions of colour resonated with me via distinct doctrinal and liturgical meanings, the deeper metaphorical readings—such as green as a symbol of photosynthetic transformation or gold as the perfection of ultimate source—could be seen as interpretative on Rohr's part (and others) while going beyond documented iconographic tradition.
3. Kelsey (2022).
4. See Kelsey (2025).
5. Rohr (2016a, 2016b, 2019a, 2019b).
6. Kripal (2020).
7. Ibid: 11–16.
8. With this foundation, we move forward. If the humanities are to be superhuman, as Kripal suggests, then they must have the courage to follow the human impulse towards transcendence—to let our fascinations, our most daring speculations, and our deepest yearnings take us where they will. My research in this book continues in that spirit, venturing into the territories where mystery and human experience collide: the liminal spaces where the unknown beckons and where the boundaries of knowledge are rewritten.
9. For an accessible introduction to the work of Karl Rahner, see Kilby (2007). For a deeper analysis of Rahner's theology, see Kilby (2004). To read Rahner's work directly, see Rahner (1965, 1975, 1981, 1996).
10. As Rohr (2016a, 2016b) points out, Karl Rahner famously suggested that the Christian of the future would either be a mystic or would cease to be Christian altogether. Central to Rahner's thought is the idea that God is not an object among others, but the horizon of all human experience—an orientation that led him to emphasize the importance of personal, mystical encounters with the divine. This deeply experiential approach has influenced many contemporary spiritual writers, including Richard Rohr, who often cites Rahner as a key voice in reclaiming mysticism as the living heart of Christian faith. Both thinkers challenge the reduction of religion to mere moralism or dogma, instead calling for a transformative spirituality rooted in wonder, inner experience, and openness to mystery. The future

of spirituality and collective psychology may lie in a post-secular ethos—one that transcends the increasingly obsolete divides between religion and science, theism and secularism. Post-secularism, in this sense, offers a holistic framework for cross-cultural and transdisciplinary research, integrating insights from social, psychological, and cosmological studies. It opens the door to a more inclusive understanding of spirituality's role in human life—one that honours diverse perspectives and remains open to the mystical dimensions of existence.

11. Rohr (2016b, 2019a).
12. Rohr (2016a: 36).
13. As Rohr points out, "History has long operated with a static and imperial image of God," a supreme (male) Monarch who is mostly living in splendid isolation as a Critical Spectator (2016a: 35). A spiritual paradigm shift enables us to rethink this premise in line with those earliest teachings recognised by the mystics.
14. Rohr (2016a, 2016b, 2016c, 2016d, 2022).
15. For more on self-proclaimed traditionalists and scriptural ideologues, see Kelsey (2025).
16. Rohr (2016a: 27).
17. Rohr (2016a) draws on this imagery in *The Divine Dance*, interpreting it as a vision of the Trinity not as a static doctrine but as a living flow of mutual giving and receiving—a divine rhythm of love in motion.
18. See Rohr (2016a) for a discussion of Young's work.
19. Ibid.
20. Marechal (2015).
21. Kuhn (1962).
22. Scott (2016).
23. Rohr (2016a).
24. Rohr (2019a, 2019b).
25. Kripal (2022).
26. This view is shared among many theologically sympathetic and intellectually respected scientists (see, for example, Meyer, 2009, 2013, 2021; Lennox, 2007, 2011, 2019, 2020).
27. For accessible sources on panentheism, see the likes of Richard Rohr (2019c) and Rupert Sheldrake (2025) sharing their thoughts through a various public platforms.
28. Goff (2023).
29. Ibid.
30. For a roundtable discussion on this topic and Goff's rationale, see Goff et al. (2024).
31. Goff (2024).

32. Azarian (2024) discusses the work of Michael Levin, a biochemist who observed what he saw as traces of agency and intelligence even at the atomic level. He was particularly fascinated by the Pauli Exclusion Principle, which governs the behaviour of electrons in atoms. According to Levin, the way electrons "choose" their positions in atomic shells—seemingly in coordination with their neighbours—suggests a kind of social behaviour or mutual awareness that standard physics doesn't fully account for. Levin didn't claim that this constitutes consciousness per se, but he saw it as a kind of proto-agency—an early expression of the same self-organizing principles that scale upward into more complex forms of life and intelligence. This idea supports a view in which agency is baked into the structure of matter itself, providing a foundation for emergent consciousness as systems assemble and evolve. In a similar vein, Ervin Laszlo's (2014, 2020) work on the self-actualising cosmos presents a similarly radical paradigm. Laszlo proposes that the cosmos is not a passive, mechanistic backdrop but an active, living system in the process of becoming—one that self-organizes, evolves, and participates in its own unfolding. This vision treats the universe as a dynamic whole in which consciousness is not an accidental by-product but a fundamental property emerging from its very structure. In doing so, Laszlo revitalizes the spirit of Bucke's mystical vision of cosmic consciousness, but grounds it in the language and logic of contemporary systems theory, quantum coherence, and cosmology. Rather than being dismissed as metaphysical speculation, such perspectives are gaining traction in transdisciplinary discussions seeking to reframe the nature of mind, matter, and meaning on a cosmic scale.
33. For Rohr, this is a spirituality that remains enchanted—enchanted by the beauty of what we can now see more clearly, and by the wonder of what still escapes us. It is a love for both the known and the unknown, rooted not in fear or superstition, but in awe. Rohr invites us to see God not as an explanation, but as the radiant presence within all things—the sacred depth of reality itself, both revealed and concealed in equal measure (see, for example, Rohr, 2019a, 2019b).
34. Kripal (2020: 12).
35. Jung (1947).
36. This is the terrain where Jung (1952) argued that synchronicities occur: meaningful coincidences that bypass causal logic and reveal a hidden coherence between psyche and world. To appreciate how synchronicities have been taken seriously in personal experiences and modern science, see Lisa Miller's (2021) work in *The Awakened Brain*. More recently, see Tara Swart's (2025a, 2025b) claims on noticing these "signs" as a meaningful language for communicating with deceased loved ones.
37. Rohr (2019a, 2019b).

38. Rohr (2016b, 2018).
39. Rohr (2019a, 2019b).
40. Rohr (2019a, 2019b).
41. Rohr (2019a, 2019b).
42. Rohr (2019a).
43. *The Shack* was first a book (Young, 2008) and then a film (Hazeldine, 2017).
44. See Rohr and Brown (2021).
45. Rohr (2013, 2019a, 2019b).
46. See Kelsey (2025).
47. This event was titled "Trinity: The Soul of Creation" and held from April 6 to 8, 2017, organized by the Center for Action and Contemplation (CAC). This conference featured Richard Rohr, Cynthia Bourgeault, and William Paul Young as the main speakers, focusing on the Christian doctrine of the Trinity.
48. Rohr (2016a).
49. *Communion* was a book (Strieber, 1987) and then a film (Mora, 1989). Streiber has talked recently about the devastating impact these experiences had on his life due to public ridicule, family stress, and personal and financial hardships arising as a result (Coulthart, 2025; Ramsay, 2025).
50. Rohr (2019a); Piedra (2025).

Bibliography

Azarian, B. (2024). Cosmic Consciousness and the Truth Beyond Simulation Theory. *Third Eye Drops with Michael Phillip*. Retrieved April 14, 2025, from https://www.youtube.com/watch?v=THNVAZEx9UM

Coulthart, R. (2025). Whitley Strieber on Abduction Experience, Extreme Medical Testing | Reality Check [YouTube video]. *NewsNation*, Published 2025. Retrieved August 20, 2025, from https://www.youtube.com/watch?v=JzS2GqSB6OI&t=20s

Goff, P. (2023). *Why? The Purpose of the Universe*. Oxford University Press.

Goff, P. (2024). I Now Think a Heretical Form of Christianity Might be True. *Aeon*. Retrieved June 13, 2025, from https://aeon.co/essays/i-now-think-a-heretical-form-of-christianity-might-be-true

Goff, P., et al. (2024). Between God and Atheism. [YouTube video] *The Sacred*. Retrieved June 13, 2025, from https://www.youtube.com/watch?v=5IiZgjuHzLQ

Hazeldine, S. (2017). *The Shack* [Film]. Summit Entertainment.

Jung, C. G. (1947). On the Nature of the Psyche. In *Collected Works, Volume 8, The Structure and Dynamics of the Psyche* (pp. 343–442). Routledge & Kegan Paul.

Jung, C. G. (1952). *Synchronicity: An Acausal Connecting Principle* (Vol. 8 of the Collected Works of C.G. Jung). Princeton University Press.

Kelsey, D. (2022). *Murmurations Podcast: Derren Brown: Illusion, Psychology, and the Art of Influence* [Podcast]. Retrieved September 10, 2024, from https://murmurationspodcast.com/derren-brown

Kelsey, D. (2025). FR RICHARD ROHR: THE MYSTIC MENTOR. *Arcane Horizons* [Substack]. Retrieved June 30, 2025, from https://dkelsey.substack.com/p/fr-richard-rohr-the-mystic-mentor

Kilby, K. (2004). *Karl Rahner: Theology and Philosophy.* Routledge. amazon.com+11fbcclassroom.com+11powells.com+11

Kilby, K. (2007). *A Brief Introduction to Karl Rahner.* SPCK.

Kripal, J. (2020). *The Flip: Who You Really Are and Why It Matters.* Penguin Books. static.fnac-static.com+3London Review Bookshop+3Blackwell's+3

Kripal, J. (2022). *Superhumanities: Historical Precedents, Moral Objections, and New Realities.* University of Chicago Press.

Kuhn, T. (1962). *The Structure of Scientific Revolutions.* University of Chicago Press.

Laszlo, E. (2014). *The Self-Actualizing Cosmos: The Akasha Revolution in Science and Human Consciousness.* Inner Traditions.

Laszlo, E. (2020). *Reconnecting to the Source: The New Science of Spiritual Experience, How It Can Change You, and How It Can Transform the World.* St. Martin's Essentials.

Lennox, J. (2007). *God's Undertaker: Has Science Buried God?* Lion Books.

Lennox, J. (2011). *Gunning for God: Why the New Atheists are Missing the Target.* Lion Hudson.

Lennox, J. (2019). *Can Science Explain Everything?* The Good Book Company.

Lennox, J. (2020). *Where is God in a Coronavirus World?* The Good Book Company.

Marechal, E. (2015). *Tears of an Innocent God: Conversations on Silence, Kindness, and Prayer.* Paulist.

Meyer, S. (2009). *Signature in the Cell: DNA and the Evidence for Intelligent Design.* HarperOne.

Meyer, S. (2013). *Darwin's Doubt: The Explosive Origin of Animal Life and the Case for Intelligent Design.* HarperOne.

Meyer, S. (2021). *The Return of the God Hypothesis: Three Scientific Discoveries That Reveal the Mind Behind the Universe.* HarperOne.

Miller, L. (2021). *The Awakened Brain: The New Science of Spirituality and Our Quest for an Inspired Life.* Random House.

Mora, P. (1989). *Communion* [Film]. Carolco Pictures.

Piedra, G. (2025). *Is Jesus an Alien? Pope Francis' Interest in UAPs Explained.* Retrieved April 10, 2025, from https://www.youtube.com/watch?v=2izhNXn1Msc

Rahner, K. (1965). *Theological Investigations, Volume I: The Relationship of the Church to Non-Christian Religions* (R. J. McInerny, Trans.). Darton, Longman and Todd.

Rahner, K. (1975). *Theological Investigations, Volume IV: More Recent Writings* (R. J. McInerny, Trans.). Darton, Longman and Todd.

Rahner, K. (1981). *Theological Investigations, Volume VI: The Church and the Sacraments* (R. J. McInerny, Trans.). Darton, Longman and Todd.

Rahner, K. (1996). *Foundations of Christian Faith: An Introduction to the Idea of Christianity* (W. V. Dych, Trans.). Crossroad.

Ramsay, C. (2025). He Has Direct Contact With Aliens—Whitley Strieber. *AREA52—DEBRIEFED* (Episode 36). YouTube. Retrieved August 20, 2025, from https://www.youtube.com/watch?v=jFqzrK8ZIjs

Rohr, R. (2013). *Immortal Diamond: The Search for Our True Self.* Jossey-Bass.

Rohr, R. (2016a). *The Divine Dance: The Trinity and Your Transformation.* SPCK Publishing.

Rohr, R. (2016b). *Divine Dance: The Trinity and Your Transformation | Richard Rohr | Talks at Google.* Retrieved April 10, 2025, from https://www.youtube.com/watch?v=U1rA_gOgcjs

Rohr, R. (2016c). *Negative Capability, Center for Action and Contemplation* [Daily Meditation], 11 January. Retrieved June 30, 2025, from https://cac.org/daily-meditations/negative-capability-2016-01-11

Rohr, R. (2016d). Resurrection: Not a One-Time Miracle. *All Saints Church Pasadena.* YouTube. Retrieved August 20, 2025, from https://www.youtube.com/watch?v=XU5f72VVvsg&t=186s

Rohr, R. (2018). The Template of Reality. *Center for Action and Contemplation*, 29 April. Retrieved April 10, 2025, from https://cac.org/daily-meditations/the-template-of-reality-2018-04-29/

Rohr, R. (2019a). *Richard Rohr on THE UNIVERSAL CHRIST.* Retrieved April 10, 2025, from https://www.youtube.com/watch?v=KD7B3wr3xeY

Rohr, R. (2019b). *The Universal Christ: How a Forgotten Reality Can Change Everything We See, Hope For, and Believe.* SPCK Publishing.

Rohr, R. (2019c). *Panentheism (False Teaching).* Popular Gospel [YouTube video]. Retrieved June 13, 2025, from https://www.youtube.com/watch?v=o7mVmvOZ1uM

Rohr, R. (2022). *Jesus' Alternative Plan: The Sermon on the Mount.* Franciscan Media.

Rohr, R., & Brown, B. (2021). The Two Halves of Life with Brené Brown. [Podcast] *Center for Action and Contemplation*, 17 March. Retrieved April 10, 2025, from https://cac.org/podcasts/the-two-halves-of-life-with-brene-brown/

Scott, A. (2016). *Shifting Stories: How Changing Their Stories Can Transform People.* Troubador Publishing Ltd.

Sheldrake, R. (2025). *Panentheism: God is in Nature.* Rupert Sheldrake Substack. Retrieved June 13, 2025, from https://rupertsheldrake.substack.com/p/panentheism-god-is-in-nature
Strieber, W. (1987). *Communion: A True Story.* Beech Tree Books.
Swart, T. (2025a). *The Signs: The New Science of How to Trust Your Instincts.* Transworld Publishers.
Swart, T. (2025b). Neuroscientist (Dr. Tara Swart): Evidence We Can Communicate After Death! *The Diary of a CEO* podcast, 14 August. YouTube. Retrieved August 20, 2025, from https://www.youtube.com/watch?v=yfEQRqFo2bI
Young, W. P. (2008). *The Shack.* Hodder & Stoughton.

CHAPTER 5

Angels and Intermediaries

Jung considered archetypal messengers to be figures that carry profound meaning from the collective unconscious.[1] In this respect, messengers served as bridges between conscious awareness and deeper, unseen layers of the psyche. These messengers often appear in myths, dreams, and cultural symbols, conveying truths or guidance from archetypal realms.

Messengers embody the idea of beings or entities that bridge realms, carrying vital information, knowledge, or warnings. They often serve as conduits between worlds, delivering messages that are intended to inform, guide, or transform those who receive them. They are liminal figures, operating at the threshold between the known and the unknown, the earthly and the transcendent.

In myth and religion, messengers frequently appear as angels, prophets, or divine intermediaries tasked with conveying wisdom, warnings, or hope. They often carry an aura of mystery, embodying both awe and uncertainty, as their messages can be cryptic, and their origins or intentions may not always be fully understood.

Once known as Flying Saucers and now referred to as UFOs or UAPs, these phenomena have long served as celestial emissaries in our collective psychology. Whether in fiction or reality, our contemplation of them has acted as a potential bridge between humanity and a greater cosmic or spiritual reality.

D. Kelsey, *Transcendence and Collective Psychology*,
https://doi.org/10.1007/978-3-032-09495-7_5

Multiple Possibilities

While UFOs have traditionally been associated with the stars and outer space, it is increasingly speculated that they might not come from distant realms but instead coexist with us—possibly through interdimensional realities on Earth, advanced technology beyond our sensory understanding, or even concealed in the unexplored depths of our oceans and Antarctica. Other claims have pointed towards technology manifested and controlled (or "summoned") by human consciousness through telepathic realms we are yet to understand.[2]

This chapter does not aim to determine the technological or biological nature of UFOs or explain what they are or where they come from. It is worth noting that we don't even know if the experiences outlined in this chapter can be explained by *one* technology, phenomenon, intelligence, lifeform, or even disinformation—there could be a multitude of explanations yet to be uncovered or aspects of reality yet to be understood in this world.

The question is: *what stories do we tell when we tell stories about UFOs?* What these two chapters will show is *how* UFO mythology (ufology) plays a transcendental role in our collective psychology. These experiences and the meanings people take from them reflect recurring patterns of thought and behaviour, taking on their own archetypal form. Here we see the transcendental realms of storytelling that arise from this phenomenon, which should be taken seriously by sceptics and seekers alike.

Maintaining Criticality

That's not to suggest we should suspend our critical faculties. As I write this chapter, serious concerns remain about the extent to which public and political attention to UFOs may be shaped by disinformation—whether through the strategic manipulation of political elites or the viral spread of belief systems that have begun to resemble a form of religiosity, complete with dogmas, rituals, and hierarchical command structures.[3] That said, we can still examine the historical and contemporary patterns in these stories with an open mind and healthy (even strategical) scepticism.

Back to the messengers. Mythological messengers convey all kinds of meanings to their recipients. Humanity's enduring hope for contact with something greater than ourselves also endures the trickster paradox of messengers: they both reveal and obscure, offering tantalizing glimpses of a larger mystery without providing complete answers.

In this way, messengers invite us to embrace the unknown as a source of wonder and transformation. However, like many transcendental realms, they reflect tensions and anxieties in the psyche—they take on a meaningful symbolic form in our culture.

Symbolic Saucers in the Sky

In *Flying Saucers: A Modern Myth of Things Seen in the Skies*, Carl Jung proposed that the UFO phenomenon should not be dismissed as mere fantasy nor accepted as literal evidence of extraterrestrial visitation.[4] Instead, he argued that UFOs were symbolic projections arising from the collective unconscious—expressions of deeply repressed psychological content emerging during times of cultural anxiety and existential threat.

Jung observed that these visions often took the form of circular, mandala-like shapes—symbols of wholeness that recur throughout mythological and religious traditions. In his view, such imagery reflected a profound yearning for unity in a fractured and disoriented world. Writing in the shadow of the post-World War II nuclear age, Jung suggested that the rise of UFO sightings coincided with a period of intense technological upheaval and spiritual dislocation. He believed that when conscious life starts to fragment under psychic pressure, the archetype of wholeness tends to emerge in response.

Rather than treating UFOs as physical objects or scientific anomalies, Jung interpreted them as modern myths—psychologically real phenomena that speak to our need for coherence, meaning, and transcendence. He believed that these experiences should be taken seriously, not in terms of literal truth, but for what they reveal about the collective psyche.

This psychological framework laid the foundation for later interpretations by scholars in scientific, theological, and psychological fields, who have continued to explore the symbolic, cultural, and mystical dimensions of the UFO phenomenon. Jung's legacy remains vital: his approach invites us to understand UFOs not simply as questions of belief or disbelief, but as mirrors reflecting the deepest structures of human consciousness and our enduring desire to reconnect with something greater than ourselves.

Sharing elements of Jung's perspective on UFOs, Terence McKenna also saw UFOs as manifestations of the psyche rather than solely physical phenomena.[5] Jung and McKenna suggested that their appearance reflected a psychological and cultural response to the anxieties of the atomic age, with UFOs symbolizing a desire for transcendence and salvation amidst existential uncertainty.

McKenna viewed UFOs as projections of the mind, emerging from altered states of consciousness to challenge rigid perceptions of reality. Jung and McKenna emphasized the interplay between inner and outer worlds, suggesting that UFOs are not just external anomalies but also catalysts for inner transformation, pushing humanity to explore its relationship with mystery, imagination, and the unknown potentials of our future.

Collective Experiences

This shared focus on UFOs as liminal phenomena resonates with the psychedelic experience I discuss later—where encounters with otherworldly imagery and entities often act as mirrors of the psyche, guiding individuals toward profound self-awareness and collective insight. In this respect, the notion of UFOs as an archetypal form has survived the test of time—especially when we consider our collective desire for wholeness in tribal times where we feel as divided, atomized, and ethically disconnected as ever before.

As discussed by the likes of Jung and, more recently, Jacques Vallée, Diana Pasulka and Jeffrey Kripal, among others, UFO and alien encounters consistently feature distinct archetypal traits that reflect and shape our perceptions of reality. These recurring themes suggest that UFO phenomena tap into deep, shared aspects of the human psyche.

One key archetypal form is the encounter with the "Other"— something unknown, mysterious, and incomprehensible, mirroring the archetype of the divine or supernatural realm, where the boundaries of ordinary reality are dissolved. Many UFO experiences are also framed as mystical or divine encounters, where individuals undergo transformative, spiritual awakenings akin to religious epiphanies.

These encounters often lead to personal transformation, as individuals report shifts in consciousness, new spiritual insights, or altered worldviews.

Celestial Messengers

Much like angels in religious traditions, who serve as messengers or intermediaries delivering profound insights or warnings, UFOs and their associated beings often take on a similar role in modern folklore. The concept of advanced, benevolent beings coming to guide humanity reflects archetypes of the saviour or liberator, seen in myths of divine intervention or the return of a messianic figure.

UFO crafts are often depicted as a wheel or circular object with powerful, mystical energy, reminiscent of divine vehicles in religious texts, representing a means of transcendence or movement between worlds. UFO communities also mirror the communal dynamics of religious practices, with shared rituals, beliefs, and authority figures, while the phenomenon blurs the lines between the material and spiritual realms, representing a crossing from the known to the unknown, and from the earthly to the cosmic.[6]

Jung's focus was on what UFOs revealed about the psyche in this respect. Although Jung didn't dismiss the physical existence outright, he did emphasize that their *apparent* impossibility made them more psychologically significant as archetypal symbols rather than objective realities.

Diana Pasulka, however, sees an evolution in our understanding, suggesting that Jung missed a critical aspect: it is precisely the potential for a physical reality behind UFOs that gives them their power as a *living myth*.[7] The interplay between myth and possible reality is what makes UFOs a unique *universal mass rumour*—a phenomenon of modern folklore, fed by sightings, government disclosures, and cultural fascination.

Writing in a time with vastly more evidence at hand, Pasulka and others have revisited and refined Jung's ideas with a serious eye toward both mythological and physical dimensions. A key figure who embodies this dual approach is Jacques Vallée, a French computer scientist and ufologist, who has integrated Jung's psychological framework with rigorous inquiry into the physical possibilities of UFOs.[8]

Vallée's work explores not only the symbolic significance of UFOs but also the material and scientific questions they pose, effectively bridging the mythic and the empirical in a way Jung might have appreciated, even if it was beyond the methodological reach of his time.

Focus on the Data

Vallée's work explores not only the symbolic significance of UFOs but also the material and scientific questions they pose—effectively bridging the mythic and the empirical in a way that Carl Jung might have appreciated, even if it lay beyond the methodological reach of his time.

Vallée emphasizes data over conclusions, remaining open to multiple hypotheses and speculative possibilities. His approach resists the temptation to leap toward interpretations shaped by personal intuition or paradigmatic assumptions, encouraging instead a disciplined openness to wherever the data may lead.

One researcher deeply influenced by Vallée in this regard is Garry Nolan, an American immunologist, academic, and inventor known for his unconventional yet rigorous engagement with UFO research. Nolan advocates for a convergence between scientific precision and openness to the metaphysical dimensions suggested by these phenomena. While grounded in analytical methods, his work also acknowledges the symbolic and transcendent potential embedded in UFO experiences.

For Nolan, understanding UFOs offers not only the possibility of insights into non-human intelligences but also a deeper comprehension of human consciousness and our place in the cosmos. By exploring the intersection of UFO phenomena, perception, and reality itself, Nolan challenges conventional frameworks and invites a form of intellectual awakening—one that could catalyse transformative shifts in how we understand the limits of knowledge and the latent capacities of the human mind.[9]

Physical *and* Symbolic?

Vallée argues that these phenomena might not be extraterrestrial in origin, but rather interdimensional, psychological, or even symbolic in nature. Likewise, Jeff Kripal proposes that instead of focusing solely on whether UFOs are extraterrestrial, they could represent an intermediary reality, existing between the physical and symbolic. These perspectives encourage a more flexible, nuanced inquiry into how humans understand these experiences, highlighting the potential for UFO phenomena to expand both scientific and spiritual understandings of reality.

Vallée is the French scientist and UFO researcher who served as the inspiration for the character of the French scientist in Steven Spielberg's

Close Encounters of the Third Kind. While this connection to Hollywood may raise the suspicion that UFO phenomena are merely a product of the media or creative imagination, Vallée himself presents a deeper interpretation.

Vallee's work suggests that UFO sightings, encounters, and other related phenomena are not just manifestations of collective fantasies but may stem from much older and deeper aspects of reality and human consciousness that we are yet to understand.

Hollywood as Symptom

This brings us to another idea: what if Hollywood is not the source of UFO stories but the symptom, like a fantastical mirror of our collective unconscious, and a modern archive for articulating ancestral knowledge? If Hollywood reflects the dreams, fears, and desires that humans have carried across generations, then it is possible that the UFO phenomena in film aren't merely fictional constructs, but an externalization of real, often unconscious, human experience.

Films like *Close Encounters* might not be entirely born of creative invention, but of an ancient, collective memory encoded in our psyche—something that has appeared throughout history in various forms, from angels to gods to extraterrestrials. However, as we shall see in the stories I account for, UFOs stimulate as many questions about ourselves than the potential for other life out there in the cosmos.

Whether they're messengers seeking to save us from ourselves or a potential threat to our cosmic safety and existence, the narratives around UFOs have historically raised questions about the conflicts we have among ourselves as humans.

A Greater Unknown

Geneva, 1985. Amid the tension and mistrust of the Cold War, President Ronald Reagan and Soviet leader Mikhail Gorbachev met at a summit to address the escalating risk of nuclear conflict. During a break from official talks, Reagan and Gorbachev took a private walk, during which Reagan asked Gorbachev if the Soviet Union would help America if it were attacked by an extraterrestrial force.[10] Gorbachev reportedly replied, "No doubt about it."

Reagan affirmed that America, too, would stand by the Soviet Union if the situation were reversed. In this brief exchange, a glimmer of shared humanity broke through the layers of tension and caution that had defined their countries' relationship for decades.[11]

While the question itself was hypothetical, it held profound implications. Despite their ideological divide, both leaders acknowledged that some challenges transcend national boundaries and differences. The existence of a potential "other"—something beyond human comprehension—was enough to unite them in a vision of cooperation against a greater unknown.

This conversation shows how even those who are seemingly most divided can recognize humanity's shared place in the cosmos. For Reagan, UFOs and alien life had always carried a sense of possibility, perhaps stemming from an encounter he'd had years earlier when, as Governor of California, he witnessed a strange object trailing his plane before whizzing off at a seemingly impossible speed and angle. The pilot that day witnessed the incident and said the experience left Reagan and his companions surprised by what they had seen, and Reagan remained curious thereafter.

Reagan's enduring fascination with UFOs, combined with the gravity of that exchange with Gorbachev, underscores the transcendental implications of the phenomenon. But the question here doesn't only concern a threat to humanity. As I will show in this chapter, UFO stories and experiences stimulate many themes and questions aroused from deep in the collective psyche, including a shared wonder, mystery, and a collective sense of "something more."

Our collective curiosity on this topic hosts an evolving dialogue that bridges science, spirituality, and the human desire to transcend our limitations. It encourages us to embrace the vastness of a universe that may hold far more than we have dared to imagine, and it's likely that by the time you are reading this book, many more whistle-blowers and disclosures will have occurred beyond the scope of my research here.

Whether UFOs are extraterrestrial entities from beyond Earth, an as-yet-unknown part of our own reality, a threat to global security, a prophetic source of wisdom, or a projection from our collective psyche, their apparent presence stirs something deep within us. They prompt us to consider what might be the greatest mystery humanity has ever encountered.

Humanity's Biggest Secret?

When speaking to the Scientific Coalition for UAP Studies (SCU), investigative journalist Ross Coulthart stated, "Nothing could transform … humanity more than the realisation that we are not alone. This is the biggest secret in human history. … If you can get this secret out, the world will change overnight."[12] Undeterred by accusations of conspiracy theories about little green men, Coulthart asserts he has credible evidence suggesting that extraterrestrial intelligence and technology have been secretly retrieved and reverse-engineered by aeronautical enterprises in the United States.

If Coulthart's claims hold any truth, the implications reach far beyond fringe speculation. This could signal a paradigm shift in how humanity understands its place in the universe, potentially opening the door to collective transcendence on a scale that humanity has never seen before. Such a discovery would not merely rewrite our scientific understanding of reality, but fundamentally alter the trajectory of human civilization, presenting opportunities for profound advancements in technology, consciousness, and our connection to the cosmos.

The current challenge lies in how we make sense of this myriad of phenomena associated with UFOs. Our mystical friends can help us out here. As I will show throughout this case study, a non-dualist ethos and contemplative reflection provides us with a nuanced lens for understanding all possibilities associated with UFOs. As Richard Rohr emphasized earlier, a Trinitarian take on the cosmic Christ sees divinity in all things throughout the universe rather than reducing divinity down to our limited perspective of Earth and humanity.

For Rohr, if we return to our mystical routes, we can be fully prepared for the revelation of other life out there in the cosmos, or perhaps even here among us on Earth.[13] Even the Vatican has stated its openness to the idea that extraterrestrial life exists, casually asserting that they probably have their own Jesus equivalent.[14]

This is contrary to the common belief that Christians would or should be nervous about the possibility of extraterrestrial life in the cosmos. Rather than undermining our faith, we can see how it could extend our mystical sense of awe, wonder, and connection with the cosmos. And many believe that instead of being some other disconnected entity in the cosmos, this phenomenon might be closely linked to human consciousness itself.

Realms of Consciousness

Returning to journalist Ross Coulthart, he considers the dimensional speculations around physical and symbolic realms of human consciousness. Based on accounts from sources that he considers credible, Coulthart hypothesizes that UFOs may be linked to human consciousness, particularly to phenomena we often describe as psychic or telepathic. The military term for such phenomena is "psionics," and despite public ridicule and scepticism, Coulthart asserts that these kinds of capabilities are real. His confidence stems not only from research but from personal encounters with evidence that he claims has convinced him of their legitimacy.

Coulthart claims that the U.S. government is aware of extraordinary human capabilities and that UFO sightings might play a role in activating or amplifying our awareness of these latent abilities. He points to speculations about quantum links between human consciousness and an external, possibly non-human intelligence or external field of consciousness associated with UFOs. This idea aligns with a growing body of thought suggesting that UFOs might not just be physical objects but manifestations of a deeper, interconnected reality.

This hypothesis challenges conventional thinking about UFOs, suggesting they aren't just extraterrestrial craft but potentially a bridge between physical and metaphysical realms. If the likes of Coulthart are correct, the phenomenon may not only point outward to the cosmos but also inward, encouraging us to reconsider the nature of consciousness, reality, and our place within it. Could UFOs be a kind of cosmic mirror, reflecting back to us abilities and dimensions of existence we have yet to fully understand?

Intuition and Pre-cognition

One of Coulthart's key insights comes from his conversations with UFO witnesses and experiencers. When he asks whether they've ever felt a strong sense of intuition or pre-cognition—an ability to access realms beyond ordinary perception—they often respond emotionally, admitting they've kept such experiences secret out of fear of ridicule. For many, these sensations of "second sight" are deeply personal, yet they may hold the key to understanding the phenomenon.

Regardless of our personal beliefs on such claims, this is a transcendental realm in which people have legitimate experiences they can't explain other than it consolidates their sense of cosmic connection. Coulthart argues that this intuitive, pre-cognitive ability might allow certain individuals to engage with external phenomena in ways that humanity has yet to consciously recognize or understand.

Coulthart suggests this untapped potential is a crucial piece of the puzzle in our growing understanding of UFOs. Far from being mere spectators, humans may possess latent abilities that not only connect us to the phenomenon but also invite us to reconsider the boundaries of our consciousness and the universe itself—the search for potential portals to other dimensions of reality and consciousness.[15]

The Pentagon Whistle-Blower

Since becoming a prominent whistle-blower, Luis Elizondo has consistently suggested that UAPs may not be fully understood within a strictly materialist framework. Across numerous interviews, and in his book *Imminent*, he points to the potential importance of consciousness, human perception, and non-traditional or altered realities when attempting to make sense of these encounters.[16]

Elizondo is the former head of the Pentagon's Advanced Aerospace Threat Identification Program (AATIP). This was a secretive U.S. Department of Defense initiative that investigated reports of unidentified aerial phenomena (UAP). The existence of AATIP has been officially acknowledged, confirming that government departments have taken the UAP issue seriously and devoted resources to its study.

Rather than dismissing UAPs as purely physical or mechanical objects, Elizondo encourages a more expansive framework—one that includes dimensions of subjectivity, awareness, and possibly even intentional interaction with human observers. Key to understanding the common features observed in this phenomenon, Elizondo has coined what he calls the five observables of UFO/UAP craft: sudden and instantaneous acceleration; hypersonic speeds without detectable signatures; low observability or active cloaking; transmedium travel across air, water, and space; and positive lift without any visible means of propulsion.

Elizondo suggests that the phenomenon may interact with human consciousness in ways that challenge conventional physics, pointing to encounters that blur the line between objective events and subjective experience. He has also referenced the U.S. government's historical interest in remote viewing programs, such as Project Stargate, to demonstrate a long-standing institutional willingness to investigate non-material or psi-based phenomena.

These suggestions frame UAP not only as a technological mystery but as a potential epistemological rupture, requiring new models of understanding that integrate consciousness and perception. Elizondo's openness to these ideas places him at the crossroads of intelligence, technoscience, and modern mysticism. And he believes that our ancestors may have been as familiar with this phenomenon as we are today.

An Ancestral Phenomenon?

Elizondo points to examples across history and cultures that he believes challenge our understanding of the unknown and raise questions about the nature of belief. In Western Australia, for instance, there are 4000-year-old Aboriginal rock paintings depicting the Wandjina, spirit beings with large white heads, big eyes, and little or no mouths.

Similarly, in Peru, there exists a 1300-year-old image of a Mayan king seated in what appears to be a spaceship. For the likes on Elizondo, these ancient depictions, separated by vast distances and centuries, suggest that different cultures and times have recorded encounters with beings or phenomena that defy explanation.

Elizondo draws attention to these kinds of stories, such as the Cherokee myth about glowing people who descended to Earth, lived briefly among the Cherokee, and then ascended to become the stars. Despite the geographic and temporal differences, the striking similarities between these myths provoke the question: Are these stories products of human imagination, and if they are, what do they tell us about our cross-generational and cross-cultural projections? Are they more than imagined projections they reflect some other deeper knowledge or shared experience? Or are modern mythologies, like the UFO movement, projecting their presuppositions onto symbology of other historical and cultural origins unrelated to technology?

Some archaeologists are rightly sceptical of claims that cave or rock art represents literal encounters with extraterrestrials.[17] Instead, such imagery is usually interpreted as symbolically or culturally rooted, emerging from masks, ritual practices, shamanic visions, and anthropomorphic fusions that carried deep meaning within their societies. Yet this does not diminish their fascination: if such motifs recur across cultures, perhaps they speak to archetypal patterns that have been inherited across evolutionary and memetic terrains.

In this sense, the figures we project as "aliens" may in fact bond us more closely to our ancestors than we realize, reflecting a shared symbolic imagination that continues to shape our responses to mystery. Our contemporary fixation on UFOs could therefore be understood less as evidence of external visitations and more as the latest manifestation of humanity's enduring techno-spiritual imagination—an imagination that adapts to each epoch's tools, fears, and longings, while still echoing ancient archetypes within our collective psychology.

Evidence of Portals?

Whether we approach these images as evidence of literal portals mediated by non-human intelligences, as symbolic thresholds into cross-ancestral consciousness, or as some elusive synergy of both, they continue to stir profound transcendental interests. In this sense, rock art does more than record the past: it gestures towards the timeless human impulse to imagine and encounter portals—doorways between worlds—that remain as compelling in our own techno-spiritual age as they were for our ancestors.

Ross Coulthart claims Native American rock art offers depictions in other ancient cultures as potential evidence of portals—or at least our conceptual awareness of portals—in symbols suggesting a connection between human consciousness and other realms. Spirals, concentric circles, and figures interacting with these "gateways" reflect a shared human curiosity about the universe and a belief in accessing alternate dimensions. These artworks, if they are preserving lost knowledge or intuitively exploring metaphysical ideas, resonate with the modern hypothesis that consciousness itself may be a key to understanding phenomena like UFOs.[18]

Jacques Vallée considered how these UFO experiences might not be evidence of alien visitation in the traditional sense, but of a phenomenon that interacts with the human mind in ways we do not yet fully understand. As he suggests, it's possible that UFOs—or the experiences and symbols associated with them—could represent some other form of consciousness or intelligence that transcends conventional understanding.

This perspective challenges the assumption that Hollywood invented UFOs purely for entertainment. Instead, and similar to my earlier points, it suggests that the archetypes in film may reflect a deeper, collective yearning for understanding, transcendence, and connection with the unknown.

The Collective Unconscious

Instead of dismissing UFOs as purely fictional constructs in popular culture, sceptical takes can still consider how they reflect a longing for connection with the unknown and a desire to explore the mysteries of existence itself. Furthermore, we can consider how they reflect a physical reality and experiential phenomena that has been either visiting us or recurring in the psyche for millennia. This suggests certain symbols and myths appear across cultures as part of the collective unconscious.[19]

Either way, Elizondo among others argues that these kinds of myths and depictions highlight a universal response to the unknown. When humans encounter something beyond their understanding, they often turn to religion or spiritual explanations to make sense of it. As a species, we have a deep tendency to interpret the unexplainable through the dual lens of belief versus non-belief, rather than simply accepting that we don't know.

Elizondo points to a historical example from World War II when American bombers and cargo planes landed on remote Polynesian islands. The islanders, unfamiliar with modern technology, interacted with the pilots and received a small portion of their cargo. After the planes departed, the islanders constructed wooden effigies of the aircraft and performed rituals in hopes of bringing the planes back with more supplies.[20]

Elizondo identifies this as a cargo cult, a phenomenon where the encounter with advanced technology inspired new beliefs and practices. He argues that this mirrors the way ancient cultures might have interpreted strange or unexplained phenomena.

The perceptual challenges of understanding unexplained phenomena are not a thing of our ancestral past. It is something humans are still grappling with today.

UFOs, Technology, and Religion

In *American Cosmic*, Diana Pasulka argues that focusing on whether UFOs are real misses the point. Instead, she suggests examining the meaning of UFO experiences for individuals, as these encounters often lead to profound personal transformations, altering belief systems and contributing to what is now a global phenomenon. Although distinct from traditional religion, Pasulka describes this belief system as "religion-like."[21]

Drawing from her research in religious studies, Pasulka notes a recurring historical theme of people interpreting unknown phenomena in the sky based on the beliefs of their time. She shows how so-called paranormal experiences are deeply embedded within the history and traditions of the Catholic Church. One example in Pasulka's research involves a nineteenth-century nun who reportedly witnessed a glowing orb hovering above her head while she lay in bed at night.

This event was not only seen by the nun herself but also by the Mother Superior of the convent, lending it a degree of credibility within the religious community. At the time, the phenomenon was interpreted through a theological lens: the orb was believed to be the manifestation of a lost soul seeking release from purgatory. Pasulka uses this story to illustrate how experiences we might today associate with UFOs or UAPs—glowing orbs, radiant lights, strange visitations—have long been present in religious settings but were traditionally understood within the framework of Catholic theology.

Pasulka's work suggests that modern language labels such as "extraterrestrial" or "paranormal" could just as easily be interpreted as divine or mystical, depending on the cultural context. In doing so, Pasulka bridges the gap between contemporary UAP phenomena and historical religious experience, arguing that the two may be more connected than they initially appear.

While analysing modern UFO encounters alongside historical religious experiences, Diana Walsh Pasulka discusses the case of St. Francis of Assisi. According to historical accounts, St. Francis experienced a powerful vision in which he was struck by a radiant, torch-like beam of light—an encounter that left him marked with the stigmata, the wounds of Christ. Within the Church, this event has long been interpreted as a miraculous sign of divine favour, affirming St. Francis' sanctity through a profoundly spiritual lens.[22]

Life-Altering Transcendence

Pasulka invites readers to consider, again, how similar this account is to descriptions of modern UFO or UAP experiences, where witnesses often report being struck by beams of light, experiencing bodily effects, and interpreting the event as life-altering or transcendent. By comparing such historical and contemporary narratives, Pasulka argues that many religious phenomena—visions, lights, bodily marks—may share a common experiential structure with what we now classify as UFO encounters.

So, these stories and phenomena needn't be deemed as mutually exclusive. As Pasulka suggests, they might be different cultural expressions of the same underlying phenomenon, filtered through the expectations, language, and cosmologies of their respective times.

People who witness UFOs often experience a shift in their understanding of the cosmos, which affects their work, relationships, and worldview at a fundamental level. Pasulka draws key parallels that align with mystical and transcendent themes that we have adopted thus far.

Pasulka also examines how technology plays a pivotal role in this modern form of spirituality, with UFOs symbolizing a new kind of transcendence through advanced technology. The individuals studying UFOs frequently adopt a techno-spiritual approach, resembling traditional religious devotion. UFO research communities, often led by charismatic figures, develop rituals and shared beliefs, mirroring the behaviours seen in religious sects or cults.

Blurring Boundaries

Furthermore, Pasulka highlights the idea that encounters with UFOs can be interpreted as contact with extraterrestrial or divine beings, blurring the lines between the sacred and the profane. These experiences invoke a search for personal and collective transformation, much like the spiritual awakenings sought in religious traditions.

In essence, Pasulka argues that UFO phenomena function as a modern form of mysticism, where the boundaries of the material, spiritual, and technological realms increasingly overlap, echoing the transformative power once attributed to religious experiences. Pasulka's research highlights the spiritual and religious dimensions of the UFO phenomenon, making the case that the way people experience and interpret UFO encounters shares many characteristics with religious experiences. This suggests that UFOs can be understood as a contemporary manifestation of humanity's search for meaning, belonging, and connection with a greater cosmic order.

Pasulka suggests that the UFO phenomenon should not be reduced to simple explanations of extraterrestrial visitation but should be viewed as a complex and significant element of our modern mythos. The transcendental nature of these experiences and the messages people take from them are transformational. Even the highest authority of the Catholic Church is aware of this.

A Prophecy for the Pope

Ufologist and theologian Gabriel Piedra claims that Pope Francis has had a long-standing and deeply personal interest in UFOs (or UAPs), rooted in experiences and relationships formed during his time in Argentina.[23] As a younger man, Jorge Bergoglio (later Pope Francis) was initially sceptical of extraterrestrial phenomena, but this changed significantly around 1988 after he became close with two prominent Argentinian ufologists, Pedro Romaniuk and Ángel Cristo Acoglanis.

The three met at a gathering where they discussed topics such as life after death and extraterrestrial intelligence. During this meeting, Acoglanis—who claimed to be in contact with "light beings" residing in a well-known UFO hotspot in Mount Uritorco, Argentina—delivered a prophecy that Bergoglio would one day become Pope. Although Bergoglio laughed it off at the time, the moment seemed to stay with him.

Over the following years, he became increasingly open to the reality of the phenomenon, eventually developing a belief that extraterrestrial intelligences are not only real but possibly divine in origin. Piedra suggests that this shift had a broader impact on Bergoglio's worldview, softening his once-conservative stance and influencing the more inclusive and progressive approach that has defined his papacy. Pope Francis's interest in UAPs is not marginal, Piedra claims, but central to his theological and philosophical outlook.

Collecting Testimonies

Within the Vatican, the Pontifical Academy of Sciences is said to be actively collecting testimonies and data on the phenomenon from around the world. These reports are reviewed and reportedly passed along to Pope Francis himself, who takes the subject seriously.

The Vatican's increasing engagement with UAPs, including internal research and quiet preparation for a possible future revelation, echoes a broader interpretation gaining traction in both religious and academic circles: that many historical supernatural events—such as visions, Marian apparitions, or glowing orbs—might actually be early encounters with non-human intelligences.

According to Piedra, Francis sees these experiences not as irrational or fringe, but as part of a deeper mystery tied to the divine, and the Church may be slowly preparing the world for this paradigm shift.

As the likes of Ralph Blumenthal and Ross Coulthart point out, the biggest challenge on the topic of UFOs is ridicule.

Paradigms Beyond Ridicule

Blumenthal's 2017 *New York Times* article, which I return to in the closing points of this case study in Chap. 6, played a pivotal role in bringing UFOs into the mainstream media.[24] The piece not only revealed unprecedented footage of unidentified aerial phenomena (UAP) but also sparked widespread public interest, making it the most viewed article in the history of the NYT website at the time. This shift in how UFOs were portrayed—no longer fringe topics or dismissed as conspiracies—opened the door for other major outlets to cover the story.[25]

As Coulthard observes, interest in UAPs has garnered attention from several high-profile figures, including former Presidents like Jimmy Carter and Donald Trump, both of whom have publicly expressed curiosity about the phenomenon. Former President Barack Obama's communication on UFOs has shifted notably over the years. Initially, he largely dismissed questions on the subject, but in more recent years, his comments have acknowledged the legitimacy of the phenomenon.[26]

Whether these leaders truly possess inside knowledge or are simply responding to public demand is unclear, but their attention to the subject signals a collective desire for transcendence and mystery. The fact that the UFO phenomenon is being discussed at such high levels indicates that society, at large, craves something greater than what we can grasp in our "ordinary" lives.

Towards a Greater Good

Matthew Roberts, a former Naval Intelligence Cryptologist, claims to have witnessed the Navy's 2015 "Gimbal" footage of a UFO—an object seen near the USS *Theodore Roosevelt* during a training exercise.[27] The footage showed a disc-shaped object rotating mid-air, lacking visible aviation surfaces like wings or rudders. Observing its unique behaviour, Roberts described his feeling of a profound, unsettling certainty that this technology was not human-made. With his intelligence background, he had access to classified information, confirming that such sightings were not isolated events but part of a broader pattern observed by the Navy.

His fascination with these sightings grew into a near-obsession, ultimately leading him to transfer to the Office of Naval Intelligence in 2017 to pursue further analysis. Shortly after this move, Roberts began experiencing disturbing, personal encounters—describing non-human entities in his room at night, accompanied by episodes of paralysis. He connected these experiences with the confirmed sightings, reinforcing his belief that he wasn't imagining it.

What's significant here is not that we jump to conclusions about *what* this experience was. For Roberts, it's the profoundness of the experience and the seeming connection with those events after that resonate with him. The potential for psychological explanation makes this no less profound when we consider the affective persuasion this has on Roberts and his perceptions of reality thereafter.

Roberts advocates for full governmental disclosure, suggesting that even admitting ignorance about these phenomena would be a step forward. He emphasizes that understanding UFOs isn't purely a defence issue but a fundamentally human one.

Roberts argues that physics can tell us *how* these objects behave, but it's the humanities that can help us explore *why*. With retirement approaching, Roberts could have enjoyed his pension and opted for a comfortable, quiet life. But he felt compelled to sacrifice his personally security and circumstances to speak out for the collective good, convinced that this is an "open secret"—known by some, hidden from many.

Casual Dismissiveness

UFOs are an archetypal phenomenon. Even if we are sceptics, we should be strategic sceptics. Beyond the casual dismissiveness of conclusions stating, "it's *just* government technology we don't know about" or "it's *merely* a figment of our collective imagination," there's more to ponder.

The language of "just" and "merely" does not suffice here. Whether UFOs are physically out there in the world, symbolic projections from the collective psyche, or some other realm that we are yet to understand, their manifestations reflect distinct and recurring patterns of thought, behaviour, and meaning in the stories we attach to them—projections from our deepest hopes and fears. They're important.

Whether these phenomena are "real" in the conventional sense or not, they represent profound experiences that tap into deep aspects of our collective psychology. They speak to our collective angst, ethical dilemmas, and the longing for transcendence. As further examples will show, they speculate on technological progress that we could make to end poverty and energy crises, and the associated mistrust for governments and private enterprise.

When I talk to sceptics about this topic, there's often a willingness to accept there is evidence of technologies in the sky that appear to be more advanced than any human-made aircraft we are aware of. Such sceptics often conclude that secret technologies, weapons, and aircraft have always been developed by governments and private military projects, so that's *all* they are.

But this is where strategic scepticism proves helpful. If these technologies are "just" or "merely" classified projects and technological developments that are kept secret from public knowledge, then profound questions arise. Those projections from UFO believers and communities seeking disclosure takes us to transcendental realms.

Many experiencers point out that if these technologies are real and human-made, then we have not only rewritten the current laws of physics behind closed doors, but we have also conquered energy conundrums that continue to leave populations in poverty and countries battling for resources. Even the worry of paying energy bills in an otherwise peaceful domestic life dissipates under the premise of technologies that could irradicate the need for expensive energy and potentially irradicate other forms of poverty in the world.

None of this is to be scoffed at. From the laws of physics to the eradication of poverty, these human endeavours and aspirations transcend the political spectrum and take us to new frontiers in how we live our lives and the flourishing we are potentially free to pursue as global populations. Those are the kind of possibilities that arise here. It's got nothing to do with "just" or "merely."

Stories, Hopes, and Fears

As I will continue to show, the stories we tell when we tell stories about UFOs are a self-evident mythos—containing our deepest hopes, fears, dreams, threats, and aspirations. These projections from our collective psychology play out across the stories and experiences explored in this case study, and far beyond it. All are noteworthy, even those I cover only in passing.

Let's consider some of the questions arising from these projections.

Are we alone in the universe? Is there a non-human intelligence living alongside us on Earth? Do we share this reality with interdimensional intelligences we will someday understand? Are they peaceful, or do they pose a threat?

Have these intelligences existed for millennia, influencing human consciousness throughout evolution? Have we been telling stories about them since prehistorical times?

Do extraterrestrial intelligences attempt to communicate moral messages or warnings about humanity? If UFOs appear around military and nuclear sites, are they here to protect us—or should we be more concerned? Have secret human advancements in technology been developed for future wars, and did we break the current known laws of physics to invent them? Did we reverse engineer non-human technologies from crash sites, and if so, how much of our taxes have been paid for this?

If new forms of energy have been discovered, why are we still fighting over resources? Are political and economic elites stifling technological progress to maximize profits—even if it maintains poverty?

If they are human made, who made them, who owns them, and can they be weaponized against us? What kind of weaponry might already exist, and who controls it? Do we trust our governments and intelligence agencies?

Are UFOs manifestations of a higher consciousness trying to guide human evolution? Are these experiences designed to initiate transformation in those who encounter them? Could encounters with UFOs be modern expressions of ancient religious or mystical phenomena?

Do these experiences reflect a breakdown between material reality and dream, myth, or the unconscious? And if they are purely psychological, what do they reveal about our collective and cross-historical psyche?

I could go on. But you get my point.

As this case study will continue to show, the questions stimulated by this transcendental realm of possibility are endless, and this growing field of interest is being taken increasingly seriously. Whether UFOs are revealed to be advanced human technology or dismissed as collective projections through hallucinatory experiences, these represent two extreme possibilities—but neither should be reduced to the language of "just" or "merely."

Even hallucinations emerge from a complex interplay of social, psychological, and physical environments, reflecting deeper truths about the collective psyche. From the perspective of strategic scepticism, we should resist dismissing any explanation outright, as each reveals significant insights into the human condition and our interaction with the unknown.

UFOs, then, are our modern folklore, and the answers to any of those questions above are significant to how we continue to live on this planet.

Exploiting Transcendence

Chase Hughes suggests that the current era of UFO speculations might represent a psychological operation designed to unify people around a common perceived "threat" or unknown presence. The patterns are familiar: while writing this book, we've seen mysterious "drones" over New Jersey, the gradual escalation of media attention to UFOs, and congressional hearings from whistle-blowers.[28]

Hughes speculates that these elements could be creating a normalization phase—a sense of public curiosity without panic. Such a phase could culminate in a dramatic event involving advanced technology, setting the stage for a major reveal. At this point, with a shared "threat" uniting the public, the narrative could pivot towards the need for a saviour, whether in the form of state legislation, increased surveillance, military operations, or even global cooperation.

These scenarios align with historically effective strategies for manipulating collective emotion, opinion, and support for state actions. From propaganda to psychological operations, governments have long exploited shared fears or mysteries to consolidate power, shift policy, or rally populations towards specific ends. The UFO phenomenon, with its mix of mystery, awe, and potential threat, provides an ideal canvas for such strategies.

Alternative Objectives

One possibility is that governments might engineer a UFO/UAP phenomenon to serve unrelated objectives, such as increasing defence budgets, advancing surveillance capabilities, or fostering international alliances. The phenomenon could be entirely staged or partially exaggerated, designed to harness the public's innate yearning for meaning, mystery, and unity.

Alternatively, the state may know of a genuine phenomenon or threat but choose to reveal it in a gradual, controlled way. Given the vast disparities in awareness and concern across populations, this approach could ensure public unity and preparedness while preventing mass panic. This scenario suggests that the government might experiment with various narratives and communication strategies to gauge and shape public reactions before any major disclosure.

In either case, these strategies exploit or manage the transcendental urges and reactions of the masses. UFOs tap into deep-seated archetypes of mystery, awe, and the unknown, offering fertile ground for collective meaning-making. For those deeply engaged with the phenomenon, it can be jarring to encounter scepticism or indifference.

Furthermore, whistle-blowers face ridicule, harassment, and potential harm for disclosing classified information and experiences—especially from within the military.

Air Force Whistle-Blower

Jake Barber is a former Air Force pilot and whistle-blower who has come forward with claims about a covert Pentagon program. Barber alleges that the U.S. government has been secretly retrieving and studying UFO craft for years—and he says he's had direct encounters with what he believes were non-human intelligences and technologies. Barber remained anonymous as one of Ross Coulthart's sources for over two years before taking the leap—in congress and on the public stage.

Barber describes his experiences with UAP and non-human intelligence (NHI) as transcendent, life-altering, and quasi-religious.[29] As a helicopter pilot in a covert craft retrieval program, Barber recounts recovering an egg-shaped craft unlike anything of human origin. The object, approximately 20 feet long—about the size of a large SUV—was metallic with a pearly white sheen. Seated within 150 feet of it, Barber couldn't identify what it was, but high-ranking officials later confirmed to him that it was of non-human origin.

Barber claims he also retrieved a gong-shaped craft. It was during this operation that he had an extraordinary experience that changed his life. As he approached the retrieval site in his helicopter, Barber began feeling an overwhelming rush of emotions—happiness, sadness, and a profound sense of beauty. The closer he got to the craft, the more intense these feelings became, as though something was tuning into his soul.

While attempting to focus on his mission, Barber felt guided by this unseen presence, which provided him with a deep understanding of the importance of his task. After securing the object beneath his helicopter, he experienced an even greater sense of connection. In flight, Barber described being possessed by the most beautiful spirit imaginable—a feminine energy he likened to the spirit of God, though not in a masculine form. He described it as a frequency or force that seemed to possess and guide him during and after the incident.

This telepathic connection to a non-human intelligence—whether from the craft itself or another entity controlling it—left Barber with a lasting sense of protection and purpose. It was, in his words, the most beautiful experience of his life, and it continues to influence him to this day.

Summoned by Psionics

Barber believes the craft he retrieved was summoned by a special "psionics" team—individuals with psychic abilities capable of telepathic and spiritual communication with UAPs. This team, he claims, could persuade or even guide craft to land through mental engagement. Such abilities, which military figures like Don Bales and Luis Elizondo have also acknowledged, suggest a deeper interplay between consciousness and these enigmatic phenomena.

Barber has recently founded Skywatcher: a newly formed research organization aiming to establish a rigorous, transparent, and scientifically valid framework for investigating this phenomenon. In August 2024, his team conducted an operation involving a psionic asset, which reportedly summoned a UAP. This event culminated in an unusual "psychic dogfight" between two unidentified craft, illustrating the team's innovative and proactive approach to studying UAPs.

Now supported by strategic adviser Matthew Pines, the group has released a structured investigative protocol known as the Skywatcher Discovery Framework. This framework outlines a six-level progression from anecdotal accounts to full scientific validation and public integration.

Beginning with preliminary observations (Level 1), Skywatcher collects structured, multi-modal sensor data in field conditions (Level 2), moving towards hypothesis testing (Level 3) and independent verification and peer review (Level 4), with the goal of eventual public dissemination (Level 5) and cultural or scientific integration (Level 6). The team insists that transparency, methodological discipline, and rigorous experimentation are essential to moving beyond the current ambiguity and towards solid, peer-reviewed scientific knowledge.

Classifications and Techniques

Skywatcher's efforts currently focus on gathering real-time evidence using both advanced instrumentation and novel interaction techniques. Their classification system divides observed phenomena into nine proprietary UAP classes, which fall under three broader categories: mechanical craft (like the well-documented "Tic Tac"), luminous or plasma-based phenomena (orbs, beams, crystal-like lights), and creature-like entities (jellyfish-like forms with electrical pulses).

According to Barber, these are not hypothetical but have been directly observed and recorded with multi-sensor corroboration. One particularly bold claim involves the "flying jellyfish," described as a purple, metallic, contracting form that has been detected and imaged under controlled conditions.

Central to Skywatcher's strategy are two experimental techniques for "interacting" with the phenomena. The first is electromechanical signalling, internally dubbed the "dog whistle"—a machine-based system that emits specific signals which reportedly correlate 100% of the time with UAP appearances during trials. This method, currently assessed at Level 3, includes radar, visual, and infrared detections from multiple vantage points, and has reportedly yielded consistent results under controlled conditions.

The second method, neuromeditative interaction (also termed "psionics"), involves human operators engaging in focused meditative states to summon or detect UAPs. This more subjective technique is currently at Level 2, showing promising but less reproducible outcomes. However, practitioners have reportedly made accurate precognitive predictions about the timing and nature of UAP events, with physiological data collection underway to help quantify their experiences.[30]

Collective Intuition and Relief

When interviewing Barber and Pines, Coulthart expresses his astonishment at such claims from the Skywatcher team.[31] He asserts that these findings could provide some of the most significant scientific findings and existential breakthroughs ever made in human history. For Barber, this is a welcomed possibility not just for his team, but for the general public and the collective psyche. He believes our transcendental senses are already onto something, and such findings would provide significant relief among the public.

Barber challenges the idea that revelations about UAPs, aliens, and telepathy would cause widespread shock among the public. Instead, he argues, they would bring ontological relief to people, affirming a collective intuition—the shared, deep knowing—that there is more to life than we currently understand.[32] Barber's work offers a profound window into the intersection of technology, consciousness, and transcendence. His experience of love, sadness, and divine connection echoes similar themes found in other encounters with UAPs and NHI.

While Barber's story involves military personnel and advanced intelligence operations, the next chapter shifts to civilian stories, beginning with a group of children in a school playground in Zimbabwe. As we shall see throughout these stories, despite the stark contrast in settings, many accounts share remarkable commonalities—telepathic communication with a non-human intelligence, profound messages about humanity, and transcendental realms that are transformative for those who experience them.

These encounters and epiphanies invite us to consider the universal significance of UFO sightings.[33]

Notes

1. Jung (1967) explored the figure of Hermes, the Greek messenger god, as a symbolic mediator between the conscious and unconscious. For Jung, Hermes embodied the trickster archetype—holding opposites together and guiding the inner journey of psychological transformation.
2. Coulthart (2025a).
3. Later in this chapter, I examine the work of Luis Elizondo, who is currently under scrutiny for multiple instances of mistaken revelation—having presented "evidence" of UFOs that was later shown to be inaccurate or fabricated (2025). That is not to discredit Elizondo entirely, but it shows why we must remain critically attuned to the political tensions of transcendental topics and anomalous phenomena. These tensions and powerplays are a recurring point I return to throughout these case studies. Likewise, while Evans (2025b) does not suggest we should stop taking the UFO topic seriously, he critically interrogates the mythology of Skin Walker

Ranch to show why this critical lens is crucial when we scrutinize the formation of collective storytelling around "infectious" topics and cases.

4. Jung (1959).
5. McKenna (1991).
6. See Pasulka (2019); Evans (2025a, 2025b).
7. Pasulka (2019, 2023).
8. Vallée (1979, 1990, 1992); Vallée and Aubeck (2010).
9. Fridman (2022).
10. Lewis (2015).
11. Jeremy Corbell (2025) has cautioned that political elites may one day fabricate or amplify a narrative of an alien threat—such as a craft approaching Earth from deep space—as a psychological operation to justify militarization, surveillance, or global control. While he maintains that UAPs are real and worthy of investigation, he warns against the exploitation of such narratives for geopolitical ends. At the time of writing, an object designated 3I/ATLAS is attracting attention as it moves through the solar system. Although most astronomers consider it likely to be a comet, its anomalous features—unusual velocity and the absence of a visible tail or other typical markers—have sparked speculation. For some, this appears to confirm Corbell's warning; for others, including Avi Loeb, it raises the possibility that the object could be an artificial craft. Either way, 3I/ATLAS illustrates how celestial anomalies readily generate transcendental narratives, entangling the political, social, cosmic, and psychological tensions of the collective psyche.
12. Coulthart (2025b).
13. Rohr (2019a, 2019b).
14. Paul Thigpen (2022) makes the point that philosophers, scientists, and theologians—from Plato to Isaac Newton and C. S. Lewis—all pontificated the existence of life beyond Earth. Perhaps surprisingly, the Vatican has continued this line of inquiry in modern life. Thigpen provides an historical overview of conversations on extraterrestrial intelligence (ETI) within Catholicism. Catholic saints, such as Pope Saint John Paul II, Saint Pio of Pietrelcina (Padre Pio), and Blessed Anne Catherine Emmerich, considered the possibility of ETI, reflecting the openness with which the Church has historically acknowledged the potential for such a discovery. See also: Rohr (2019b) and Piedra (2025).
15. See Coulthart (2025a) for a detailed conversation on these claims from Skywatcher—a team of scientists systematically investigating psionics.
16. Elizondo (2024). See also Coulthart (2024).
17. Lewis-Williams and Dowson (1988) make the case that cave art derives from shamanic visions, ritual, and altered states of consciousness. Lewis-Williams (2002) further explores rock art as symbolic, visionary, and

culturally rooted rather than literal. Bahn (2010) provides a critical overview of rock art interpretations, emphasizing caution against "pseudoscientific" alien readings.

18. Coulthart (2023).
19. See also: Jung (1959) for UFOs as projections of archetypal imagery onto modern skies; Kripal (2016) exploring UFOs and anomalous phenomena as modern expressions of sacred mythmaking; Partridge (2005) arguing that UFO beliefs belong to wider contemporary re-enchantment and "techno-spiritual" currents.
20. Elizondo (2024).
21. See also Fridman (2021) for a long-form conversation on this research.
22. Pasulka (2019); Fridman (2021).
23. Piedra (2025).
24. Cooper et al. (2017)
25. This is not to suggest more truths have been exposed about the phenomena—there could be multiple levels of misinformation circulating or being strategically disseminated, and we should remain aware of that possibility. Nonetheless, it is the case that the reporting on this topic has shifted and public discourse has gained traction in recent years.
26. See Obama (2015) followed by Obama (2021). This chapter was written before the more recent UFO statements between Trump and Obama in 2026, which led to Trump suggesting he will release all files relating to the phenomenon.
27. Motskin (2023).
28. Hughes (2025).
29. For a full account of Barber's profile and the profiles of Skywatcher team members, see Coulthart (2025a) and the Skywatcher (2025); SkywatcherHQ (2025).
30. Skywatcher carefully distinguishes between correlation and causation but highlights that ongoing, structured fieldwork is starting to produce data that goes beyond simple anecdotes. According to Barber and his team, their approach uses controls, comparisons, and attempts to disprove findings, following standard scientific methods. They combine video, sensor readings, and visual sightings, assessing each with different levels of confidence rather than claiming absolute proof. The goal is not just to record unusual events, but to encourage scientists, public institutions, and policymakers to take the reality—and possible consequences—of unexplained aerial phenomena seriously (Skywatcher, 2025; SkywatcherHQ, 2025).
31. Coulthart (2025a).
32. Barber (2025).
33. However, despite the sacred nature of his experience, Barber explains that he and his team have experience physical injuries from this work (see

Barber, 2025). In one incident, after transporting sealed boxes—contents unknown to them—the entire team was hospitalized. They had been authorized to use lethal force if anyone attempted to interfere. The aftermath was alarming: Barber lost all his body hair, his skin began peeling, and he developed a heart murmur he'd never had before. Immunologist Garry Nolan reviewed his medical records and found strong signs of radiation exposure. With the whole team experiencing the same symptoms simultaneously, Nolan concluded it was unlikely to be a coincidence or unrelated to their work. But for Barber, the biggest concern isn't just the toll on his health—it's his safety. During a mission involving the recovery of hard drives, those fears only deepened.

Bibliography

Bahn, P. (2010). *Prehistoric Rock Art: Polemics and Progress.* Cambridge University Press.

Barber, J. (2025). UFO Whistleblower Jake Barber Would '100% Testify' under Oath to Congress. *Reality Check.* [Online video]. Retrieved April 11, 2025, from https://www.youtube.com/watch?v=t37-SKj4rtY

Cooper, H., Blumenthal, R., & Kean, L. (2017). Glowing Auras and 'Black Money': The Pentagon's Mysterious U.F.O. Program. *The New York Times*, 16 December. Retrieved April 11, 2025, from https://www.nytimes.com/2017/12/16/us/politics/pentagon-program-ufo-harry-reid.html

Corbell, J. (2025). Jeremy Corbell's 2027 UFO Threat Warning: Disinformation or Disclosure? *UnexplainedIE.* YouTube. Retrieved August 20, 2025, from https://www.youtube.com/watch?v=8xIW3yr0GL8

Coulthart, R. (2023). *In Plain Sight: An Investigation into UFOs and Impossible Science.* HarperCollins.

Coulthart, R. (2024). Confessions of a UFO Hunter: Ross Coulthart Interviews Lue Elizondo. *Reality Check.* [Online video]. Retrieved April 11, 2025, from https://www.youtube.com/watch?v=wgM5V44eQHU

Coulthart, R. (2025a). Jake Barber: Skywatcher is 'Finding Things That Are Not Known Objects'. *Reality Check.* [Online video]. Retrieved April 11, 2025, from https://www.youtube.com/watch?v=t5e5z1bcBgQ

Coulthart, R. (2025b). *Ross Coulthart Reveals the Night That Convinced Him to Investigate UFOs.* Retrieved April 10, 2025, from https://www.youtube.com/watch?v=VuCPbavls0U

Elizondo, L. (2024). *Imminent: Inside the Pentagon's Hunt for UFOs.* William Morrow.

Evans, J. (2025a). Psychedelic Policy: Speed Up or Slow Down? *Ecstatic Integration.* Retrieved June 30, 2025, from https://www.ecstaticintegration.org/p/psychedelic-policy-speed-up-or-slow

Evans, J. (2025b). Fake UFOs in Congress, and Nine Other Stories I'm Following. *Ecstatic Integration*, 6 May. Retrieved June 16, 2025, from https://www.ecstaticintegration.org/p/fake-ufos-in-congress-and-nine-other

Fridman, L. (2021). *Lex Fridman Podcast: Diana Pasulka: UFOs, Religion, and the Search for Meaning* [Podcast]. Retrieved September 10, 2024, from https://www.lexfridman.com/diana-pasulka

Fridman, L. (2022). *Lex Fridman Podcast: Garry Nolan: UFOs, Science, and the Search for Extraterrestrial Intelligence* [Podcast]. Retrieved September 10, 2024, from https://www.lexfridman.com/garry-nolan

Hughes, C. (2025). Society and Psy-ops: Drone UFOs, Cognitive Manipulation and the Rise of Public Threat Narratives. *Behavior Panel/YouTube Channel*, published c. 6 months ago. Retrieved June 30, 2025, from https://www.youtube.com/

Jung, C. G. (1959). *Four Archetypes: Mother, Rebirth, Spirit, Trickster*. Princeton University Press.

Jung, C. G. (1967). *Alchemical Studies* (R. F. C. Hull, Trans.). Routledge. (The Collected Works of C.G. Jung, Vol. 13).

Kelsey, D. (2025). FR RICHARD ROHR: THE MYSTIC MENTOR. *Arcane Horizons* [Substack]. Retrieved June 30, 2025, from https://dkelsey.substack.com/p/fr-richard-rohr-the-mystic-mentor

Kripal, J. J. (2016). *Secret Body: Erotic and Esoteric Currents in the History of Religions*. University of Chicago Press.

Lewis, D. (2015). Reagan and Gorbachev Agreed to Pause the Cold War in Case of an Alien Invasion. *Smithsonian Magazine*, 25 November. Retrieved April 10, 2025, from https://www.smithsonianmag.com/smart-news/reagan-and-gorbachev-agreed-pause-cold-war-case-alien-invasion-180957402/

Lewis-Williams, D. (2002). *The Mind in the Cave: Consciousness and the Origins of Art*. Thames & Hudson.

Lewis-Williams, D., & Dowson, T. (1988). The Signs of All Times: Entoptic Phenomena in Upper Palaeolithic Art. *Current Anthropology, 29*(2), 201–245.

McKenna, T. (1991). *The Archaic Revival: Speculations on Psychedelic Mushrooms, the Amazon, Virtual Reality, UFOs, Evolution, Shamanism, the Rebirth of the Goddess, and the End of History*. HarperSanFrancisco.

Motskin, Y. (2023). Messengers. *Encounters*, Season 1, Episode 3. [Netflix series episode]. Netflix.

Obama, B. (2015). *President Barack Obama Denies Knowledge of Aliens*. [YouTube video] *Jimmy Kimmel Live*, 12 March. Retrieved June 30, 2025, from https://www.youtube.com/watch?v=EYzRY2XpLBk

Obama, B. (2021). Obama Says UFO Sightings Are Real. [YouTube video] *FOX59 News*, published circa 2021. Retrieved June 30, 2025, from https://www.youtube.com/watch?v=u1hNYs55sqs

Partridge, C. (2005). *The Re-Enchantment of the West: Alternative Spiritualities, Sacralization, Popular Culture and Occulture*. T&T Clark.

Pasulka, D. (2019). *American Cosmic: UFOs, Religion, Technology*. Oxford University Press.

Pasulka, D. (2023). *Encounters: Experiences with Nonhuman Intelligences*. St. Martin's Press.

Piedra, G. (2025). *Is Jesus an Alien? Pope Francis' Interest in UAPs Explained*. Retrieved April 10, 2025, from https://www.youtube.com/watch?v=2izhNXn1Msc

Rohr, R. (2019a). *Richard Rohr on THE UNIVERSAL CHRIST*. Retrieved April 10, 2025, from https://www.youtube.com/watch?v=KD7B3wr3xeY

Rohr, R. (2019b). *The Universal Christ: How a Forgotten Reality Can Change Everything We See, Hope For, and Believe*. SPCK Publishing.

Skywatcher. (2025). *Defining the Future of Aerial Intelligence*. Retrieved April 11, 2025, from https://skywatcher.ai/

SkywatcherHQ. (2025). *SkywatcherHQ*. YouTube channel. Retrieved April 11, 2025, from https://www.youtube.com/@SkywatcherHQ

Thigpen, P. (2022). *Extraterrestrial Intelligence and the Catholic Faith: Are We Alone in the Universe with God and the Angels?* TAN Books.

Vallée, J. (1979). *Messengers of Deception: UFO Contacts and Cults*. Harper & Row.

Vallée, J. (1990). *Dimensions: A Casebook of Alien Contact*. Contemporary Books.

Vallée, J. (1992). *Confrontations: A Scientist's Search for Alien Contact*. Contemporary Books.

Vallée, J., & Aubeck, C. (2010). *Wonders in the Sky: Unexplained Aerial Objects from Antiquity to Modern Times*. Penguin.

CHAPTER 6

Encounters and Epiphanies

This case study can only skim the surface of the countless UFO stories, experiences, and phenomena found in the vast and growing datasets available to us. This chapter will offer further examples that capture some of the recurring transcendental themes tied to UFO encounters: awe and wonder; a sense of unity and connectedness; altered perceptions of time or timelessness; intense curiosity coupled with a surprising fearlessness; reverence for the unknown; and experiences of personal transformation and insight.

As we'll see, these themes aren't unique to UFOs; they appear frequently across various transcendental experiences, themes that I'll continue to explore in later chapters. Beyond these themes, this chapter reveals two broader insights.

Firstly, through non-dual thinking and contemplative practice, a mystical approach offers a way to remain open to possibilities, while honouring unique experiences that contribute to a greater whole. Rohr's prelude already briefed us to avoid seeing the possibility of extraterrestrial life as a threat to religion—Catholicism and Islam are preparing to break the news that we are not alone to their followers.[1]

This mystical approach helps us understand our existence and our place in the universe more holistically and live comfortably with mystery and paradox.

D. Kelsey, *Transcendence and Collective Psychology*,
https://doi.org/10.1007/978-3-032-09495-7_6

Second, transcendental experiences, even when personally transformative, are often steeped in tension and conflict. People may fear ridicule, and social or political powers sometimes suppress or control our understanding and access to transcendental realms. As we continue, the characteristics of transcendence and its role in collective psychology will become even more apparent.

Terrestrial Neighbours

Our cosmic gaze, while often directed outward to the skies and stars, also looks closer to home. While writing this book, and during the latest UAP congressional hearings from whistle-blowers in the U.S., it has become an increasingly accepted possibility that UFOs are not only real, but currently unknown lifeforms live here among us rather than travelling here from other planets.

Given we have only explored 5% of Earth's oceans, there is a growing suspicion that these craft live somewhere under the sea rather than "out there" in the cosmos. Or as we shall see later, the portal to those alternative intelligences might be accessed via our own consciousness with the help of mind-altering substances.

Whether they are from out space, deep in the oceans, currently unknown dimensions, or symbolic and intelligential dimensions in our collective psyche, they are framed through the celestial wonder of our cosmic gaze and sense of celestial connection with all that is known and unknown in the universe.

A School in Zimbabwe

September 16, 1994, Ariel School, Zimbabwe. While teachers were in a meeting, a group of children playing outside spotted a bright light descending into the school field. Witnesses reported seeing a strange craft land and a being emerge—described as having a large head, oversized black eyes, and a suit-like body.[2]

One student recounted that, although the being never physically touched her, its penetrating gaze felt as if it connected with every part of her being. Multiple students described experiencing telepathy, receiving overwhelming messages about the importance of caring for the environment. They collectively expressed a sense of responsibility, voicing concerns that technology was harming wildlife and the planet, and acknowledging that humanity's long-term safety depended on a change in our priorities.

As the incident unfolded, chaos erupted in the playground. The children soon faced disbelief and ridicule from teachers, reporters, and even their parents, who were afraid of the stigma associated with such claims. The aftermath was traumatic, and many children felt ostracized by authority figures who dismissed their experiences.

Over thirty years later, many witnesses publicly stand by their accounts. Recently, the headteacher revealed her own experiences, including an alleged alien abduction where she felt something being inserted into her abdomen. After leaving her deeply troubled and contemplating suicide, she claims the aliens returned more than once, offering the opportunity for her to go with them. She said she chose to stay, driven by her commitment to the school and its students.

In the wake of the incident, witnesses have come together to reclaim their stories, fostering a sense of solidarity and pride. One former student reflected on how the experience helped him understand his African identity and spirituality. Another emphasized the importance of acknowledging such experiences as human stories that cultivate empathy, regardless of differing beliefs about the event's veracity. They suggest that the question should not be "Are we alone?" but rather "Who are we?"—inviting reflection on how others might perceive us.

What's significant about these stories are those experiences and meanings that such young people took from them. Even if a sceptic claims they were all influenced by their immersion in popular culture and shared similar accounts due to the shared influence of television and Hollywood, the fact that such deep and profound meanings occurred then, and they collectively maintain them to this day, is significant.

The transcendental themes of connection, shared experience, environmental responsibilities, and technological warnings are recurring traits of UFO stories—the idea that a superior form of intelligence seeks to prophesize messages to us for collective safety and wellbeing.

One Lie Creates Chaos?

Amidst these testimonies, a more critical voice also emerged. One of the former students claimed he fabricated the entire incident to escape lessons, pointing to a shiny rock as the catalyst for the ensuing excitement when he said it was a UFO.[3] He speculated on why the story gained such traction, suggesting it might have stemmed from children's imaginations running wild. If he had indeed witnessed an alien encounter, he said he would have seized the opportunity to communicate with it, firmly asserting that the other students had conspired to lie.

This former student also questioned why aliens would travel such vast distances from other galaxies only to land in a school playground and then leave shortly after. However, this criticism operates within a limited and presumptuous scope: it overlooks the potential for symbolic, psychological, and interdimensional interpretations that can enrich our understanding of what UFOs might be. We cannot definitively assert that these beings are extraterrestrial visitors from another galaxy; they may represent aspects of our own reality on Earth that remain shrouded in mystery beyond our perceptual capacities.

Moreover, these encounters could be manifestations of psychological projections arising from collective experiences and cultural narratives, as discussed earlier. By limiting the conversation to a straightforward interpretation of alien visitation, we risk dismissing the deeper meanings and implications that such experiences might hold for our understanding of consciousness, interconnectedness, and the nature of reality itself.

Pause for a Moment

Let's apply some strategic scepticism here and imagine the former student who claims to have lied is telling the truth. That could make these profound accounts *more* significant when we consider the children's psychological states that were assessed at the time (which I return to below), the consistency of their accounts, and the fact that they've collectively maintained those claims without wavering to this day. The messages these children took from this experience were not only profound and consistent across a large group, but they've stuck with them into adulthood with clarity and consistency.

Regardless of what this phenomenon might be, the experiences reported by so many witnesses who maintain their accounts to this day reflect distinct transcendental themes—an "unselfing" and connection with an unknown other, prophesying messages and meanings related to collective well-being, the common good, and existential preservation.

This was a remarkably consistent collection of shared stories from witnesses who remain adamant on what they saw, and there are good reasons to take this seriously from a psychological perspective.

The Ostracized Professor

Professor John Mack was a Harvard psychiatrist and Pulitzer Prize--winning author who established the psychiatric department at Cambridge Hospital. Mack became interested in the Ariel School incident following reports of the children's accounts and the surrounding media and public scepticism.[4]

Mack approached the phenomenon with both an open mind and a critical lens, drawing on his previous experience interviewing over 150 individuals who claimed to have experienced alien abductions.[5] He consistently claimed to find no evidence of psychosis among these individuals; instead, he identified genuine trauma and emotional distress, prompting him to explore the implications of their experiences further. He did not try to explain exactly what these experiences were, but he was open to the possibility that traditional methods were failing to offer sound conclusions.

Mack's investigation at Ariel revealed striking consistency in the children's accounts and drawings they provided independently after the incident. Mack noted what he termed "suitable affect," observing fear and emotional responses that aligned with their narratives, which further validated their testimonies from his perspective. He began to question why individuals are often labelled as delusional for experiencing connections with unknown intelligences.

However, Mack's commitment to this line of inquiry came at a significant cost. While increasingly vocal about his findings, a faction of his colleagues at Harvard sought to have his tenure revoked, a move that had not occurred in the university's history for over 350 years.[6] This campaign against him was fuelled by accusations of gross malpractice for treating those who reported alien encounters as credible witnesses rather than mentally ill. His peers grew frustrated by his rising popularity in mainstream media, where he shared insights about the psychological experiences of those claiming abduction.

Despite this pressure, Mack remained resolute in his belief that these experiences warranted serious consideration. He argued that the reality of these encounters—whether understood through conventional means or not—should be respected.[7] Mack was particularly concerned about the impact of dismissing these experiences on the individuals involved; he noted that some witnesses had expressed suicidal thoughts and indicated that his willingness to listen and take their experiences seriously had been crucial in saving their lives.

As the scrutiny against him intensified, the situation evolved into what many viewed as a witch hunt, prompting Harvard to reassess its stance. Ultimately, the university dropped its case against Mack, recognizing the merit in his approach and the importance of considering the subjective experiences of those who felt alienated and misunderstood.

Mack's work highlighted the need for open-mindedness in the exploration of complex phenomena, reflecting a broader inquiry into the nature of reality itself.

Testimonies and Vindication

Daniel MacLeish is a lawyer renowned for his role in winning a landmark case against the Catholic Church on behalf of abuse survivors. He was contacted about John Mack's case.[8] Seeing similarities between the children's testimonies at Ariel and the credible survivor accounts in abuse cases, MacLeish argued that the consistency and emotional detail in the children's statements warranted serious attention.

MacLeish noted that if the legal system accepted the accounts of five or six teenagers against a single authority figure as credible evidence, then the corroborated accounts from over sixty children at Ariel should be taken seriously, regardless of the phenomenon's unusual nature. His arguments shifted perspectives on Mack's work, lending legal weight to the idea that witness testimonies—even those describing extraordinary experiences—deserve respect and careful consideration.

MacLeish helped to reshape public discourse around the case, highlighting the value of understanding experiences that fall outside typical frameworks of reality.

Today, the Ariel School incident is remembered as a profound case study in belief, trauma, and the complexities of the human experience. Many witnesses have reclaimed their stories, finding personal meaning in their encounters and a renewed sense of agency over what they experienced. For some, the incident was transformative, inspiring a sense of responsibility towards the environment and a deeper understanding of humanity's place within the cosmos.

Empathy and Connection

As they reflect on their shared experiences, witnesses emphasize empathy, connection, and the importance of respecting diverse interpretations of reality. This respect is deemed essential to understanding more about who we are within a vast and mysterious universe.

But the trials and tribulations of witnesses and professionals involved in this case demonstrate the sensitivities of transcendental realms and alternative understandings of reality beyond our current comprehension. The social and psychological burden that witness face after these experiences should be approached with as much care as the topic itself.

Mack's experience alone provides a compelling account of those hemispherical disparities in our personal and collective lives, which bring tensions and tribulations to the ontological possibilities of modern life and culture. Transcendental experiences and their associated data lurk into territories that make hierarchies of tradition, institutional principles, and the gatekeepers of intellectual paradigms nervous.

As the next encounter shows, this is especially the case when the military are involved.

Mass Sightings in Texas

Stephenville, Texas, 2008. A smalltown community drew attention from across the country when over 300 witnesses reported seeing strange lights in the sky.[9] These sightings were unlike anything they had experienced before, and they described the objects as large, silent, and moving at speeds far beyond what conventional aircraft could achieve. The mass of reports shared commonalities in their descriptions, adding credibility to the event and raising questions about what these sightings might have been.

Steve Allen, a successful businessman and seasoned pilot, seemed to have it all—a thriving trucking company, a happy marriage of over 16 years, and a stable, comfortable life. His fascination with technology was a defining part of his identity, and his career in aviation gave him a grounded understanding of flight and aerodynamics. Yet his experience would ultimately redefine his sense of self and reality.

One evening, Steve was with friends on a hillside near his home in Stephenville enjoying a campfire. It was a clear night. Bright, blinding lights suddenly appeared in the sky. As they approached, Steve observed a massive object gliding silently overhead.

Steve described the craft as a ship about a mile long and a mile and a half wide—an enormous, solid structure that moved with an eerie quietness, unlike anything he had ever encountered in his years as a pilot. There were no sounds, no wind, just what Steve describes to this day as an *overwhelming silence*. As the lights passed overhead, Steve described the experience as *peaceful, like a religious or spiritual encounter.*

Steve felt as though he were at one with whatever this entity or object was. It was a sensation of transcendence, something he had never experienced before and would never forget. When the object suddenly disappeared, two F-16 fighter jets appeared in pursuit.

A Life-Altering Moment

For Steve, the sighting was more than a UFO event—it was a profound, life-altering moment that reshaped his understanding of reality. Despite the challenges he faced after speaking out, Steve remains certain of what he saw and feels an enduring connection to the mystery that continues to drive his search for answers.

After the event, Steve went home and shared his experience with his wife, who urged him to keep it to himself, fearing the consequences of public exposure. People would think they were crazy, she said. But Steve was resolute. He knew what he had seen.

The next day, he contacted the local newspaper and shared his account. The aftermath was intense. The media pressure, the dismissiveness from others, and the strain it put on his personal life eventually cost him his marriage and professional stability.[10]

Yet, despite these challenges, Steve continued to view the experience as a "blessing." He felt profoundly connected to something beyond himself, something far greater than the confines of his everyday life. He became committed to a quest for truth, determined to uncover one day what it was he had witnessed in the sky that night.

Stephenville in the Press

Angelia Joiner, a local journalist in Stephenville, took Steve's call about the UFO sightings and started working on the story. Sara Vanden Berge was Angelia's managing editor. As the youngest ever managing editor at the *Stephenville Empire-Tribune*, and only the second woman to hold that role, Sara was relatively new and still treated as an outsider.[11]

Understandably then, Sara was nervous about including a story on UFOs—especially when she picked the paper up the following day and saw that her publisher had pulled rank. Sara's front page was rearranged, with the UFO story as a central front-page feature. Sara rushed to the publisher's office, furious and upset, fearing the end of her career. The publisher reassured Sara that her fears were misplaced, pointing out that every copy of the paper across the county had sold out.

The community cared about this and had plenty to say about it.

Meanwhile, Angelia Joiner was determined to follow the leads and contact the local air force base to verify the presence of F-16 fighter jets in the area during the time of the sightings. Initially, the air force denied any such activity, but later military officials contradicted themselves, suggesting that the witnesses had simply misidentified the jets, and that there had been a communication error.

This contradiction only fuelled the frustration of Steve Allen and his friends, who had seen the lights firsthand. In defiance of the official explanations, they took to the skies themselves in their private planes, searching for more answers. As the sightings became less frequent and government responses dwindled, Vanden Berge decided it was time for the paper to move on to other stories.

Editorial Tensions

For Angelia Joiner, the UFO story was no longer just another article. She had become personally invested in the witnesses and their accounts—the story represented something bigger than the typical reporting she had done. Joiner understood the psychological impact of the events on the witnesses, noting how shaken they were, some to the very core of their belief systems, by what they had seen. The story became more than just news; it was a cause she felt compelled to pursue.

This growing rift between Joiner's deepening investment in the story and Sara's desire to let it go eventually led to tensions between the two. Joiner became frustrated when it seemed the management had shut the story down. Angelia sent emails to her contacts suggesting that the paper's management had suppressed the story due to government interference. This was untrue, and when Sara found out she terminated Angelia's contract.

Nine months later, Sara herself had an encounter with the strange lights in the sky. She saw them from her own home—separate lights that merged and then disappeared. The sighting connected her in a personal way to the story the paper had covered months earlier. This experience caused her to reflect on the earlier tensions with Angelia.

Sara now regrets the way their professional relationship ended and wishes she could praise Angelia for her bravery in standing by the witnesses and the story itself.

Angelia passed away in 2021. Sara carries that sense of connection and regret to this day. But Angelia and Sara's willingness to cover the story made a major contribution in the support it provided to witnesses and the experiences that brought the community together.

The Local Sheriff

Lee Roy Gaitan, a constable in Erath County, Texas, was another key witness to the strange events surrounding the UFO sightings in 2008.[12] One night, while standing outside his house with his son, Gaitan saw what appeared to be a giant red orb in the sky. As he watched, he says the orb split into 11 or 12 smaller lights before quickly shooting off into the distance. He believed that these lights were the same ones seen by Steve Allen and his friends, with their timelines matching up.

Like many of the other witnesses, Gaitan was initially hesitant to speak publicly about his experience. As a respected figure in his community, he feared ridicule. However, Steve Allen, who had already gone public with his own sighting, convinced Gaitan to come forward and share his experience as part of the investigation led by journalist Angelia Joiner.

Gaitan's involvement in the case deepened when he was called to a local farm one evening. Upon arriving, he observed an orb hovering in the sky. This time, he took out his camera and filmed the object. When he later reviewed the footage at home, he was startled to find that it appeared as though something had tampered with the camera. The footage was distorted in a way that he had never experienced before or since.

Gaitan was baffled by the anomaly, as he had used the camera countless times without issue. This strange occurrence added to the growing collection of inexplicable events that surrounded the UFO sightings in Stephenville, further suggesting a transcendental element to the phenomenon—one that appeared to defy normal physical explanations.

The School Principal

Dr. Norma Briseno was a school principal in Stephenville at the time.[13] Originally from Mexico, Norma shares a unique perspective to the sightings, explaining how Mexican culture shaped how she interpreted unexplained phenomena, contrasting it with the highly fact-centred approach she observed in the United States: "What we don't understand, we try to explain, but our culture is also very open to accepting things we cannot see or understand. We do not rely on facts constantly like here in the U.S. The inexplicable does not necessarily mean that it is not reality or fact."

Norma's experiences with unexplained lights spanned decades. The 2008 lights reminded her of a similar event from her past. In 1989, her mother had observed unusual lights in the sky, an occurrence that repeated the following night, witnessed this time by both Briseno and her sister. These memories resurfaced as she watched the lights again in 2008, recognizing that their movement and speed were far beyond what she believed human technology could achieve, such as that of a plane or helicopter.

Norma's recounting added a cultural layer to the resonance of these sightings, highlighting how interpretations of the unknown can vary widely across cultural backgrounds. Our cross-cultural boundaries vary in terms of what is accepted as reality, and what is ridiculed. When the Stephenville story broke on national television, the town and its witnesses faced more than their share of ridicule and criticism.

But for Norma, mystery is a welcome guest in the collective psyche, inviting a more receptive and even transcendent view of phenomena that defy immediate explanation. Likewise, other witnesses had their worldviews shaken to the core—even the mechanistic mind of an avid machine enthusiast like Steve was suddenly open to the mystery and wonder of what he described as a religious experience and a blessing.

Despite their different backgrounds and unique personal insights, they shared a common connection in the transcendent.

From Homeland Security

Another Stephenville witness was Eddie Wiess, a homeland security consultant and threat analyst.[14] As a father, Weiss teaches his children about Bible stories, including the vision of Ezekiel, which he believes describes a UFO.[15] Ezekiel's vision of fiery, winged creatures with multiple faces, accompanied by mysterious, rotating wheels that move in all directions without turning, has similarities to modern UFO descriptions. The glowing, metallic appearance, rapid movement, and unidirectional travel of the wheels echo reports of unidentified flying objects.

Eddie uses these biblical accounts to show his kids that the experiences of ancient civilizations have a deep, lived connection to present-day UFO stories. By drawing these parallels, Eddie helps his children see that the so-called supernatural and the technology are intertwined, illustrating that these shared, arcane experiences stretch across time and offer a direct ancestral connection to the mysteries of the cosmos.

Eddie also critiques the rigid worldview of certain "Christian populists," who, in his view, reject the reality of UFOs because it challenges their established understanding of the universe. Unlike the mystical perspective that is open to such phenomena, this fixed mindset limits transcendental potentials and the ability to explore the deeper, more nuanced, and arcane horizons of reality.

Eddie argues that such a worldview is incapable of engaging in mature reflection on mystery and the unknown. For him, the acceptance of UFOs as part of the natural world is not a theological threat but an expansion of human consciousness—inviting us to consider the universal nature of Christ and divinity across the cosmos, rather than confining these concepts to humanity alone.

In this context, Eddie raises a profound question: who is the Bible really for? Is it solely for humans, or is it also meant to be shared with "them"—the beings from other worlds? This notion dovetails with his view that the existence of life beyond Earth is not a challenge to Christian faith but rather an extension of it.

Eddie's conclusion resonates with a similar sentiment from Lee Roy Gaitan, who is open to the possibility that God created other life forms beyond humans. The likes of Eddie and other Stephenville witnesses see transcendental realms as opportunities, not limitations. They open possibilities for understanding our place in the universe, rather than closing them down to the orders of religious or intellectual authorities.

Suspicion and the State

As a threat analyst, Eddie is also deeply critical of government responses to UFO sightings. He believes the government has lied about the phenomena, particularly regarding the unexplained objects seen over Stephenville. From his perspective, the technology and movements of these craft are so advanced that they seem "otherworldly," and the refusal to acknowledge them points to a deep discomfort in confronting the implications of such technology.

Many people, Eddie believes, cannot accept the reality of UFOs because it challenges their perception of who they are in relation to the vastness of the universe. This fear of confronting the larger unknown reflects a broader reluctance to embrace transcendental experiences that challenge self-centred, limited worldviews.

While Eddie acknowledges the existence of UFOs and believes in life on other planets, he holds a distinct view on their origins. He does not think that these technologies are extraterrestrial in nature. Instead, he believes they are manifestations of angels—beings that have always been part of our reality.

These "messengers," Eddie argues, have been among us for centuries, and their appearances are not a harbinger of alien invasion but an invitation to communicate. For Eddie, the arcane horizons represented by UFOs are a critical part of our reality, one that should be respected and explored, regardless of personal beliefs or differing experiences.

The transcendental nature of these encounters calls for a broader cultural acceptance of the unknown, and a willingness to engage with the mysteries that lie beyond the (currently) observable world.

Unsettling Experiences

Robert Powell, a nanotechnology engineer with a dedication to studying UFOs scientifically, was a lead researcher at the Mutual UFO Network (MUFON) when the reports from Stephenville began to flood in. Powell's approach was to apply scientific rigor to the phenomenon, aiming to make sense of the many reports that defied conventional explanation.

The reports were numerous, with more than twenty accounts surfacing from the area in a short period, leading Powell to initiate an investigation into the sightings. Powell, who had studied similar cases extensively, observed a consistent reaction among witnesses who encountered UFOs, noting that these experiences often unsettled their fundamental understanding of reality, leaving them questioning how they perceived the world and its possibilities.

One witness Powell interviewed was a local deer hunter named Ricky, who recounted a remarkable encounter in the woods. While alone, Ricky says he saw an enormous craft hovering above, seemingly defying our current understanding of physics with its size and silent movement. In an instant, the craft vanished, so swiftly that, by natural laws, it should have created a disturbance—yet, like so many encounter stories, there was no sound, no rush of air, only a surreal calm, and unimaginable speed upon disappearance.

Following this incident, Ricky described disturbing occurrences such as low-flying helicopters over his house and a bullet placed on the dashboard of his car. Journalist Angelia Joiner speculated that Ricky may have been targeted due to the unusually detailed view he had of the craft, which had appeared in daylight. Using the scope on his rifle, Ricky claimed to observe an insect-like figure inside the craft, a detail that set his account apart from others in both proximity and insight.

Gathering the Data

As part of his investigation, Powell consulted with a former army radar specialist who recommended he submit a Freedom of Information Act (FOIA) request to obtain radar data, which could substantiate the sightings.[16] Powell's findings were compelling: he discovered radar evidence of unidentified, non-military aircraft operating in the Stephenville area during the times witnesses had reported sightings.

These radar recordings showed craft without transponders, indicating they were not associated with any known military operations, as military aircraft are typically equipped with transponders for identification. Notably, the radar data aligned with accounts provided by Lee Roy Gaitan and Steve Allen, precisely matching the locations and times of their experiences.

Powell's conclusions were significant. Based on the technological capabilities demonstrated—silent, rapid disappearance and reappearance, and other advanced behaviours—he posited that these craft did not belong to any human government. The technology exceeded what he believed could be covertly developed, even by the most advanced earthly agencies.

In Powell's view, these performances suggested a non-human origin, or at least an origin beyond any known terrestrial source, placing the events within a realm that challenged both scientific understanding and the boundaries of human knowledge.[17] It's these boundaries that determine how experiencers choose to make sense of what they see, and the stories they tell as a result.

Tragedy and Mythos in Japan

In Kimitsu, Japan, Chief Monk Tomonori Izumi and several residents of the Enmyoin Temple have reported seeing UFOs.[18] Izumi himself says he witnessed a large UFO hovering near the temple and was struck by its size, describing how the sight nearly caused his legs to give out from shock.

This occurred shortly before the 2011 earthquake off Japan's east coast, a magnitude 8.9 event that triggered a devastating tsunami. The disaster caused thousands of deaths and significant destruction, including a meltdown at the Fukushima nuclear power plant.

Following the explosion at the nuclear power plant, multiple witnesses reported seeing orbs hovering over the site, and videos captured these lights. In the days after the event, hundreds of people reported sightings of these lights.

Interpretations varied: some believed the lights were the souls of those who had died, some believed they were extraterrestrial messengers looking out for humanity, while others saw them as something totally unexplained and beyond material reality. Whatever they were, it is not uncommon to see this link between nuclear sites and UFO sightings.

UFOs and Nuclear Sites

According to researcher Robert Hastings, the link between UFOs and nuclear sites has been well-documented through declassified government files and accounts from hundreds of U.S. military veterans.[19] Hastings has interviewed over 150 veterans about these incidents, including events where nuclear missiles mysteriously malfunctioned after UFOs were observed near launch sites. A notable case from March 1967, detailed by Hastings, involved missile silos in Montana being disabled as a disc-shaped craft hovered nearby, a story shared during a 2010 press conference streamed by CNN.

Hastings notes that UFO activity near nuclear sites dates back to January 1945 at a plutonium processing plant in Washington State. Other incidents include a massive cigar-shaped craft disrupting communications at a missile base in Wyoming in 2010 and Soviet nuclear sites being targeted during the Cold War. A Soviet case from 1982, as documented by Hastings, involved missiles initiating an unauthorized launch sequence while a disc-shaped UFO hovered overhead before the system reverted to standby mode.

According to Hastings, these events suggest a sustained interest in humanity's most destructive technologies by unknown entities with advanced capabilities. He argues that this connection may be a central reason for UFO sightings since the advent of nuclear weapons during World War II. While this link might be significant, UFO sightings precede the birth of nuclear technology.

Ancient Protectors?

Dr. Jensine Andresen, a scholar in religious studies specializing in mysticism, consciousness, and cultural phenomena, has examined the connection between UFOs and nuclear sites. She suggests that advanced, non-human technology may have existed on Earth even before the development of nuclear weapons. Andresen notes a rise in UFO sightings after the first nuclear bombs were dropped on Japan, with repeated reports of UFO activity near nuclear weapon facilities and disaster sites.

Andresen highlights an incident at Chernobyl in 1986, where during the peak of the Unit 4 reactor fire, a UFO reportedly hovered over the site for three minutes, shining a light towards the reactor. According to some accounts, radiation levels dropped significantly following this event. Andresen interprets this as a deliberate attempt to minimize the danger from the explosion, reflecting a concern for humanity's well-being.

Andresen also references Robert Salas, a former missile launch officer in Montana, who reported that a UFO entered restricted airspace, shining a light over the launch site and disabling the nuclear missiles. This incident is one of multiple similar reports from nuclear facilities. Andresen believes these cases demonstrate a pattern of intervention, with the intelligence behind these phenomena wanting to prevent human self-destruction. She describes this intelligence as caring, urging humanity to open its mind and foster greater understanding and connection.

The Monk and the Temple

Returning to Japan, Chief Monk Tomonori Izumi says that although he and others fled the area after the tsunami, Enmyoin Temple remained intact, earning the nickname "the miracle temple." He believes in "unseen forces" such as divine power or the power of UFOs and thinks that they may have played a role in protecting the area. He describes the temple as a place with a special spiritual energy, which he believes may be attractive to UFOs.

Tomonori Izumi suggests that the UFOs appeared to help, potentially adjusting the nuclear radiation around Fukushima to reduce ongoing harm. He encourages others not to fear UFOs, suggesting that they may be benevolent forces, and believes that these events prompt us to work towards a peaceful world.

The accounts from Fukushima highlight how cultural traditions can embrace contradiction and paradox without the tension or conflict often seen in other cultures. Witnesses interpret these phenomena through metaphorical and existential lenses, uncovering deeper truths about what matters most to them. Their interpretations reflect their relationship with the world, encompassing both the living and the dead.

Souls of the Dead

Keisuke Udagawa, a newspaper editor in Japan, felt compelled to help after witnessing the Fukushima nuclear plant explosion. Despite losing a friend who lived near the plant, Udagawa remained committed to supporting the recovery.

Days after the tsunami, he stood on a beach observing the destruction, with houses still floating out to sea. In the distance above the water, he noticed blue-white orbs of light, which he describes as floating above the ocean.

Five years after the disaster, Keisuke Udagawa reflects on the many mysterious occurrences since then. He frequently visited the exclusion zone within three miles of the nuclear plant, noting that orbs, or "hitodama," often appeared in specific spots, sometimes above vehicles or isolated areas, which he felt were sites of death. In Japanese tradition, hitodama are thought to be souls of the deceased, appearing as bright floating balls of light.

Keisuke Udagawa does not believe these lights are extraterrestrials but rather views them as the souls of those who died in the disaster. He suggests that the survivors find comfort in these sightings, seeing them as signs that lost friends and family may be returning in some form. Seeing the presence of these souls and orbs as messengers teach him to see the beauty in people's hearts. For Keisuke Udagawa, these orbs have become a meaningful and significant part of daily life, especially for those affected by the tragedy.

Peaceful Messengers

Jiyo Sakuma, a visual artist, regularly visits the abandoned elementary school where his mother once worked, which was destroyed in the tsunami. Although he doesn't claim to understand why UFOs appeared near the site, he reports that many locals saw vivid, glowing orbs after the Fukushima explosion—many orbs floating near each other before merging into a single light. He also notes that reports often link UFO sightings with nuclear sites.

Three months after the tsunami, Jiyo Sakuma and his wife experienced what they believe was a close encounter. His wife woke in the middle of the night, feeling as though they were being watched. Looking out the window, they saw a bright, golden UFO hovering over the hills near their apartment. The UFO seemed to emit a deep pink light, flashing intermittently. Jiyo Sakuma recalls feeling reassured, as though the UFO was communicating a message of safety and welcome.

Reflecting on this experience, Jiyo Sakuma suggests that if humans, like children, experiment with powerful tools like nuclear energy, then more advanced beings may feel a responsibility to watch over them. Although the disaster deeply affected him, he felt the UFO encounter provided him with a sense of healing and support, reinforcing his belief that these entities are benevolent.

In 2016, Jiyo Sakuma reports having an "astral abduction," where he experienced his astral body, rather than his physical self, being taken into a UFO. During this experience, he saw images of Earth and felt a message that trauma and negativity cloud human consciousness. He suggests that every individual has a responsibility to clear these biases to restore a balanced, peaceful psyche—akin to a newborn's unclouded state, and perhaps alluding to the True Self that the mystics speak of.

Jiyo Sakuma interprets this message as a call for collective consciousness to evolve, suggesting that if humanity can overcome inner negativity, a cosmic future lies ahead, with Earth eventually glowing with a symbolic golden light. This, he says, marked the end of a profound lucid dream. Jiyo Sakuma, like the Mexican headteacher in Stephenville, is less concerned with finding concrete answers and more focused on the exploratory meanings that derive from these experiences, believing that the mystery of aliens and UFOs simply exists—and that alone is enough.

Evidence and Folklore

From another perspective, computer scientist Dr. Tanaka Kazou is open to the possibility of UFOs but remains committed to evidence-based research. His interest lies in the diverse views surrounding this phenomenon, which many people are eager to understand, though interpretations vary.

Tanaka Kazou finds it challenging to verify UFO sightings, especially when he feels most reports began in the 1940s in the United States. However, in Japan, he has discovered artefacts that may suggest earlier UFO-like encounters.

One such story is the legend of the *Utsuro-bune*, or "hollow ship," recorded in *Kawaraban*, a newsprint equivalent from the early 1800s. In 1803, multiple accounts describe a mysterious vessel that washed ashore with a woman on board. The vessel was round with three windows or similar openings, but it didn't resemble the known ships of the Edo period.

For many years, the location of this event was considered fictional until, in 2014, a discovery was made by the Ban family, known for their archival records. Their documents mentioned "Hitachihara" and "Sharihama," with Sharihama located about 117 miles from the Fukushima nuclear site. It was here that locals allegedly found the *Utsuro-bune* and the woman inside.

Tanaka Kazou suggests that this could be one of the earliest records of a visitor in a disc-shaped craft, though he notes that drawings with similar depictions exist from even earlier periods, raising the possibility that such imagery has long been part of human culture. Unlike artist Jiyo Sakuma, who doesn't require physical proof and focuses on the emotional resonance of his experiences, Tanaka Kazou believes that credible evidence is essential to understanding the UFO phenomenon. For him, verifying each claim and witness account is a way to guard against deception, despite his hope that these encounters could one day be confirmed as real.

Either way, both witnesses take deep meaning from the historical and modern folklore in which they are immersed.

Trauma and Popular Culture

Journalist Roland Nozomu Kelts analyses UFOs and aliens in Japanese pop culture, linking the fascination to postwar Japan's complex relationship with technology and trauma. He examines Astro Boy, a character powered by atomic energy, created by his "father" after the death of his real son—an implicit reference to Japan's World War II losses.

Kelts suggests Astro Boy symbolizes Japan's postwar belief in technology as a hopeful future while grappling with atomic destruction, reflecting the nation's effort to reconcile with and transcend beyond collective trauma through aspirations to progress.

Kelts also points to Ultraman, an extraterrestrial superhero who merges with a human scientist, Shin Hayata, after a tragic accident that results in Ultraman inadvertently causing Hayata's death. In an act of redemption, Ultraman revives him by fusing their beings, symbolizing how alien and human elements can unite for a benevolent purpose. This fusion not only grants Hayata the ability to transform into Ultraman but also reflects a deeper theme of reconciliation and responsibility—suggesting that transcendence and heroism emerge not from power alone, but from the human and technological will towards peace and justice.

This narrative suggests that aliens might have good intentions, subtly embedding messages of harmony and coexistence into Japanese pop culture. Kelts observes that Japan, unlike the West, has no dominant institutionalized religion; instead, ethics and morals often stem from family, social roles, and cultural pedagogy. This allows narrative capacity for paradox and fluid identities.

Miho's Space Language

Miho Ninagawa, a drama teacher in Japan, claims she can communicate through a "space language" with extraterrestrials, seeing herself as an alien due to her belief in reincarnation from many stars. While such views might attract scepticism, Kelts explains that Japanese society's flexible approach to identity and social roles makes this self-perception relatively uncontroversial.

Kelts emphasizes that Japanese culture doesn't typically distinguish between the natural and supernatural; they are seen as parts of a singular reality. Miho Ninagawa's experiences with extraterrestrial entities, which she interprets as beings of light bringing spiritual balance to reality, illustrate this view. In her eyes, the "aliens" symbolize a need to restore harmony in an imbalanced world. Kelts highlights how Japanese people often approach the mystery of UFOs with acceptance, allowing these experiences to remain mysterious rather than insisting on clear explanations.

While Kelts acknowledges that not all Japanese people are without uncertainty regarding alien beliefs, he suggests that Japan's cultural framework allows for a unique integration of mystery and spirituality. Kelts notes that understanding these differences enhances our appreciation of the cultural significance these stories hold across societies.

Our Modern Mythos

This is where the "micro" and "macro" intersect—the personal accounts of individuals who have witnessed inexplicable phenomena often connect in such a way that they form a collective data set. This shared storytelling, from ancient myths to modern UFO encounters, reveals patterns and resonances that transcend individual experiences.

By acknowledging the interplay between large-scale events and individual experiences, we begin to form a fuller, more nuanced understanding of the phenomena shaping our world. The personal and collective tapestry of stories that have brought us to this point suggests something profound: we are immersed in experiences we cannot fully explain, pointing to the presence of a phenomenon that is itself equally mysterious.

In *The Myth Gap*, Alex Evans explains that our collective psychology and well-being rely not only on the grand stories of macro mythologies or individual grandstanding but on a healthy balance of personal stories.[20] These stories should reflect our lived experiences while resonating in a wider tapestry of collective sense-making that provides common ground through diverse yet interconnected and relatable experiences.

UFO stories are a good example of this. Experiential accounts vary in almost endless ways, but within universal patterns of seeing and feeling. They are all part of a transcendental realm that stimulates dynamics of shared consciousness and curiosities that pontificate some of the deepest wonders of our existence.

UFOs are a mythos of our times, sharing common features and similarities but preciously unique to every individual who experiences that transcendental contact with the arcane. The political and public discourse around this topic is shifting and attitudes are changing.

While I have focused on stories and cases reflecting themes relating to transcendental experiences, the broader topic of UFOs from collective, psychological, historical, technological, and military perspectives is significant to the multi-contextual evolution of this mythos. The collective resonance here is evident in the congressional context of military whistle-blowers testifying under oath.

In recent years, UFOs (or UAPs) have entered mainstream political discourse, particularly through testimonies in the U.S. Congress. What was once confined to fringe belief has taken on institutional legitimacy, driven by credible military witnesses, investigative journalism, and a slow drip of declassified material. Among the central figures in this shift are Commander David Fravor and intelligence official David Grusch.[21]

The Tic Tac Incident

Commander David Fravor, a retired U.S. Navy pilot, is widely regarded as one of the most credible witnesses in the UAP discourse. In 2004, during a training exercise off the coast of Southern California, Fravor encountered a white, oblong object—later dubbed the "Tic Tac." He described it as having no visible propulsion system, wings, or rotors, and said it made abrupt manoeuvres that defied known aeronautical capabilities. The object reportedly descended from 80,000 feet to sea level in under a second before vanishing.

Fravor's credibility stems not only from his military rank and expertise but from the corroboration of other pilots and radar operators involved in the incident. His calm, measured testimony before Congress in July 2023 emphasized the object's unexplainable behaviour, which he suggested was "not of this world." Unlike more speculative voices, Fravor does not claim to know the origin of the phenomena, only that it is far beyond current human capability.

In contrast, David Grusch, a former intelligence officer with the National Geospatial-Intelligence Agency, catapulted the UAP discussion into more controversial territory during the same time period. Grusch testified that he had access to classified information indicating that the U.S. government possesses retrieved non-human craft and possibly biologics. He claimed this material was part of a long-standing, secret crash retrieval program operating outside proper governmental oversight or accountability for spending.

Grusch's testimony was insightful but polarizing. He did not claim to have personally seen the craft or bodies but said he had spoken to dozens of officials with direct knowledge. Predictably, and understandably, his claims attracted intense scrutiny.

Though he had passed a Department of Defense Inspector General complaint process and had a high-level security clearance, he was subjected to the usual state and media antics: character attacks, vague insinuations of mental instability, and attempts to discredit his military record.[22] These tactics reflect a recurring trend of institutional behaviours when whistle-blowers challenge national security orthodoxy.

Despite the smearing, Grusch has maintained consistency, composure, and a willingness to testify under oath, pointing out the oversight gap between the intelligence community and congressional authority. That said, many of Grusch's critics see the "hearsay" of his account as highly dubious and potentially cynical with a deliberate intention to dupe or confuse public discourse.[23]

Secrets at the Pentagon

A significant turning point in public and political discourse on this topic came via the *New York Times* in 2017.[24] An article, co-authored by Leslie Kean, Helene Cooper, and Ralph Blumenthal, titled, "Glowing Auras and 'Black Money': The Pentagon's Mysterious U.F.O. Program," revealed the existence of the Advanced Aerospace Threat Identification Program (AATIP), a secret initiative within the Department of Defense that investigated UAPs.[25]

The article included declassified videos from Navy pilots showing strange aerial objects performing impossible manoeuvres—footage that was later authenticated by the Pentagon. This marked a watershed moment: *mainstream media and governmental authorities were acknowledging that something was happening in the skies that science and military engineering could not yet explain.*

Following the 2017 article, congressional interest intensified. Key figures like Senator Marco Rubio and Representative Tim Burchett have voiced concerns about national security implications and the lack of transparency. A series of recent hearings have seen several ex-military, intelligence, and Pentagon employees provide evidence to congress under oath.

As we see throughout these case studies into the arcane, transcendence is a messy subject, and collective transcendence is a realm that the state would like to keep a close eye on. Despite bipartisan support for more disclosure, many commentators and investigators feel that progress has been too slow, hindered by bureaucratic stonewalling, and deeply embedded secrecy. Legislative proposals like the UAP Disclosure Act have faced pushback from defence and intelligence sectors.

Understandably, these factors motivate those sceptics who feel this is all smoke and mirrors with other agendas served by a sophisticated, or at least discombobulating, disinformation campaign.

Transcendental realms are messy and full of tension. But the public interest won't go away.

While congressional figures are being accused of hesitancy, backtracking, and obedience to power, the public knows there's trickery involved—whether that's concerning the actions of governments or the phenomenon itself.

The Celestial Psyche

One cold, clear night in London, broadcaster Danny Robins looked up in awe at the vastness of the universe and wondered, "Is there anybody out there?" While introducing stories about UFO experiences, he posed three possibilities: could these encounters come from other beings beyond our world, secret military experiments here on Earth, or perhaps the most mysterious source of all—the human mind?[26]

Our celestial psyche is fundamental to what we are as humans.

Some have looked much closer to home and suggested the interdimensional terrains of extraterrestrial life can be accessed "in here," in our minds, through altered states of consciousness. As we shall see, deep within our unconscious minds lies a celestial landscape of the psyche—an inner universe (or perhaps beyond) that can be explored through altered states of consciousness.

For millennia, humans have turned to plants and chemicals from the Earth to stimulate these expansions of consciousness, unlocking psychocosmic realms that reveal insights into the self and seemingly universal connections through unselfing. This inward exploration mirrors our outward journey into the stars, suggesting that the cosmos, in its vastness and mystery, can also be explored from within.

Notes

1. Elizondo (2024); Piedra (2025).
2. Motskin (2023a). Nickerson (2022).
3. Motskin (2023a).
4. Motskin (2023a); Nickerson (2022).
5. Mack (1994).
6. Motskin (2023a).
7. See also Mack (1994) for more on his research into the experiences of people claiming to have been abducted.
8. Motskin (2023a); Nickerson (2022).
9. Motskin (2023b).
10. Several formal support networks exist for individuals reporting anomalous contact or UFO-related experiences. The Consciousness and Contact Research Institute (formerly the Foundation for Research into Extraterrestrial Encounters, or FREE) provides a platform for experiencers to share their stories and participate in consciousness-based research into contact phenomena, combining academic inquiry with community engagement (CCRIT, 2024). The MUFON Experiencer Resource Team (ERT) offers confidential support and access to trained specialists for those reporting abduction or contact encounters (MUFON, 2024). Similarly, the Organization for Paranormal Understanding and Support (OPUS) provides psychological resources, peer forums, and research pathways for those undergoing anomalous experiences across UFOs, near-death, and psi domains (OPUS, 2024). Meditation-led outreach is also popular, with CE-5 (Close Encounters of the Fifth Kind) groups forming worldwide around consciousness-initiated contact protocols, inspired by Dr. Steven Greer's work and supported through digital tools like the CE5 Contact App (Greer, 2020). In Australia, ACERN (the Australian Close Encounter Resource Network), founded by Mary Rodwell, offers professional counselling and research support, with a focus on psychological integration and the broader implications of contact (ACERN, 2024). Alongside these formal networks, informal communities have rapidly emerged across platforms such as Reddit, Discord, and Facebook, offering peer-based, grassroots support for experiencers in more accessible and often anonymous environments.
11. Ibid.
12. Ibid.
13. Ibid.

14. Ibid.
15. "I looked, and I saw a windstorm coming out of the north—an immense cloud with flashing lightning and surrounded by brilliant light. The center of the fire looked like glowing metal, and in the fire was what looked like four living creatures. In appearance their form was human, but each of them had four faces and four wings. Their legs were straight; their feet were like those of a calf and gleamed like burnished bronze. Under their wings on their four sides they had human hands. All four of them had faces and wings, and the wings of one touched the wings of another. Each one went straight ahead; they did not turn as they moved. Their faces looked like this: Each of the four had the face of a human being, and on the right side each had the face of a lion, and on the left the face of an ox; each also had the face of an eagle. Such were their faces. They each had two wings spreading out upward, each wing touching that of the creature on either side; and each had two other wings covering its body. Each one went straight ahead. Wherever the spirit would go, they would go, without turning as they went. The appearance of the living creatures was like burning coals of fire or like torches. Fire moved back and forth among the creatures; it was bright, and lightning flashed out of it. The creatures sped back and forth like flashes of lightning. As I looked at the living creatures, I saw a wheel on the ground beside each creature with its four faces. This was the appearance and structure of the wheels: They sparkled like topaz, and all four looked alike. Each appeared to be made like a wheel intersecting a wheel. As they moved, they would go in any one of the four directions the creatures faced; the wheels did not change direction as the creatures went. Their rims were high and awesome, and all four rims were full of eyes all around." (Ezekiel 1:4–18)
16. Ibid.
17. Notably, since the Stephenville case, requests for radar data from the FAA under the Freedom of Information Act have reportedly been more restricted, adding to the frustration of those like Roberts who believe the public has a right to know.
18. Motskin (2023c).
19. Hastings (2017).
20. Evans (2017).
21. Grusch and Fravor (2023). For further interviews, see Grusch (2024) and Fravor (2020).
22. Coulthart (2024).
23. See West (2023a, 2023b) for critical takes on Grusch's testimony. For West's critical response to UFOs along with what he considers to be other forms of conspiracy theory, see West (2023c, 2025).
24. Cooper et al. (2017).

25. Kean, a journalist with a long history of careful, evidence-based reporting on anomalous phenomena, has continued to champion responsible inquiry. Kean and Blumenthal (2023) later published follow-ups in *The Debrief* and elsewhere, often focusing on whistle-blowers and testimonies that suggest deeper layers of secrecy.
26. Robins (2021).

Bibliography

ACERN. (2024). *Australian Close Encounter Resource Network*. Viewed 2 June 2025. http://www.acern.com.au

CCRIT. (2024). *Consciousness and Contact Research Institute*. Viewed 2 June 2025. https://www.consciousnessandcontact.org

Cooper, H., Blumenthal, R., & Kean, L. (2017). Glowing Auras and 'Black Money': The Pentagon's Mysterious U.F.O. Program. *The New York Times*, 16 December. Retrieved April 11, 2025, from https://www.nytimes.com/2017/12/16/us/politics/pentagon-program-ufo-harry-reid.html

Coulthart, R. (2024). Coulthart: Grusch Health Records Should Not Have Been Released or Published. *Reality Check*. Retrieved April 11, 2025, from https://www.youtube.com/watch?v=ozIZeEbexjU

Elizondo, L. (2024). *Imminent: Inside the Pentagon's Hunt for UFOs*. William Morrow.

Evans, A. (2017). *The Myth Gap: What Happens When Old Stories Fade and New Stories Are Needed*. Fourth Estate.

Fravor, D. (2020). David Fravor: UFOs, Aliens, Fighter Jets, and Aerospace Engineering. *Lex Fridman Podcast* #122. YouTube. Retrieved August 20, 2025, from https://www.youtube.com/watch?v=aB8zcAttP1E

Greer, S. (2020). *CE5 Contact*, iOS/Android mobile app, CE5 Contact Inc. ICER 2024, *International Coalition for Extraterrestrial Research*. Viewed 2 June 2025. https://www.icer.network

Grusch, D. (2024). Joe Rogan Experience #2065—David Grusch. *Powerful JRE*. YouTube. Retrieved August 20, 2025, from https://www.youtube.com/watch?v=R8TqBrrqL4U&t=7400s

Grusch, D., & Fravor, D. (2023). House Holds Hearing on UFOs, Government Transparency | Full Video. *CBS News*. YouTube. Retrieved August 20, 2025, from https://www.youtube.com/watch?v=SNgoul4vyDM

Hastings, R. L. (2017). *UFOs & Nukes: Extraordinary Encounters at Nuclear Weapons Sites* (2nd ed.). CreateSpace Independent Publishing Platform.

Kean, L., & Blumenthal, R. (2023). Intelligence Officials Say U.S. Has Retrieved Craft of Non-Human Origin. *The Debrief*, 5 June. Retrieved April 11, 2025, from https://thedebrief.org/intelligence-officials-say-u-s-has-retrieved-non-human-craft/

Mack, J. (1994). *Abduction: Human Encounters with Aliens*. Scribner.

Motskin, Y. (2023a). Believers. *Encounters*, Season 1, Episode 2. [Netflix series episode]. Netflix.

Motskin, Y. (2023b). Messengers. *Encounters*, Season 1, Episode 3. [Netflix series episode]. Netflix.

Motskin, Y. (2023c). Japan. *Encounters*, Season 1, Episode 4. [Netflix series episode]. Netflix.

MUFON. (2024). *Experiencer Resource Team.* Mutual UFO Network. Viewed 2 June 2025. https://www.mufon.com

Nickerson, R. (2022). *Ariel Phenomenon* [Documentary Film]. String Theory Films.

OPUS. (2024). *Organization for Paranormal Understanding and Support.* Viewed 2 June 2025. https://www.opusnetwork.org

Piedra, G. (2025). *Is Jesus an Alien? Pope Francis' Interest in UAPs Explained.* Retrieved April 10, 2025, from https://www.youtube.com/watch?v=2izhNXn1Msc

Robins, D. (2021). The UFO in the Playground. *Uncanny*, Series 1, Episode 8. BBC Sounds. Retrieved August 20, 2025, from https://www.bbc.co.uk/sounds/play/p0b8j7hx

West, M. (2023a). *Escaping the Rabbit Hole: How to Debunk Conspiracy Theories Using Facts, Logic, and Respect* (2nd ed.). Skyhorse Publishing.

West, M. (2023b). A Conversation with UFO Skeptic Mick West. *Tangle News.* Retrieved June 30, 2025, from https://www.readtangle.com/conversation-with-mick-west-ufo-skeptic

West, M. (2023c). Claims Made by 'UFO Whistleblower' David Grusch are Pure Science Fiction. *Forbes*, 13 June. Retrieved June 30, 2025, from https://www.forbes.com/sites/danidiplacido/2023/06/13/claims-made-by-ufo-whistleblower-david-grusch-are-pure-science-fiction

West, M. (2025). UFOs, Disclosures & What's Really Going On? *The Asa Park Podcast.* Retrieved May 13, 2025, from https://www.youtube.com/watch?v=j6xN3lfkZx8

CHAPTER 7

Chemical Tricksters

The trickster archetype is intimately connected to portals. Tricksters embody the ability to disrupt boundaries, create new possibilities, and force transitions. By their very nature, tricksters challenge the established order of things, opening metaphorical or literal doors to uncharted territories.[1] This role makes them central figures in mythologies, rituals, and psychological narratives that involve transformation or crossing thresholds.

Psychedelics are chemical tricksters. These substances disrupt ordinary patterns of perception, cognition, and selfhood—dismantling egoic boundaries and opening access to states of consciousness that are typically inaccessible. Like mythological tricksters, psychedelics introduce chaos into the psyche, breaking down order through disorder. Yet this disruption carries the potential for reordering—catalysing profound personal change, heightened creativity, or spiritual insight.

Psychedelics often act as portals to inner worlds or alternate dimensions, offering glimpses into experiences that are at once transformative and disorienting. The dynamic between the trickster and the portal reveals a deeper truth about human growth: thresholds are rarely crossed without a destabilizing force to challenge the familiar. Tricksters personify this force—luring us to the edge, inviting us to step through, and confronting us with the unknown.

D. Kelsey, *Transcendence and Collective Psychology*,
https://doi.org/10.1007/978-3-032-09495-7_7

In this way, psychedelics resemble their archetypal counterparts: unpredictable, multifaceted, and charged with both the risk of psychic disintegration and the promise of renewal.

Celestial Common Ground

Like UFO stories, psychedelics share a capacity to evoke experiences that transcend familiarity and challenge our understanding of consciousness and reality. Both phenomena often involve encounters with the unknown, whether through vivid, otherworldly visions during a psychedelic trip or sightings of anomalous phenomena. These experiences frequently include reports of strange beings, profound messages, and an altered sense of time and space, suggesting a bridge between the psyche and a broader cosmic reality.

For many, the visionary nature of psychedelics mirrors the transcendent themes of those UFO encounters discussed in the previous chapter. Psychedelics can elicit archetypal imagery and cosmic motifs that resonate with narratives surrounding UFO phenomena. These substances enable individuals to explore realms that feel both deeply personal and profoundly other or alien, reflecting the psychological and spiritual dimensions often described by those who report UFO encounters.

Other Intelligences

Neuroscientist Andrew Gallimore explores the idea that psychedelics may function as a communication technology, enabling humans to interface with non-human intelligences.[2] He views this possibility as both extraordinary and transformative, suggesting that psychedelics open doorways to realms that appear "lived in," brimming with beings and consciousness that seem independent of the user's mind.

These experiences, often characterized by hyperbolic geometry and otherworldly beauty, challenge conventional understandings of reality and invite deeper philosophical inquiry.

Gallimore's research focuses on enabling individuals to remain in psychedelic states for extended periods—compared to the typically brief trips associated with substances like dimethyltryptamine (DMT). He argues that sustained immersion could allow more structured interactions with these intelligences and deepen our understanding of their nature. His books, *Reality Switch Technologies* and *Alien Information Theory*, expand on these ideas, proposing that DMT not only alters perception but may also reveal fundamental insights about the nature of reality and humanity's place within it.

Communication Technologies

By treating DMT as a technology for communication, Gallimore pushes the boundaries of how psychedelics are understood, suggesting they might play a role in uncovering deeper truths about consciousness and reality. He suggests that psychedelics have been part of human evolution for far longer than we previously thought, providing a pathway into arcane knowledge and transformative experiences.

This makes them not just tools but symbolic guides in humanity's ongoing exploration of transcendence and the mysteries that lie beyond familiar horizons. However, as we see in this chapter, they offer a profound example of the tensions that transcendental realms cause for those in power.

Of course, there are significant risks and requirements for caution in how we approach regulate and legislate the potential induction of psychedelics in health and medicine, with the likes of Jules Evans among others providing rigorous insight in this sense.[3] But this case study is concerned with the transcendental nature and potentials of these substances and what they teach us about the human experience, collective psychology, and the unconscious mind.

Get the Politicians Tripping

Bodybuilder Dorian Yates made a profound point when he shared his desire to force a group of politicians into a room and have them take psychedelic drugs.[4] He argued that such an experience could prevent the careless and self-centred behaviour he believes is typical of the political class. That's because psychedelics can create new possibilities for positive change, shifting our perception of reality in profound ways—including that dissolution of ego that can prohibit our empathetic and altruist potentials of a humanness.

Psychedelics are natural, plant-based compounds that are generally non-toxic. These substances can drag repressed memories, emotions, and unresolved complexes from the shadows into conscious awareness, often with startling intensity. In this chaos, they open pathways to insights previously inaccessible, offering glimpses into dimensions of consciousness that defy ordinary states of perception.

For many, they enable profound transcendence through what can be described as radical unselfing—a temporary dissolution of the ego that allows individuals to step beyond their limited sense of self. This unselfing creates space for a deep sense of connection with something greater, whether it is nature, humanity, or the cosmos itself.

Reimagining Inner Worlds

For many, this archetypal trickster energy has proven invaluable, particularly in alleviating depression and other mental health challenges. By breaking down the ***known***, they create fertile ground for the ***unknown*** to emerge, offering not only personal transformation but a profound sense of unity with the cosmos. In these altered states, individuals often feel a dissolving of the barriers that separate them from the universe, experiencing an interconnectedness that is both humbling and awe-inspiring, pushing the boundaries of what we believe is possible.

Many psychedelic experiencers report encountering visions of the cosmos or perceiving a reality so vivid and profound that it feels "more real" than real life itself. Joe Rogan describes DMT trips as encounters with a divine reality, likening the experience to meeting God or stepping into another dimension where divinity is made manifest.[5]

Due to these kinds of experiences, psychedelics like DMT have even been likened to spiritual gateways; DMT's nickname, "the spirit molecule," reflects the profundity of the experiences it can catalyse. DMT is not only found in various plants but is also produced naturally in animals and humans. DMT has been detected in the pineal gland, cerebrospinal fluid, and peripheral tissues such as the lungs and blood. However, its exact role in human physiology—whether functional, incidental, or related to altered states of consciousness—remains the subject of ongoing debate and research.

Psychedelic Ufology

Terence McKenna's psychedelic ufology explores the intersection of mystical and extraterrestrial experiences through altered states of consciousness.[6] McKenna argued that psychedelics, such as psilocybin and DMT, open visionary realms where alien intelligences can be encountered through these experiences he describes as phenomenologically real. Like Jung, McKenna saw these encounters as projections of the collective unconscious, with UFOs symbolizing the psyche's quest for wholeness and integration, which, for McKenna, could be found through non-physical realms.

McKenna extended Jung's idea of UFOs as modern myths that reflect the cultural anxieties and collective aspirations of their time.[7] McKenna saw psychedelic ufology and extraterrestrial experiences as opportunities for personal transformation, individuation, and self-realization. He adds speculative elements, suggesting that psychedelics might facilitate interdimensional communication and that mushrooms themselves could represent alien intelligence.

Psychedelic ufology more broadly examines narratives emerging from altered states of consciousness and their interplay with cultural myths of the unknown. Three key interpretations emerge: these experiences might be purely endogenous products of the mind; they could represent contact with exogenous, independent entities; or they might blur the line between the two, offering gnostic revelations that transcend distinctions between inner and outer realities.

Mystical Traditions

Terrence McKenna and Richard Rohr might seem worlds apart—one a psychedelic advocate critiquing modern culture, the other a Franciscan priest reshaping Christian theology—but both are rooted in mystical traditions that challenge mainstream thinking and offer paths to transcendence. While their methods and emphases differ, both share an interest in connecting people to deeper realities within *and beyond* the confines of the ego and the material world.[8]

McKenna believed psychedelics offered unparalleled access to other realms of consciousness. He described these substances as tools for breaking through the barriers of ordinary perception and connecting with a living, intelligent cosmos. For McKenna, this experience was not simply escapism; it was an urgent critique of "dominator culture," a modern mindset he saw as disconnected from nature and the sacred. Psychedelics, he argued, could heal this rift by revealing the profound interconnectedness of life, opening individuals to transformational insights that transcend cultural conditioning.[9]

As we saw earlier, Rohr's theological paradigm offers a parallel but distinct path to McKenna's claims here. Instead of turning to chemical tools, Rohr turns inward, emphasizing contemplative practices like prayer and meditation as a means of achieving direct, non-dual awareness of God. For Rohr, this connection isn't confined to moments of chemically stimulated ecstasy or revelation, but is a lifelong journey of surrender, healing, and participation in the divine flow of love, rooted in the Trinity.

But these approaches share some common ground too. Rohr's critique of dogmatic religion mirrors McKenna's critique of modernity: both argue that dominant spiritual and material paradigms respectively obscure humanity's potential to connect with the transcendent wholeness of reality.

The earliest pioneers in Western psychedelic science discovered the profound benefits of these compounds back in the 1940s—but only after an accident in a lab and a bike ride that ensued thereafter.

The Curious Chemist

Sandoz Laboratories, Basel, 1938. The Swiss chemist Albert Hofmann synthesized a compound called lysergic acid diethylamide (LSD) while researching substances to stimulate circulation and respiration. Initially, the compound showed little promise, and it was set aside for several years.

It wasn't until 1943 that Hofmann revisited LSD, conducting further tests on the substance. In what he later described as an unintentional self-experiment, Hofmann accidentally consumed a small amount of LSD, believing it to be harmless but unaware of its potent psychoactive effects.[10]

Almost immediately after taking the compound, Hofmann began to experience intense changes in perception. His world transformed, with colours becoming more vivid and his sense of time and space altering dramatically. Disturbed by these effects, Hofmann, who was alone in his lab at the time, attempted to return home.

Bicycle Day

As he bicycled through the streets of Basel, his altered state of consciousness intensified, making the journey a surreal and disorienting experience, which would later become known as "Bicycle Day." When Hoffmann woke the next morning he said he felt born again, like he was starting a new life.

Hofmann's discovery was a turning point in psychedelic science. By the mid-twentieth century, psychedelics were widely regarded as a revolutionary development in psychiatry. Between 1950 and the mid-1960s, they became the focus of intense scientific interest, with over a thousand research papers published on their effects and therapeutic potential. The excitement culminated in six major conferences dedicated to LSD alone, as many in the field viewed these compounds as the future of psychiatric medicine.

This accident led to an explosion of scientific interest in psychedelics, with researchers across the globe beginning to explore their potential for altering the mind, treating psychological conditions, and understanding consciousness itself. Hofmann had unwittingly opened a door to a new frontier of scientific inquiry, one that would captivate the imagination of both the academic world and the counterculture movements of the 1960s.

Atomic Happenings

An interviewer once asked Albert Hofmann to comment on the striking coincidence that LSD was discovered around the same time as the scientific breakthroughs that created the atomic bomb. Hofmann himself hesitated to dismiss this as mere chance.

Carl Jung would encourage us to reflect on this profound synchronicity and paradox in human progress: the simultaneous unlocking of unprecedented power in both the physical and mental realms.

The atomic bomb shattered physical barriers, marking a turning point in humanity's ability to harness nature's forces, and at a catastrophic cost. At the same time, LSD shattered mental barriers, offering a tool to explore the hidden depths of consciousness and transform our understanding of the self, others, and the planet. Both discoveries represent the trickster archetype in action: disrupting order through chaos to pave the way for new possibilities. Yet, this disruption carries dual potential—descent into destruction or ascent into transformation—depending on how we wield these forces.

LSD's capacity to dissolve the ego mirrors how the atomic bomb dissolved the illusion of global security, confronting humanity with existential vulnerabilities. Both breakthroughs demanded a reckoning with the shadow side of transcendence: one threatening annihilation, the other offering the peril and promise of profound inner change.

This synchronicity, Jung might suggest, reflects a deeper, collective intuition. The psyche is a vulnerable terrain of paradox, which is why we seek order to help make sense of the world around us. Yet, the collective psyche often confronts us with paradoxes that are difficult to grasp.

They Called It Trinity

This is especially true when we consider that the first nuclear weapon test, on July 16th, 1945, at the Alamogordo Bombing Range in New Mexico, was named "Trinity." The choice of Trinity for such a weapon shows how sacred symbols can be co-opted to justify actions that destory life, rather than celebrate its profound mystery.

Psychedelics have long been intertwined with spiritual traditions and religious symbolism. From the Ayahuasca churches of Brazil, which merge Christian rituals with shamanic practices, to hypotheses about psychedelic influences on early Christianity, these substances reveal a deep and ancient connection between altered states of consciousness and collective spirituality.[11]

Brian Muraresku and John Allegro both argue that psychedelics have played a significant role in shaping religious practices and the development of spiritual traditions throughout history.[12] Their analyses provide a provocative lens through which to understand the intersection of altered states of consciousness, divine revelation, and the sacred, challenging conventional views on religious origins.

Psychoactive Influences

Allegro presented his controversial thesis in *The Sacred Mushroom and the Cross.*[13] Allegro advanced the highly controversial claim that psychoactive mushrooms may have shaped aspects of early religious symbolism and ritual, including elements later embedded in Christian narrative.

Allegro claimed that long before Christianity, secret cults worshipped the Amanita Muscaria mushroom, viewing it as a symbol of God on earth due to its distinctive appearance and powerful psychoactive properties. When the practices of these cults needed to be recorded, they were supposedly hidden within folk tales in ways that only the initiated would understand. For Allegro, the stories in the New Testament were designed as a literary tool to pass on the rituals and teachings of mushroom worship to followers.

Allegro believed that these substances enabled practitioners to enter altered states of consciousness where they could experience direct, transcendent contact with the divine. He suggested that these psychedelic experiences were essential to the spiritual practices of early religious figures because they provided access to divine knowledge and transformation.

Although his ideas have been widely criticized and rejected by other scholars, Allegro's work has stimulated further inquiry into the role of psychedelics in ancient spiritual traditions.[14]

Mysterious Religions

More recently, Muraresku's book, *The Immortality Key* builds on similar ideas but takes a broader historical approach.[15] Muraresku argues that the use of psychoactive substances like *kykeon*—the sacred drink of the Eleusinian Mysteries—was central to the mystery religions of ancient Greece and early Christianity. He suggests that these substances, which could induce altered states of consciousness, played a significant role in early Christian spirituality via the bridging of physical and spiritual realms.

Muraresku speculates that, before the rise of Christianity, the Ancient Greeks might have incorporated a secret psychedelic substance into their most famous and widely attended religious ceremonies. He suggests that this sacramental tradition may have been handed down to early Greek-speaking Christians, raising the possibility that the original Holy Communion, or Eucharist, was influenced by these earlier psychedelic practices.

Muraresku's analysis situates psychedelics as a possible key to understanding the profound mystical experiences described in Christian texts, pointing to their role in shaping the development of religious practices and beliefs that transcended the institutional authority of the early Church. Both Allegro and Muraresku challenge the conventional narrative of religious history, proposing that the sacred and the psychedelic were intertwined in the quest for transcendence, divine knowledge, and the search for the sacred.

Despite early Church authorities attempting to repress the use or sacred recognition of psychedelic mushrooms, they lived on and would eventually grow (quite literally) beyond the control of institutional rigidity.

Paganism, Magic, Heresy

The rise of monasticism and the development of Christian dogma contributed to the marginalization of alternative spiritual practices. The Church actively suppressed practices associated with paganism, magic, and heresy, extending this suppression to rituals and substances used in those contexts.

While speculations on the Church systematically targeting psychedelics or similar substances are up for debate, the incidental prohibition of such practices—due to efforts to standardize Christian practices, eliminate paganism and magical rituals, and pursue witch-hunts—would have inevitably impinged upon spiritual explorations involving psychedelics.

Yet, the influence of mystical traditions persisted in underground or marginal forms, especially in regions or communities beyond the full reach of the institutional church. Gnostic texts—which emphasize esoteric knowledge (*gnosis*) and personal spiritual experience—reflect a longstanding tension between formalized Christianity and more experiential, inward forms of spirituality. While there is no direct evidence that early Christian Gnostics used psychedelics, some scholars have speculated that such substances may have been used in certain heterodox or mystery traditions to access altered states of consciousness and divine knowledge, potentially outside the authority of the church.

Despite those historical and institutional pursuits for rigidity, the legacy of this alternative spirituality continued to resurface in modern Christian mysticism and other spiritual movements. Returning to recent history, the countercultural movement of the 1960s was marked by this recurring counter-institutional pursuit of sacred exploration and encounters with God-like realms—a distinctly human and trickster-like pattern of behaviour seeking change beyond order. This movement rejected traditional authority, including religious institutions, and sought direct, personal experiences of the divine, often through the use of psychedelics.

But this rejection of order would also come at certain costs, which the Mazatec people of Mexico found out when the small town of Huautla de Jiménez became a global, psychedelic hotspot through the rediscovery of what would become known as magic mushrooms.[16]

Mushrooms and Curanderas

Michael Pollan reminds us how the Spanish conquistadors and Catholic Church violently eradicated indigenous Mexican rituals involving psilocybin. The Mazatec people described mushrooms as "the flesh of the Gods," drawing a distinct parallel to the Christian Eucharist. This similarity was so threatening to the Catholic Church that it brutally suppressed the practice.

However, rather than disappearing, the use of mushrooms went underground.[17] While still illegal today, authorities in Mexico often turn a blind eye, and "curanderas" (healers) continue to apply traditions passed down for over 1000 years.

The curandera embodies the archetype of the *wounded healer* and the *mystic guide*. Rooted in Indigenous, African, and Catholic syncretic traditions, she channels ancestral knowledge to heal physical, emotional, and spiritual wounds. As an archetype, the curandera represents embodied wisdom, often passed through oral traditions, ritual, herbs, dreams, and spiritual insight.[18]

Unlike institutional healers or priests, the curandera operates outside formal systems of power, often in marginalized spaces—making her a symbol of resistance, care, and cultural survival. She draws power not from hierarchy but from connection: to land, lineage, spirits, and the suffering of her community.

The curandera archetype also carries a liminal role: bridging worlds—between the seen and unseen, science and spirit, body and cosmos. In Jungian terms, she resonates with both the wise elder and the magician, offering transformation through altered states, ritual, and symbolic language.

In contemporary discourse, the curandera has been reclaimed as a feminist and decolonial figure, challenging dominant medical, religious, and political paradigms. She calls us back to a form of healing that is communal, intuitive, and grounded in sacred relationality.

Underground Survival

Despite repression from the Catholic Church, these traditions survived underground, passed down through curanderas like María Sabina—a wise elder who oversaw the rituals and ingestion of mushrooms for psychedelic experiences.

In the 1950s, mycologists R. Gordon Wasson and Valentina Wasson travelled to Mexico, where they met the Mazatec curandera María Sabina and participated in an indigenous mushroom ceremony.[19] Their experience introduced them to the psychoactive mushrooms later popularly known as "magic mushrooms." Gordon Wasson's ecstatic description of the experience, published in *Life* magazine in the 1950s, introduced millions of readers to psilocybin and sparked widespread interest.

This attention eventually led to the chemical isolation of psilocybin by Albert Hofmann—the Swiss chemist best known for synthesizing LSD. Wasson and Hofmann later returned to Mexico with synthesized psilocybin tablets, which María Sabina ingested and reportedly affirmed contained the same spirit as the natural mushrooms.

However, the influx of Western visitors devastated Sabina's community, transforming her quiet hometown of Huautla de Jiménez into a chaotic destination for hippies, seekers, and celebrities. As resentment grew over what many locals saw as the disrespectful intrusion and commodification of sacred traditions, María Sabina was blamed for attracting unwanted attention. She was ultimately ostracized by her community and died in poverty.

But Sabina's legacy lives on, and she is widely considering the grandmother of psychedelics—with her knowledge and wisdom of mushrooms replicated by experts around the world.

The Mystical Mycologist

Paul Stamets, a contemporary mycologist, recalls his own introduction to psilocybin in the 1970s.[20] His brother's experiences inspired him to explore mushrooms growing in his garden, igniting a lifelong fascination.

Stamets has since discovered several new species and describes psilocybin as a "great unifier" that dissolves cultural and temporal boundaries. For him, mushrooms are *portals to primordial origins*, and he blames human arrogance for outlawing a species that holds such a profound connection to our consciousness. Stamets championed the psychoactive mushroom renaissance through conferences like the Millennium Mushroom Conference in 1999, which aimed to establish scientific legitimacy for research.

Roland Griffiths, a psychopharmacologist, joined this movement after his own spiritual crisis. Meditation had introduced him to altered states of consciousness, but psilocybin deepened his understanding. Collaborating with Richards, Griffiths conducted groundbreaking studies at Johns Hopkins University, where participants reported mystical experiences with profound long-term effects.[21] Many described these as among the most significant events of their lives, comparable to the birth of a child or the death of a parent.

Biblical Symbolism

In a conversation with Joe Rogan, bodybuilder Dorian Yates recounted a moment during a psychedelic trip when he found himself trapped in a dark tunnel filled with frightening, negative images. Instinctively, he decided to relax, started laughing, and said, "Fuck you, you're not even real."[22] Immediately, the images disappeared. Yates reflected that he had just passed through the "valley of the shadow of death," a reference from the Lord's Prayer. He realized that he had escaped that negative place in the trip because, as the prayer suggests, we should fear no evil—God is by our side.

A well-known story from scripture is Moses' encounter with God through the burning bush in Exodus. As Moses approached, the bush was on fire but not consumed by the flames, and from it, God called out to him. Marked by both awe and fear, this encounter with the divine is one of the most iconic mystical experiences in the Bible.

Some scholars speculate that this vision could have been influenced by the use of psychoactive substances, such as those native to the region. These substances may have facilitated an altered state of consciousness that allowed Moses to perceive the burning bush as a divine revelation.

In a similar vein, the manna described in *Exodus*—the mysterious substance that appeared each morning to feed the Israelites—has also sparked speculation. Some researchers have proposed that this manna may represent a form of visionary or altered-state food, potentially linked to psychoactive plants or fungi. Just as Moses' encounter with God has been interpreted by some as a possible experience of altered perception, the manna has been hypothesized as a psychoactive substance—offering sustenance not only for the body, but also for the mind and spirit during a time of hardship and transformation.[23]

Ezekiel's vivid vision of angels and divine glory, often described in surreal and symbolic terms, has led some to suggest that he may have experienced a psychedelic encounter, possibly through the inhalation of smoke from burning sacred plants. The Transfiguration of Jesus, where he is seen in radiant glory by his disciples, is another example where some have drawn parallels to mystical experiences that could involve altered states, possibly triggered by psychedelics.[24]

In early Christianity, there were alternative forms of spirituality that were more experiential and less focused on institutionalized practices. Early Christians, especially those in rural or isolated areas, might have continued spiritual practices involving altered states of consciousness, which were seen as a direct connection to God or divine realities.

These practices would have existed outside the knowledge or control of church authorities as the institutional church began to establish its hierarchy and doctrines.

Beyond the Authorities

Pollan marvels at the mushroom's extraordinary power to inspire creativity, heal emotional wounds, and help people confront profound existential fears, such as the terror of death. He recounts the story of Kathleen Krall: a 78-year-old Catholic woman with a terminal cancer diagnosis, whose life had been overshadowed by negativity and deepened by her illness. Defying expectations of someone her age and religious background, she was open to trying psilocybin, despite warnings from friends. Her goal was simple but urgent: to lift her depression.[25]

During her psilocybin trip, she described conducting an imaginary orchestra to beautiful music. She saw ancestors at their weddings, including her own, reflecting on the joys and challenges of marriage. Then came frightening and ferocious waves, like a storm at sea, which she interpreted symbolically as her cancer. Instead of resisting, she embraced the waves, asking them to reveal whatever they needed to teach her.

The experience turned dark, plunging her into blackness and memories of a miscarriage 44 years earlier. She felt inept and burdened, but then a radiant golden light appeared. The Virgin Mary, bathed in this light, reassured her that the miscarriage was cared for and no longer her burden. This profound vision brought her tremendous relief, as though a hidden weight had been lifted. She emerged with a renewed sense of spiritual reality: a cosmos interconnected across past, present, and future.

Systematic Evaluation

Roland Griffiths explains how mystical experiences reported in psychedelic studies are systematically evaluated using the Mystical Experience Questionnaire (MEQ). Pollan asks Kathleen a series of questions about her experience. The MEQ is designed to assess subjective experiences across specific domains commonly associated with mysticism experiences.

Examples include feelings of unity, where individuals report a profound sense of interconnectedness with all things; transcendence of time and space, where participants lose awareness of past, present, and future or feel they exist beyond physical dimensions; and perceptions of sacredness, where the experience is imbued with deep spiritual significance. Additionally, the questionnaire examines reports of ineffability—moments that participants find impossible to fully articulate in words—and positive mood, characterized by overwhelming joy, peace, or love.

Studies show that high scores on the MEQ, particularly in the domains of unity and sacredness, correlate with enduring positive effects on spiritual well-being, life satisfaction, and prosocial behaviour over the following year. This scientific approach provides a structured way to analyse the subjective and transformative aspects of mystical experiences, further melding the investigative architecture between personal spirituality and empirical research.

Psychologist Bill Richards sees these experiences not as anomalies but as encounters with the same sacred realm that religions describe as revelation. He argues that science and spirituality are not in conflict here but are instead converging through the study of psychedelics. For some, the spiritual depth of these experiences is so profound that the substances themselves are perceived as gifts from God.

The Polarizing Prophet

Timothy Leary, a psychiatrist and countercultural icon, believed psychedelics could revolutionize collective psychological development and spiritual growth. He envisioned their use becoming widespread, moving from laboratories into everyday life. His work and advocacy ignited a counterculture that challenged authority, conformity, and the structures of war and corporate power.[26]

Leary championed psychedelics as a pathway to spiritual and psychological liberation. Leary made the point that: "Most of us see the world through a very small set of filters. When you take LSD and your consciousness is expanded, the number of possibilities and perspectives dramatically multiplies." For Leary, psychedelics marked the beginning of a major religious renaissance, as he stated he didn't make LSD, but God did.[27]

After leaving Berkeley, Leary travelled to Mexico, where he tried psilocybin mushrooms for the first time. He described the experience as transformative, claiming it taught him more about the mind than his 15 years of psychological study.

In 1960, Harvard recruited Leary, and he developed a research program on psychedelics. Alongside colleague Richard Alpert (later Ram Dass), Leary conducted studies exploring how psychedelics could induce mystical experiences. One notable study in a church setting found that 9 out of 10 participants reported profound spiritual revelations during the experiment.

Controversy soon arose around their methods, particularly accusations that they encouraged students to take psychedelics. Leary and Alpert denied coercing anyone, arguing that researchers needed personal experience with psychedelics to understand their effects. However, their program drew criticism for breaching academic boundaries. When Alpert gave psychedelics to an undergraduate, Harvard dismissed him outright. Though Leary wasn't formally fired, his contract was not renewed in 1963, effectively ending his tenure at the university.

Leary's departure marked the start of his transformation into a public advocate for psychedelics. He developed the concepts of "set and setting" for safe psychedelic use—principles still foundational in modern research—and moved from psilocybin to LSD. Establishing retreats like Millbrook in New York, he invited participants to explore psychedelics in controlled environments.

However, as his fame grew, so did public scrutiny. His mantra, "Turn on, tune in, drop out," became a rallying cry for the countercultural movement, which was increasingly seen as a threat by the establishment.[28]

A Typical Trickster

With their ability to induce altered states of consciousness and profound experiences of transcendence that intersected with the resistance to mainstream American politics (and war) at the time, psychedelics posed a trickster-like challenge to the establishment. For young people, these substances offered a sense of liberation, connection, and resistance to the hierarchical systems of power. For the authorities, however, they represented chaos—disrupting the social order, encouraging dissent, and undermining conformity.

Leary embodied this trickster dynamic, championing psychedelics as tools to expand consciousness and break free from the constraints of traditional authority. Yet, this same ethos made him a scapegoat. Losing the battle for public opinion during the Vietnam War, the establishment could not tolerate the counterculture's opposition to war, corporate greed, and institutional power.

Leary's mantra, "Turn on, tune in, drop out," was seen as a direct threat to the values of productivity, discipline, and obedience that upheld the system. To the establishment, he was not a visionary but a corrupter of the youth, whose embrace of transcendence was reinterpreted as recklessness and anarchy.

Like a typical trickster figure, Leary's actions sparked systemic reactions that ultimately ensnared him. His chaos—deliberate or not—provoked fear and repression from those in power, culminating in his criminalization and vilification. Yet, the very forces that sought to silence him also amplified his message, ensuring his place as a polarizing figure in the cultural psyche. Leary's undoing reflected the trickster's paradox: by challenging the rules, he forced transformation, but he also bore the consequences of the chaos he unleashed.

Arrested multiple times, he received a 10-year sentence for cannabis possession in 1970. While in prison, Leary escaped with the help of countercultural allies, fleeing to Algeria. There, tensions with the Black Panthers soured his exile; his focus on psychedelic mind expansion was seen as a bourgeois distraction from radical, political, and armed revolutionary goals. Leary was later recaptured in Afghanistan and cooperated with the FBI to reduce his sentence, a move that alienated many of his supporters.

The Reborn Futurist

In the 1970s, Leary reinvented himself as a futurist, embracing emerging technologies. He saw the internet as a tool for human evolution and catalogued his life on *leary.com* to preserve his legacy. By the 1990s, as he faced terminal cancer, Leary openly confronted death, planning to livestream his final moments and cryogenically preserve his head.

Even shortly before death, he rejected mainstream wisdom, opting against orthodox painkillers while using marijuana and laughing gas for pain management. After his death in 1996, Leary's ashes were launched into space, symbolizing his lifelong desire to transcend boundaries—social, spiritual, and physical.

Despite his rebellion against authority, a friend recalled how Leary sought reassurance that he had "been a good boy" during his life, suggesting he never fully relinquished the baggage of his strict Catholic upbringing. Leary remains a polarizing figure, embodying both the promise and peril of psychedelics and countercultural revolution.

Chemical Warfare

Michael Pollan highlights how Timothy Leary became a convenient scapegoat for the backlash against psychedelics in the 1960s. While Leary's role in shaping public perceptions of psychedelics is undeniable, Pollan suggests this narrative overshadows the CIA's significant, if shadowy, contributions to the spread of psychedelics in American culture.[29]

During the 1950s and early 1960s, the CIA conducted extensive experiments with psychedelics, particularly LSD, as part of *MK-Ultra*, a covert program aimed at exploring their potential as bioweapons, mind control agents, or interrogation tools. These experiments often involved non-consensual dosing of unwitting participants, including prisoners, mental patients, and even ordinary civilians.

The CIA hoped to uncover ways to manipulate the human mind, induce compliance, or break enemy agents. While much of this research was unethical and secretive, it inadvertently contributed to the popularization of psychedelics. The agency's experiments leaked into the broader culture when some participants—aware or otherwise—began sharing their experiences, sparking curiosity and experimentation in artistic, intellectual, and countercultural circles.

One such participant was Ken Kesey, an author and cultural icon who took part in a CIA-funded experiment at Stanford University. Kesey later became a pivotal figure in the West Coast psychedelic movement, forming a loose collective known as the *Merry Pranksters*. This group became famous for their cross-country bus tour in 1964 aboard a psychedelic-painted vehicle called *Further*.

The Pranksters, inspired by Kesey's vision, embraced LSD as a tool for spiritual exploration, creative expression, and communal experiences.

They hosted *Acid Tests*, multi-sensory parties featuring live music, light shows, and communal LSD trips, which laid the groundwork for the West Coast counterculture and the rise of the psychedelic rock scene, including bands like the Grateful Dead.

In contrast to Leary's academic persona and East Coast intellectualism, Kesey and the Merry Pranksters represented a more anarchic, freewheeling approach to psychedelics. They emphasized the experiential and celebratory aspects of the drug, rejecting institutional authority and encouraging people to "freak freely."

While both Leary and Kesey contributed to the cultural entrenchment of psychedelics, their philosophies and styles diverged significantly, reflecting the multifaceted nature of the psychedelic revolution.

Pollan makes the point that while Leary's advocacy for recreational use made him a convenient scapegoat, it was the CIA's covert experiments—marked by ethical violations and unintended cultural spillover—that fuelled public fears about psychedelics. Ironically, the agency's inability to control the narrative around their use contributed to the need to suppress the very movement they had inadvertently helped ignite, propagating fear and stigma to cover up their own missteps.

Fear and Suppression

Despite initial optimism among psychiatry envisaging a bright future with psychedelics, and the alternative cultural thinking on possibilities for collective consciousness and spiritual connection, the fear generated among governments and institutions proved costly for psychiatric research. By the late 1960s, psychedelics were outlawed, with Leary blamed for their recreational misuse and fostering a reckless counterculture. A government propaganda campaign ensued. Psychedelics were demonized as a source of life-threatening harm and danger to society.

After their prohibition, research on psychedelics virtually disappeared from mainstream academic settings for about thirty years. Several decades later, they were reintroduced into university labs for serious scientific study.

This period marked the beginning of scientific studies on the therapeutic potential of substances like MDMA and psilocybin, with the FDA approving certain studies. A significant milestone came in 2000 when Johns Hopkins University launched its first modern study on psilocybin, examining its effects on mystical experiences.

By the 2010s, psychedelic research was expanding, with institutions like Imperial College London and the Multidisciplinary Association for Psychedelic Studies (MAPS) leading investigations into psychedelics' potential for treating conditions such as depression, PTSD, and addiction.[30] Today, psychedelics are increasingly recognized as valuable tools in mental health treatment, signalling a dramatic shift in how these substances are viewed in both scientific and medical communities.[31]

Notes

1. Hollis (2007); Hynes and Doty (1993); Hyde (1998); Jung (1959); Moore and Gillette (1990); Radin (1956); Kelsey (2017).
2. Gallimore (2019, 2022).
3. See Evans (2025) for a cautious intervention on political approaches to psychedelic medicines. Also see Evans et al. (2023) for a study on long-term adverse effects on psychedelics: "Long-term adverse experiences following psychedelic use can persist for weeks, months, or even years, and are relatively unexplored in psychedelic research. Our convergent mixed-method study gained quantitative and qualitative data from 608 participants who reported extended difficulties following psychedelic experiences. Data was gathered on the context of use, the nature and duration of the challenges they experienced (including a written description of these), plus a range of possible risk factors and perceived causes. The most common forms of extended difficulty were feelings of anxiety and fear, existential struggle, social disconnection, depersonalization and derealization. For approximately one-third of the participants, problems persisted for over a year, and for a sixth, they endured for more than three years. It was found that a shorter duration of difficulties was predicted by knowledge of dose, drug type and lower levels of difficulty reported during the psychoactive experience, while a narrower range of difficulties was predicted by taking the drug in a guided setting. Implications for psychedelic harm reduction are discussed."
4. See Rogan (2017).
5. Rogan (2018).
6. For further insights on psychedelic ufology, see Partridge (2020).
7. McKenna (1993).
8. When juxtaposed with Richard Rohr's mystical theology, which emphasizes the sacredness and unity of physical reality as an expression of God's presence, the gnostic and esoteric elements in psychedelic ufology and spirituality move in a slightly different ontological direction. Rohr's theology is grounded in an incarnational worldview that celebrates creation as

inherently good and views the material world as a vehicle for divine revelation. This perspective aligns with the Christian affirmation of the Incarnation, where physical reality is not something to be *escaped* through transcendence but to be embraced as part of spiritual growth and transformation. Rohr would still encourage the revelatory explorations of reality and consciousness in all forms within and beyond the material world, but they're all equally accommodated through that Trinitarian flow through which he adopts panentheism. Gnostic sensibilities can emphasize hidden knowledge (gnosis) and elevate non-material or "higher" realities *over* the physical. McKenna speculates about interdimensional realms, alien intelligences, and the idea that substances like psilocybin may themselves be extraterrestrial in origin, offering insights into alternate dimensions of existence. While these ideas are compelling, they can risk diminishing the significance of the physical world by framing it as a mere stepping stone to other, supposedly superior planes of reality.

9. McKenna (1991, 1992).
10. See Pollan (2018) for a full account of Hofman's experience and work.
11. Alverga (2010); Barnard (2019); Labate and MacRae (2010).
12. Allegro (1970).
13. Muraresku (2020); Allegro (1970).
14. For counterarguments to Allegro's claims see: Pervo (1971); Brown & Brown (2019).
15. Muraresku (2020).
16. See Pollan (2018a, 2022).
17. Ibid.
18. For more on curandera figures and cultural context, see: Anzaldúa (1987); Behar (1993); Caballero (2017); Delgadillo (2011); Lara (2005); Ortiz and Davis (2009).
19. Wasson (1957).
20. See Stamets (2008, 2018).
21. Griffiths et al. (2006); Griffiths et al. (2008); Griffiths (2015).
22. See Rogan (2017).
23. McKenna (1992); Merkur (2001); Shanon (2008).
24. McKenna (1992); Merkur (2001); Shanon (2008).
25. Pollan (2018b, 2022).
26. Leary (1968); Leary et al. (1964); Leary (1983, 1994).
27. Pollan (2018b, 2022).
28. Ibid.
29. Ibid.
30. See also Nutt (2023).
31. For examples of current clinical research on psychedelic treatment for clinical depression, see: Carhart-Harris et al. (2016, 2021, 2023).

Bibliography

Allegro, J. M. (1970). *The Sacred Mushroom and the Cross: A Study of the Nature and Origins of Christianity within the Fertility Cults of the Ancient Near East.* Doubleday.

Alverga, A. (2010). *The Religion of Ayahuasca: The Teachings of the Church of Santo Daime.* Park Street Press.

Anzaldúa, G. (1987). *Borderlands/La Frontera: The New Mestiza.* Aunt Lute Books.

Barnard, G. (2019). *Liquid Light: Ayahuasca Spirituality and the Santo Daime Tradition.* Columbia University Press.

Behar, R. (1993). *Translated Woman: Crossing the Border with Esperanza's Story.* Beacon Press.

Brown, J. B., & Brown, J. M. (2019). Entheogens in Christian art: Wasson, allegro, and the psychedelic gospels. *Journal of Psychedelic Studies, 3*(2), 142–163.

Caballero, C. (2017). Curanderismo: Soul Retrieval, Energy Healing and the Body as Medicine. *Journal of Latina/o Psychology, 5*(3), 187–199.

Carhart-Harris, R. L., et al. (2016). Psilocybin with Psychological Support for Treatment-Resistant Depression: An Open-Label Feasibility Study. *The Lancet Psychiatry, 3*(7), 619–627. https://doi.org/10.1016/S2215-0366(16)30065-7

Carhart-Harris, R. L., et al. (2021). Trial of Psilocybin Versus Escitalopram for Depression. *The New England Journal of Medicine, 384*(15), 1402–1411. https://doi.org/10.1056/NEJMoa2032994

Carhart-Harris, R. L., et al. (2023). Effect of Psilocybin Versus Escitalopram on Depression Symptom Severity: A Randomized Clinical Trial. *eClinicalMedicine, 59*, 101954. https://doi.org/10.1016/j.eclinm.2024.101954

Delgadillo, T. (2011). *Spiritual Mestizaje: Religion, Gender, and Ethnicity in Latina/o Borderland Narratives.* Duke University Press.

Evans, J. (2025). Psychedelic Policy: Speed Up or Slow Down? *Ecstatic Integration.* Retrieved June 30, 2025, from https://www.ecstaticintegration.org/p/psychedelic-policy-speed-up-or-slow

Evans, J., Robinson, O. C., Argyri, E. K., Suseelan, S., Murphy-Beiner, A., McAlpine, R., et al. (2023). Extended Difficulties Following the Use of Psychedelic Drugs: A Mixed Methods Study. *PLoS One, 18*(10), e0293349. https://doi.org/10.1371/journal.pone.0293349

Gallimore, A. R. (2019). *Alien Information Theory: Psychedelic Drug Technologies and the Cosmic Game.* Strange Worlds Press.

Gallimore, A. R. (2022). *Reality Switch Technologies: Psychedelics as Tools for the Discovery and Exploration of New Worlds.* Strange Worlds Press.

Griffiths, R. R. (2015). *Psilocybin: Unlocking the Unconscious, Opening the Mind.* TEDMED. Retrieved April 28, 2025, from https://www.youtube.com/watch?v=AifzF2BJxEE

Griffiths, R. R., Richards, W. A., McCann, U., & Jesse, R. (2006). Psilocybin Can Occasion Mystical-Type Experiences Having Substantial and Sustained Personal Meaning and Spiritual Significance. *Psychopharmacology, 187*(3), 268–283.

Griffiths, R. R., Richards, W. A., Johnson, M. W., McCann, U., & Jesse, R. (2008). Mystical-Type Experiences Occasioned by Psilocybin Mediate the Attribution of Personal Meaning and Spiritual Significance 14 Months Later. *Journal of Psychopharmacology, 22*(6), 621–632.

Hollis, J. (2007). *Tracking the Gods: The Place of Myth in Modern Life*. Inner City Books.

Hyde, L. (1998). *Trickster Makes This World: Mischief, Myth, and Art*. Farrar, Straus and Giroux.

Hynes, W. J., & Doty, W. G. (Eds.). (1993). *Mythical Trickster Figures: Contours, Contexts, and Criticisms*. University of Alabama Press.

Jung, C. G. (1959). *Four Archetypes: Mother, Rebirth, Spirit, Trickster*. Princeton University Press.

Kelsey, D. (2017). *Media and Affective Mythologies: Discourse, Archetypes, and Ideology in Contemporary Politics*. Palgrave.

Labate, B., & MacRae, E. (2010). *Ayahuasca, Ritual and Religion in Brazil*. Routledge.

Lara, I. (2005). Healing Multiculturalism: The Politics of Emotional Translations in Chicana Feminist Narratives. *Hypatia, 20*(1), 88–103.

Leary, T. (1968). *High Priest*. New American Library.

Leary, T. (1983). *Flashbacks: A Personal and Cultural History of an Era*. Jeremy P. Tarcher, Inc..

Leary, T. (1994). *Chaos and Cyber Culture*. Ronin Publishing.

Leary, T., Metzner, R., & Alpert, R. (1964). *The Psychedelic Experience: A Manual Based on the Tibetan Book of the Dead*. University Books.

McKenna, T. (1991). *The Archaic Revival: Speculations on Psychedelic Mushrooms, the Amazon, Virtual Reality, UFOs, Evolution, Shamanism, the Rebirth of the Goddess, and the End of History*. HarperSanFrancisco.

McKenna, T. (1992). *Food of the Gods: The Search for the Original Tree of Knowledge—A Radical History of Plants, Drugs, and Human Evolution*. Rider.

McKenna, T. (1993). *True Hallucinations: Being an Account of the Author's Extraordinary Adventures in the Devil's Paradise*. HarperOne.

Merkur, D. (2001). *The Mystery of Manna: The Psychedelic Sacrament of the Bible*. Park Street Press.

Moore, R. L., & Gillette, D. (1990). *King, Warrior, Magician, Lover: Rediscovering the Archetypes of the Mature Masculine*. HarperCollins.

Muraresku, B. (2020). *The Immortality Key: The Secret History of the Religion with No Name*. St. Martin's Press.

Nutt, D. (2023). *Psychedelics: The New Frontier of Psychiatry*. [Publisher].

Ortiz, A. Y., & Davis, C. A. (2009). *Women's Healing Traditions: The Politics of Medicine and Cultural Knowledge*. Routledge.

Partridge, C. (2020). Inner Space/Outer Space: Terence McKenna's Jungian Psychedelic Ufology. *Nova Religio*, *23*(3), 31–59. Retrieved April 11, 2025, from https://doi.org/10.1525/nr.2020.23.3.31

Pervo, R. I. (1971). Review of *The Sacred Mushroom and the Cross*. *Journal of Biblical Literature*, *90*(1), 116–118.

Pollan, M. (2018a). *How to Change Your Mind: What the New Science of Psychedelics Teaches Us About Consciousness, Dying, Addiction, Depression, and Transcendence*. Penguin Press.

Pollan, M. (2018b). Joe Rogan Experience #1121—Michael Pollan. *The Joe Rogan Experience*, 24 May. Retrieved April 28, 2025, from https://www.youtube.com/watch?v=tz4CrWE_P0g

Pollan, M. (2022). *How to Change Your Mind*. Directed by L. Walker and A. Ellwood. [TV series]. Netflix.

Radin, P. (1956). *The Trickster: A Study in American Indian Mythology*. Columbia University Press.

Rogan, J. (2017). Joe Rogan experience #989—Dorian yates. YouTube video, added by PowerfulJRE. Accessed April 11, 2025, from https://www.youtube.com/watch?v=cu-7WSjaVyU

Rogan, J. (2018). *Joe Rogan's DMT Experiences*. YouTube video. Viewed 28 April 2025. https://www.youtube.com/watch?v=DEsCPOdPTM4

Shanon, B. (2008). *The Antipodes of the Mind: Charting the Phenomenology of the Ayahuasca Experience*. Oxford University Press.

Stamets, P. (2008). Going Underground: Paul Stamets on the Vast, Intelligent Network Beneath Our Feet. *The Sun Magazine*, February. Retrieved April 28, 2025, from https://www.edrosenthal.com/the-guru-of-ganja-blog/going-underground-paul-stamets-on-the-vast-intelligent-network-beneath-our-feet

Stamets, P. (2018). *Joe Rogan Experience #1035—Paul Stamets*. YouTube. Viewed 28 April 2025. https://www.youtube.com/watch?v=mPqWstVnRjQ

Wasson, R. G. (1957). Seeking the Magic Mushroom. *Life*, *49*(19), 100–102, 109–120.

CHAPTER 8

Psychedelic Renaissance

Michael Pollan describes how LSD has undergone a dramatic cultural re-evaluation. Once celebrated as a miracle drug that expanded consciousness and enabled transcendental experiences, it was later demonized as a substance that destroyed young minds and destabilized societal norms. The psychedelic experience, which transported individuals beyond the constraints of "realpolitik" and institutional rigidity into a realm of cosmic consciousness governed by different values, was seen as too threatening to the established order.

This led to decades of prohibition and a halt in research—a "dark age" for psychedelics.

The resurgence of LSD began in Switzerland, spearheaded by Peter Gasser, who believed in its potential to heal. Gasser's efforts coincided with the 100th birthday of Albert Hofmann, LSD's discoverer, in 2006. The event drew over 1000 attendees and included an open letter urging global authorities to reopen psychedelic research. Only Switzerland responded.[1]

Gasser treated patients like a woman suffering from terminal cancer and depression, whose experience with LSD was transformative. It did not intoxicate her; instead, it reconnected her with the cosmos, restoring a sense of meaning and transcendence that had been buried in her unconscious. This reflects Carl Jung's insight that the shadow contains not only

D. Kelsey, *Transcendence and Collective Psychology*,
https://doi.org/10.1007/978-3-032-09495-7_8

our darkest traits but also our divine potentials. For this patient, LSD unearthed that potential and provided profound psychological healing.[2]

A Cosmic Dance

Neuroscientists have taken such accounts seriously. Brain scans reveal that LSD diminishes the brain's usual filtering mechanisms, allowing regions that rarely communicate to work together. This has been described some as a "cosmic dance," reflecting the fluidity and interconnectedness of brain activity under LSD. The effect illuminates how the sense of self—our experience of "me" and "my" thoughts—is shaped by brain structures we rarely notice.

By softening the ego's defence mechanisms, psychedelics create a more flexible neurolandscape that enables insights and perspectives inaccessible in ordinary consciousness.[3]

The therapeutic applications of this phenomenon are profound. One patient, who suffered from chronic cluster headaches, described his pain as akin to an ice pick piercing his eye. After enduring a year without a single pain-free day, he saw LSD as a last resort before considering assisted suicide through Switzerland's Exit programme. Remarkably, the treatment gave him five consecutive pain-free days. He not only found relief but also a renewed sense of life's beauty, describing LSD as a pathway to healing and transcendence.

Despite such promising outcomes, research into LSD remains contentious, particularly in the United States. However, microdosing—taking sub-perceptual doses of LSD—has gained popularity, largely through the work of Jim Fadiman, often called the "father of microdosing." This practice involves taking a fraction of a recreational dose, with 80% of users reporting relief from depression that is distinct from traditional antidepressants.

Ayelet Waldman, a mother struggling with suicidal ideation, experienced immediate transformation through microdosing. For the first time in years, she was joyful and present, a change so striking that her children were amazed. Pollan, initially sceptical, experimented with microdosing himself and found it rekindled a profound sense of love. He felt as if he were experiencing love for the first time, reminded of its centrality in human life—a truth long emphasized by mystics and theologians, who describe God and divinity as rooted in love.[4]

Mystery and Wholeness

Pollan suggests that psychedelics also lead us towards the ultimate mystery of existence. As Einstein noted: "The most beautiful and profound emotion we can experience is the sensation of the mystical. It is the sower of all true science."[5] Psychedelics invite us into this unexplainable realm, where efforts to articulate or define fall short. Richard Rohr's earlier reflections on the Trinity—"it's like, it's like, it's like"—mirror the shared language of psychedelic experiences, which rely on metaphor to gesture towards what cannot be fully expressed.[6]

Pollan also compares two types of consciousness: the focused "spotlight" of adult cognition, which is goal-oriented and deliberate, and the expansive "lantern" of childhood, which illuminates everything and invites awe. Psychedelics temporarily restore this lantern-like consciousness, evoking a sense of wonder often lost in adulthood. While Pollan notes that such states are not sustainable for everyday life, they offer a glimpse into a richer, more connected mode of being.

Ultimately, psychedelics open pathways to healing, transformation, and deeper insights into the nature of consciousness. They reveal not only the mysteries of the mind but also the profound potential for awe, love, and connection—qualities essential for a meaningful life.

Now, in the mid-2020s, we are seeing a renaissance in scientific research on psychedelics, particularly in the treatment of mental health conditions such as depression and PTSD. Ground-breaking studies at institutions like Imperial College London's Centre for Psychedelic Research have demonstrated their potential to catalyse profound psychological and emotional healing.[7]

Research and Therapy

Can Magic Mushrooms Unlock Depression? That's the question Rosalind Watts addressed in her 2017 Tedx talk on those studies at Imperial College London.[8] Watts shared findings on the potential of psilocybin, the active compound in magic mushrooms, as a treatment for depression. Through the cases of two individuals, Kirk and Ben, she highlighted the transformative effects of psilocybin on those suffering from severe, treatment-resistant depression.

Kirk had been battling depression for five years with no success from antidepressants or therapy, but after a single dose of psilocybin at Imperial

College in 2015, he experienced lasting relief. Similarly, Ben, who had struggled for thirty years, found his depression lifted after psilocybin therapy in 2015. Beyond alleviating symptoms, Ben's life flourished—he pursued creative endeavours, took acting courses, and even flew on a plane for the first time in a decade. His story was a testament to psilocybin's potential not only for healing but for opening new doors in life. However, his identity remained anonymous due to the illegal status of magic mushrooms.

Watts, a clinical psychologist at Imperial's psychedelic research group, explains that psilocybin doesn't just suppress symptoms but works on the root causes of depression. In a study of twenty individuals with treatment-resistant depression, patients were given psilocybin in a controlled, therapeutic setting.

The results showed symptoms of depression significantly decreased, with some patients remaining in remission for up to six months. The effects were much more immediate and lasting than conventional treatments, which can take weeks to show results and often come with side effects.

Unlocking the Box

Watts explains that for many people, depression feels like a "locked box"—an emotional prison. Patients in the study had often tried multiple medications and therapies without success, but psilocybin unlocked something deeper in them. The treatment process involved brain scans that showed increased brain flexibility and connectivity after the psilocybin dose. More importantly, patients reported profound personal experiences.

Psychedelic experiences allow unconscious material—repressed memories, emotions, and traumas—to surface. Watts compares this to crumpled clothes pushed to the back of a wardrobe, which, under the influence of psilocybin, come to the forefront, demanding to be felt and processed. Like Carl Jung's concept of the shadow, Watts' crumpled clothes (metaphor) were the hidden, repressed aspects of the psyche that, when confronted, can lead to profound transformation.

The psilocybin experience was not always easy, however. Patients faced painful and overwhelming emotions, but the therapeutic release was transformative. Many patients reported processing long-buried trauma for the first time.

Revisiting Trauma

One patient, John, had suffered childhood abuse that he had never been able to confront. During his psilocybin session, he visualized a large cask filled with pain and shame. Through the experience, he was able to confront and accept his past, leading to a cathartic release. Many participants in the study described similar emotional breakthroughs, with some crying for the first time in years—a profound shift that could take years in traditional therapy.

Watts notes that psilocybin facilitates an inner unlocking, akin to the process of integrating the shadow. It helps people move from emotional avoidance to emotional acceptance. This is critical because many individuals with depression are emotionally numb, unable to feel or process their pain. Through psilocybin, they can access and experience emotions they've been avoiding for years. The therapeutic process is unique in that the insights and healing don't come from the therapist but from within the patients themselves, guided by their inner wisdom.

The transformative potential of psilocybin therapy, as Watts describes, is not just about symptom relief but about enabling people to reconnect with their emotions and confront their past. In this way, it offers a deeper and more lasting path to healing, one that mirrors the Jungian journey of individuation, where integrating repressed aspects of the self leads to greater wholeness and understanding.

The Wise Seeker

Journalist Michael Pollan didn't need to travel to a mountain in Peru at the age of sixty. A successful author who wrote about food, nature, and the environment, Pollan could have wound down to a quiet retirement. But due to Pollan's research that I've already discussed, he was curious about the "mystical experience" and transcendent state often described by those who take psychedelics, where the boundaries between self and the world dissolve.[9]

Pollan reflects on his own psilocybin experience, where his sense of self dissolved into a cloud of blue post-it notes. He saw his grandfather's face meld with his own and urinated diamonds into a fractal sea. The experience reconciled him with mortality, revealing death as a natural merging with something greater. He envisions a revolution in mental health care, where psychedelics help treat addiction, depression, and anxiety. Yet, he acknowledges the challenges posed by a pharmaceutical industry driven by profit, questioning how it can adapt to treatments rooted in ancient, natural compounds.

Pollan's decision to experiment with these drugs was partly motivated by a desire to challenge the cultural stigma surrounding psychedelics. As a journalist, he wanted to engage with these substances beyond the stereotypes, seeking to understand their risks and rewards from a more informed perspective. Primarily, he was driven by a deep intellectual curiosity about the nature of consciousness and the ways in which psychedelics might alter it.

Pollan was fascinated by the possibility of gaining profound insights into the mind and self-awareness, and he wanted to experience firsthand how these substances could expand or shift consciousness. Additionally, Pollan was intrigued by the growing body of research highlighting the therapeutic potential of psychedelics, particularly in treating mental health conditions—like those studies at Imperial—seeing psychedelics as a means of unlocking repressed emotions or trauma, offering a different approach to healing than conventional therapies.

On a personal level, Pollan also sought to explore the potential for growth and transformation, believing that by breaking down ego barriers and providing access to unconscious material, psychedelics could lead to insights and healing that might not be possible through traditional methods of self-exploration.

Pollan revisits Humphry Osmond as one of the foundational figures in psychedelic science, highlighting his transformative role in the field. Initially viewing psychedelics as mimicking psychosis, Osmond discarded this theory after personally experiencing their effects. He described the profound clarity they brought, noting how "everything was vivid and sharp," with the potential to spend endless time contemplating even the smallest object.[10]

This intense focus, Osmond observed, paralleled mindfulness techniques that attune attention to seemingly mundane details. Recognizing the unique potential of these substances, he coined the term psychedelic—meaning "mind manifesting"—to capture their ability to reveal otherwise inaccessible aspects of the mind.

Osmond's collaboration with Aldous Huxley was also pivotal, sparking an exchange of ideas and creativity, including Osmond's now-famous rhyme: "To fathom hell or go angelic, just take a pinch of psychedelic."

This inference to heaven and hell was a metaphor familiar to Huxley himself.

Heaven and Hell

Aldous Huxley's book, *The Doors of Perception* followed by a later paper called *Heaven and Hell* provided pivotal discussions of psychedelics and their potential to unlock transcendent states of awareness.[11] Huxley's work drew inspiration from William Blake's assertion in *The Marriage of Heaven and Hell*, which suggested that "if the doors of perception were cleansed everything would appear to man as it is, Infinite." Huxley explored how mescaline could temporarily dissolve the constraints of ordinary perception.

For Huxley, these altered states revealed dimensions of existence typically obscured, offering what he described as both "purely aesthetic" and "sacramental" visions—experiences that could inspire profound insights into the nature of reality, art, and the divine.

Neuropsychopharmacologist Robin Carhart-Harris explains how these shifts in perception and perspective stem from psychedelics disrupting the brain's Default Mode Network (DMN), the seat of the ego and self-narratives. By dissolving the DMN, psychedelics allow individuals to perceive reality beyond their constructed stories, offering profound reframing opportunities.[12]

Pollan provides the example of a patient with crippling OCD described his psilocybin trip as a journey through death, rebirth, and interconnectedness. He became a tree, experienced the seasons, and watched himself interact with family. This transformation helped him detach from obsessive thoughts, rendering his OCD powerless in the months and years following his treatment.

While praised for his bold advocacy, Huxley also faced criticism. Detractors questioned whether mescaline-induced experiences could be equated with objective mystical insight. These critics suggested that such states might merely reflect subjective, neurochemical phenomena rather than authentic encounters with ultimate reality.

Whether through chemical catalysts, meditative practices, or embodied, relational experiences, the pursuit of the infinite takes many forms. By embracing this diversity, we gain a richer understanding of transcendence as a dynamic and inclusive field, rather than a fixed or narrowly defined concept. As Michael Pollan suggests, it is for us to work out what practices make most sense for our cultures and spiritual needs.

Ritual and Mythology

In a conversation with Joe Rogan, Pollan advised on the safest way to use psychedelics.[13] He suggested they should not typically be taken alone, there should always be a sense of purpose and intention prior to any trip, a "wise elder" should be present to provide guidance, and the process should be ritualized.

This approach reflects ancient traditions where plant medicines were used ceremonially under the stewardship of shamans or elders. These figures acted as mediators between worlds, guiding participants through transformative experiences with wisdom and care.

The mythological conventions here are quite apparent. The ritual creates a ceremony that becomes a container for transcendence, providing structure, meaning, and safety as individuals navigate the unpredictable and often chaotic terrain of altered states.

Here we see the wise elder once again embodying the archetype of the guide or mentor who helps the hero navigate the unknown. The ritual typically mirrors the mythological descent into the underworld and the subsequent return, offering a framework for understanding and integrating the experience.

Pollan's advice taps into the deep functionality of myth across cultures and generations—where it offers the psychological and spiritual scaffolding for navigating mystery and the unknown. Pollan is not suggesting that we should directly transplant rituals from other cultures into our own as literal templates. Rather, he emphasizes the value of integrating ritual and shared experiential knowledge as foundational elements that can inform safer and more appropriate psychedelic practices in a Western context.

As Pollan and Rogan agree, without this guidance, the experience risks becoming untethered and potentially harmful. While government propaganda and cultural scaremongering has compromised public education on psychedelics and their associated research, this is not to suggest that psychedelic experimentation comes without its risks.

Reasons for Caution

While the transformative potential of psychedelics does offer great hope for future medicine and psychiatry, there are reasons to be cautious across the varied experiences and contexts of psychedelic practices. Philosopher Jules Evans offers a critical reminder that these substances are not without risks.[14] Evans argues that much of the contemporary enthusiasm for psychedelics tends to gloss over their darker aspects.

Psychedelics can open doors to profound insight and healing, but they can also lead to disorientation, psychological distress, and even trauma if not approached with care.

Evans warns that the chaotic nature of psychedelic experiences—the same quality that makes them powerful agents of change—can also destabilize individuals who are unprepared or vulnerable. Encounters with repressed memories, shadow elements of the psyche, or overwhelming mystical phenomena can lead to lasting emotional challenges if not integrated properly. The very dissolution of ego that many find liberating can, for others, result in confusion or a sense of loss of identity.

We cannot overlook the value of balanced perspectives on psychedelics. Their trickster-like nature means they are not inherently good or bad but must be approached with respect, caution, and appropriate care. In the same way that psychedelic trips require care and integration, our cultural accommodation of psychedelics also requires care and integrations.

The concerns raised by the likes of Evans explore the importance of preparation, context, and integration during and after psychedelic journeys. By acknowledging these potential pitfalls, ethical practitioners can advocate for a responsible and informed engagement with psychedelics, ensuring that their capacity for transcendence does not come at the cost of psychological or physical safety.

These concerns are evidenced in a *Vice* documentary based in Tulum, where tourists experience the most powerful psychedelic trip currently known to humanity: from a toad venom called Bufo Alvarius.

The Shadow Shaman

Journalist Matt Shea provides a firsthand account of a retreat in Tulum to assess whether the profound risks associated with using such a powerful substance are justified by the claimed benefits.[15] Tulum has become a hotspot for psychedelic tourism, with an increasing number of people seeking Bufo Alvarius, also known as "speed-toading," a potent hallucinogen derived from the venom of the Sonoran Desert toad.

The substance, considered the most powerful hallucinogen in the world, is smoked during ceremonies that have become legally available in Tulum. While many tourists come in search of transformative, life-changing experiences, there are growing reports of serious negative outcomes, including lasting psychosis. Some tourists express their deep regrets after visiting Tulum because it has only made their psychological trauma worse after the intensity of their trip that seemingly lacks the guidance and aftercare required to manage and integrate the experience.

There are also allegations of sexual assault during ceremonies. Some have reported instances where individuals in positions of spiritual authority, such as shamans or facilitators, have exploited their roles. Women have reported experiences of abuse and manipulation during psychedelic ceremonies, raising serious ethical concerns about the vulnerability of participants.[16]

As Jules Evans points out, many aspiring psychedelic practitioners are entering the field with noble intentions—but they need to approach it with caution.[17] Politically, the space risks being co-opted by market opportunists and political elites and commodified before ethical safeguards are in place. Communally, Evans argues the culture often leans towards the cultic and Dionysian, where blurred boundaries and spiritualized permissiveness can enable harm.[18]

Precarious Practices

As Evans points out, despite the proliferation of over 160 training programmes, the legal market remains small and precarious. Many assume expensive certificates grant legal authority to practice—but this is rarely the case. Most training graduates either work underground or at retreats, where conditions are often unregulated, exploitative, or unsafe. Pay is low, infrastructure weak, and accountability lacking.[19]

The broader psychedelic scene can be intoxicating—permissive, boundary-less, and full of spiritual romanticism. This "Dionysian bubble" can destabilize newcomers, with guru-figures and gatekeepers wielding disproportionate power. The so-called Psychedelic Village is a tight-knit, sometimes toxic network claiming moral authority but disconnected from the actual grassroots practice, which is mostly informal and peer-based.[20]

Responsible engagement requires humility, self-awareness, and a clear-eyed view of the sector's legal, ethical, and psychological risks. Without this, practitioners may become complicit in the very harms they hoped to heal.

Power dynamics inherent in shamanic and ceremonial settings can sometimes lead to the predatory behaviour discussed earlier. Some argue that the romanticization of indigenous traditions in Western psychedelic culture may inadvertently shield these issues from scrutiny, as participants assume the infallibility of the shamanic figure.

Journalist Matt Shea confronted a shaman about the troubling accusations surrounding Bufo ceremonies, including reports of abuse and exploitation. The shaman responds by suggesting that both participants in a shared ceremonial space are equally responsible for whatever occurs during the process.

Taken aback by this, Shea offers the shaman a chance to clarify his statement, but the shaman reiterates his point, indicating that this was not simply a misunderstanding or translation issue. This response raises serious ethical concerns about the dynamics of responsibility and power within such ceremonies.[21]

There are also environmental concerns on the impact that "speed-toading" is having on wildlife populations, which can be addressed by scientific progress in labs producing replicant compounds.

Science and Sustainability

Contrary to occidentalist critiques of mechanistic Western culture or the belief that lab-based substances are "impure" compared to "natural" ones, laboratory science has much to offer in terms of ethics, particularly in areas of sustainability and wildlife conservation.

Commenting on the documentary, one viewer pointed to the ecological harm caused by the growing demand for Bufo venom, which is pushing the Sonoran Desert toad toward extinction. They suggest this environmental catastrophe is unnecessary, as the active compound in the venom (5MeO DMT) can be synthesized easily and cheaply using legally available chemicals.

Despite this, the viewer suggests that many within the psychedelic community continue to prioritize the natural toad venom over its synthetic counterpart. This preference persists even though both forms are chemically identical, much like Maria Sabina's earlier approval of Hoffman's psilocybin compound.

Another viewer shared concerns about overharvesting the venom for psychedelic ceremonies. They also highlighted the significant cultural and spiritual value of Sonoran Desert toads to the Yaqui tribes, who have been advocating for the use of a synthetic alternative to help the toad population recover.

These issues raise important questions about environmental ethics and the sustainability of psychedelic practices, urging a shift towards more responsible, eco-conscious alternatives. In terms of psychological and physical well-being, integration and guided treatment through ethical practice, other practitioners have emphasized these aspects at the core of their psychedelic pedagogy.

Guided Treatment

Rosalind Watts stresses the importance of longitudinal care and support in the psychedelic space, with a particular emphasis on integration, harm-reduction, and inclusion. What sets Watts apart is her focus on building tools and structures that foster connectedness after psychedelic experiences, drawing inspiration for their design from nature.

Throughout her work, Watts' main learning has been that the safe and effective use of psychedelics requires substantial integration support. As a result, she co-founded the UK's first psychedelic integration group and, in 2022, launched ACER ('Accept, Connect, Embody, Restore') Integration, a global online community where participants follow a thirteen-month process to connect more deeply to the self, others, and nature.[22]

ACER offers a unique approach to psychedelic integration, blending evidence-based psychological theories with ancient wisdom, particularly the concept of "nature codes"—the patterns inherent in nature. ACER emphasizes reconnecting with oneself, others, and the natural world, inviting participants to explore a deeper sense of belonging.

Watts articulates this mission by stating, "As we recognise the many ways that we have become disconnected from ourselves, each other, and the natural world, we are called to build new structures and tools that help us come home to our innate belonging together."[23]

What is particularly intriguing about ACER is its alignment with the contemplative mysticism of traditions discussed earlier—like Franciscan mysticism and Rohr's incarnational theology. These systems of thought emphasize an ongoing, nature-based connection with reality, which contrasts with the more esoteric, often intense, pursuits found in other psychedelic circles. While this is not to suggest that Watts is directly drawing from the same theological or mystical foundations as Rohr, her approach emphasizes cyclical, nature-based growth.

This ontological perspective encourages participants to return to a grounded relationship with the world, using psychedelics as a tool to reconnect more deeply with nature and their sense of self. Psychedelics might propel experiencers into cosmic realms that are seemingly "out there" on some other plain, but it's how they enable the exploration of self and nature that reveals the universal dwelling and interconnected terrains of cosmic consciousness.

Guiding Mystical Journeys

Psychologist James Fadiman's encounter with the psychedelic mescaline, derived from the peyote cactus, exemplifies the profound sense of cosmic consciousness often reported during such experiences. Participating in a guided session during his graduate studies, Fadiman sought to deepen his understanding of consciousness and explore the transformative potential of psychedelics.[24]

Reflecting on his experience, Fadiman recognized that his personal traits, strengths, and imperfections were merely aspects of a much greater whole, a larger being to which he was inherently connected alongside all other life. For Fadiman this was a classical mystical experience of awareness and universal connection—a revelation that fundamentally reshaped his view of the self and its connection to the wider cosmos.

Users often describe these experiences as "more real" than everyday life, involving encounters with vivid, otherworldly realms, strange entities, and a deep sense of interconnectedness. Some psychedelics enable radical unselfing, dissolving the ego and facilitating mystical states that many interpret as encounters with the divine. The timeless, infinite dimensions reported by users are key features of transcendence and expanded consciousness.

Fostering Interconnection

By fostering a sense of interconnectedness with the cosmos and enabling profound spiritual experiences, these substances offer new ways of understanding consciousness. Their role in confronting the shadow and dissolving egoic boundaries suggests that psychedelics could provide avenues for integrating holistic, expansive perspectives into modern life, potentially fostering a deeper connection with the universe and each other.

Some psychedelics unlock deep layers of the psyche for personal therapy, while others connect us to entities or realms we don't fully understand. Some offer glimpses of divine wholeness, while others are claimed to act as communication tools for extraterrestrial contact through altered states of consciousness. The same goes for navigating our spiritual lives through religious guidance.

There are many different religions and many different movements within religious institutions. When they operate healthily, they offer diversity of experience in transcendental realms. It's transcendence and the fundamental cruciality of transcendence for humans that offer the thread of constancy and meaning that we can take from such complex phenomena.

Like UFOs in the previous case study, the phenomena of psychedelics transcend time and societal contexts—with evidence to suggest that both phenomena have been part of the human experience for thousands of years. They present a shared "problem" in that they challenge conventional thought in ways that go beyond a simple, unified narrative. Just as UFO experiences are not a monolith—they could be in the sky, underwater, demonic, angelic, psychologically symbolic, or even projections from another dimension—psychedelic chemicals and experiences also vary greatly.

While psychedelic realms share mystical qualities with other arcane cases and sacred symbology, they also confront themes around death and dying. Whether it's the death of self and ego on a trip, contemplating imminent death through terminal diagnoses, or managing the process of dying itself, psychedelics appear to offer us pathways to a more comfortable conception of the inevitable outcome we will all face one day.

In this respect, psychedelics shed light on a collective shadow in Western culture: the discomfort and denial we feel when we contemplate the most universal fact of life that we all have in common. Death.

Confronting Death

Psychologist Bill Richards believes that the main goal for psychedelic treatments and further research in medicine is to change how Western society approaches death. He recounts his own transformative experience with psilocybin in his twenties, which steered him from theology to clinical research.[25]

At the Spring Grove Clinic, he worked with cancer patients, using psilocybin to facilitate transcendental experiences. Many patients emerged with a newfound curiosity about death and a calm confidence that "all will end well." Given his wife worked closely alongside him at the clinic, her own diagnosis of terminal cancer saw them practise what they preached, and their shared understanding of psilocybin's insights brought peace to her passing.

Stanislav Grof identified the links between altered states of consciousness, such as those induced by psychedelics, and near-death experiences (NDEs).[26] His research explores the distinct parallels between these two phenomena, highlighting shared features like ego dissolution, mystical insights, and encounters with what many interpret as the divine. Grof suggests that both psychedelic experiences and NDEs offer windows into the nature of consciousness, where the boundaries between the self and the universe dissolve, allowing for profound spiritual and existential revelations.

Grof's work with altered states—through both psychedelic therapy and spontaneous NDEs—raises fundamental questions about consciousness and its relationship to reality. Grof observed that in these states, the ego, or the individual sense of self, often dissolves, giving way to a profound sense of unity with the universe. This dissolution of ego, far from being a solely psychological phenomenon, hints at the possibility that consciousness is not bound by the brain or individual identity but is instead part of a larger, interconnected whole.

Inducing Altered States

Dr. Rick Strassman also posited that DMT may play a role in facilitating profound mystical experiences, such as those associated with near-death experiences (NDEs) and reports of contact with non-human intelligences, including UFO-related phenomena.[27] Strassman's hypothesis suggests that endogenous DMT could act as a biological mechanism for inducing altered states of consciousness, potentially explaining the vivid, otherworldly visions and heightened sense of reality reported during these experiences.

Both Strassman and Grof highlight the transformative insights that can arise from these states. During NDEs people often report a sense of oneness with the universe, encounters with divine or transcendent realms, and an understanding that challenges traditional notions of life and death. These shared elements might suggest that NDEs, like psychedelic states, may be tapping into similar dimensions of consciousness—ones that transcend the physical and psychological boundaries of ordinary perception.[28]

The phenomena invite a rethinking of consciousness, not as a fixed, isolated process but as a fluid, dynamic state potentially capable of bridging non-material spirituality and science. Grof's concept of consciousness as a holistic phenomenon aligns with Strassman's suggestion that DMT might act as a gateway to these broader realms. Both perspectives propose that altered states of consciousness reveal a more expansive framework for understanding reality, offering insights into the nature of life, death, and the possibility of the divine.

The likes of Grof and Strassman provide a foundation for exploring deeper questions about the thresholds between life, death, and consciousness. Are these altered states strictly neural and material phenomena, or do they point to some other transcendent reality? This growing field of interest encourages us to look beyond the materialist assumptions of science and consider the profound implications of these experiences for understanding what it means to be alive—and what might lie beyond.

Near-Death Experiences

Often sharing the psychedelic description of being *more real than reality itself*, NDEs are profound psychological and spiritual events reported by individuals close to death or in life-threatening situations. Experiencers report a euphoric sense of arriving home in a place where they never want to leave due to the infinite love, light, and wholeness that they feel.

While no single experience is the same, they share common traits. These intense transcendental journeys often change people's view and worldview—evoking a sense of universal connection, duty to others, and belief in a divine or higher power long after the event.

Strassman did not present DMT's connection to Near-Death Experiences (NDEs) from a strictly materialist perspective.[29] While he acknowledges the brain's active role in producing and transporting DMT, he also entertains the idea that the brain may function more like a receiver of consciousness—potentially tuning into hidden dimensions or alternate realities. This view allows for a broader interpretation of NDEs, where DMT might facilitate access to realms of existence that extend beyond the confines of brain chemistry alone.

Rather than limiting visionary experiences to neurochemical events, Strassman leaves open the possibility that such states reveal something real, though difficult to measure, about the nature of consciousness and reality itself. In the next chapter I'll consider the extraordinary possibilities for materialist, post-materialist, and dualistic perspectives.

Whatever the truth might be, the mystical lens takes great value from the possibilities here. Again, rather than rushing to conclusions for pseudo-certainty, the question is, ***what stories do we tell when we tell stories about NDEs?***

Whatever worldview we apply here—from reductive materialist paradigms through to dualist notions of consciousness, souls, and speculations on other worldly dimensions—NDEs provide profound insights to some of the deepest transcendental experiences we have reports of. They're about the threshold between life and death—our portals to wherever we go or whatever happens when we die. This is the focus of my final case study.

Notes

1. Pollan (2018a, 2022); Gasser (2014); Gasser et al. (2015).
2. Ibid.
3. See Preller et al. (2019); Varley et al. (2020) for more on psychedelic brain function, interconnectedness, and "cosmic dance".
4. Pollan (2018a, 2022).
5. Einstein (1949).
6. See Rohr (2016: 27).
7. For examples of current clinical research on psychedelic treatment for clinical depression, see: Carhart-Harris et al. (2016); Carhart-Harris et al. (2021); Carhart-Harris et al. (2023).
8. Watts (2017).
9. Pollan (2018a, 2022).
10. Pollan (2022); Osmond (1957); Aaronson and Osmond (1970).
11. Huxley (1945, 1954).
12. Carhart-Harris et al. (2012).
13. Pollan (2018b).
14. Evans (2017).
15. Shea (2021).
16. Ibid.
17. Evans (2025).
18. Ibid.
19. Ibid.
20. Ibid.

21. In the documentary, Shea (2021) engages with multiple shamans to explore growing concerns about the darker side of bufo ceremonies—particularly accusations of malpractice and the lasting psychological distress some participants report following these powerful experiences.
22. Watts (2022).
23. Ibid.
24. Fadiman (2011).
25. Richards (2015), Pollan (2022).
26. Pollan (2022), Grof (1988).
27. Strassman (2001).
28. Luke (2011a, 2011b) provides an interdisciplinary study of the entities frequently reported during DMT experiences. He notes that DMT is present in numerous plant species and occurs naturally in the brains of humans and other animals. Some researchers, such as Strassman (2001), have proposed that the pineal gland might synthesize the compound, perhaps playing a role in dreaming, but this remains a hypothesis. More recent work has identified the necessary enzymes for DMT biosynthesis in mammalian tissue (Dean et al., 2019), yet whether this results in significant production or functional roles in the brain is still uncertain. Speculative links have also been drawn between DMT and mystical states, near-death experiences, psi phenomena, and psychosis, but these remain intriguing rather than settled claims. In Amazonian shamanic practice, DMT is traditionally consumed as part of ayahuasca, a Quechua term often translated as "vine of the spirits" or "vine of the dead." The brew is valued for inducing visionary states with shamanic and therapeutic dimensions, including synaesthesia, apparent extra-dimensional perception, out-of-body journeys, and encounters with discarnate beings. An intriguing aspect Luke points to is the recurring description of similar entities, regardless of the user's background or expectations, with striking cross-cultural consistency in user reports: mischievous machine-elves, insectoid mantis-like surgeons, and ornate reptilian figures. The recurrence of such imagery across independent testimonies raises profound ontological questions—whether these beings are archetypal projections, products of neurochemistry, or indicative of something beyond conventional psychology. Luke approaches the issue by blending parapsychology, ethnobotany, and psychopharmacology with anthropology, folklore, and cultural studies, producing an eclectic but substantial analysis that takes these experiences seriously without dismissing their strangeness.
29. Ibid.

Bibliography

Aaronson, B., & Osmond, H. (1970). *Psychedelics: The Uses and Implications of Hallucinogenic Drugs*. Anchor Books.

Carhart-Harris, R. L., et al. (2012). Neural Correlates of the Psychedelic State as Determined by fMRI Studies with Psilocybin. *Proceedings of the National Academy of Sciences, 109*(6), 2138–2143.

Carhart-Harris, R. L., et al. (2016). Psilocybin with Psychological Support for Treatment-Resistant Depression: An Open-Label Feasibility Study. *The Lancet Psychiatry, 3*(7), 619–627. https://doi.org/10.1016/S2215-0366(16)30065-7

Carhart-Harris, R. L., et al. (2021). Trial of Psilocybin Versus Escitalopram for Depression. *The New England Journal of Medicine, 384*(15), 1402–1411. https://doi.org/10.1056/NEJMoa2032994

Carhart-Harris, R. L., et al. (2023). Effect of Psilocybin Versus Escitalopram on Depression Symptom Severity: A Randomized Clinical Trial. *eClinicalMedicine, 59*, 101954. https://doi.org/10.1016/j.eclinm.2024.101954

Dean, J. G., Liu, T., Huff, S., Sheler, B., Barker, S. A., Strassman, R. J., Wang, M. M., & Borjigin, J. (2019). Biosynthesis and extracellular concentrations of N,N-dimethyltryptamine (DMT) in mammalian brain. *Scientific Reports, 9*, 9333.

Einstein, A. (1949). *The World As I See It*. Philosophical Library.

Evans, J. (2017). *The Art of Losing Control: A Philosopher's Search for Ecstatic Experience*. Canongate.

Evans, J. (2025). Skinwalker Ranch and the Rise of UFO Political Religion. *Ecstatic Integration*, 17 April. Retrieved June 16, 2025, from https://www.ecstaticintegration.org/p/skinwalker-ranch-and-the-rise-of

Fadiman, J. (2011). *The Psychedelic Explorer's Guide: Safe, Therapeutic, and Sacred Journeys*. Park Street Press.

Gasser, P. (2014). Safety and Efficacy of Lysergic Acid Diethylamide-Assisted Psychotherapy for Anxiety Associated with Life-Threatening Diseases. *The Journal of Nervous and Mental Disease, 202*(7), 513–520. https://doi.org/10.1097/NMD.0000000000000113

Gasser, P., Kirchner, K., & Passie, T. (2015). LSD-Assisted Psychotherapy for Anxiety Associated with a Life-Threatening Disease: A Qualitative Study of Acute and Sustained Subjective Effects. *Journal of Psychopharmacology, 29*(1), 57–68. https://doi.org/10.1177/0269881114555249

Grof, S. (1988). *The Adventure of Self-Discovery: Dimensions of Consciousness and New Perspectives in Psychotherapy and Inner Exploration*. State University of New York Press.

Huxley, A. (1945). *The Perennial Philosophy*. Harper & Brothers.

Huxley, A. (1954). *The Doors of Perception*. Chatto & Windus.

Luke, D. (2011a). Discarnate Entities and Dimethyltryptamine (DMT): Psychopharmacology, Phenomenology and Ontology. *Journal of the Society for Psychical Research, 75*(902), 26–42.

Luke, D. (2011b). *Otherworlds: Psychedelics and Exceptional Human Experience.* University of Exeter Press.

Osmond, H. (1957). A Review of the Clinical Effects of Psychotomimetic Agents. *Annals of the New York Academy of Sciences, 66*(3), 418–434. https://nyaspubs.onlinelibrary.wiley.com/doi/10.1111/j.1749-6632.1957.tb40738.x

Pollan, M. (2018a). *How to Change Your Mind: What the New Science of Psychedelics Teaches Us About Consciousness, Dying, Addiction, Depression, and Transcendence.* Penguin Press.

Pollan, M. (2018b). Joe Rogan Experience #1121—Michael Pollan. *The Joe Rogan Experience*, 24 May. Retrieved April 28, 2025, from https://www.youtube.com/watch?v=tz4CrWE_P0g

Pollan, M. (2022). *How to Change Your Mind.* Directed by L. Walker and A. Ellwood. [TV series]. Netflix.

Preller, K. H., Razi, A., Zeidman, P., Stämpfli, P., Friston, K. J., & Vollenweider, F. X. (2019). Effective Connectivity Changes in LSD-Induced Altered States of Consciousness in Humans. *Proceedings of the National Academy of Sciences, 116*(7), 2743–2748.

Richards, W. A. (2015). *Sacred Knowledge: Psychedelics and Religious Experiences.* Columbia University Press.

Rohr, R. (2016). *The Divine Dance: The Trinity and Your Transformation.* SPCK Publishing.

Shea, M. (2021). The Toad Venom That's Stronger Than DMT: Bufo. *High Society*, VICE. Retrieved April 28, 2025, from https://www.youtube.com/watch?v=0RonFMPnZq8

Strassman, R. (2001). *DMT: The Spirit Molecule.* Park Street Press.

Varley, T. F., Carhart-Harris, R. L., Roseman, L., Menon, D. K., & Stamatakis, E. A. (2020). Serotonergic Psychedelics LSD and Psilocybin Flatten the Brain's Energy Landscape: Insights from Receptor-Informed Network Control Theory. *NeuroImage, 220*, 117049.

Watts, R. (2017). Can Magic Mushrooms Unlock Depression? *TEDxOxford.* Retrieved April 28, 2025, from https://www.youtube.com/watch?v=8kfGaVAXeMY

Watts, R. (2022). *ACER Integration.* Retrieved April 28, 2025, from https://acerintegration.com/

CHAPTER 9

Transcending Death

Playwriter and podcast host, Danny Robins makes the point that while some people find God, he found ghosts.[1] His transcendental fix revolves around one of humanity's deepest desires: to transcend death and explore our curiosity about the afterlife. Whether we are sceptics or believers, we are drawn to the thrill of a ghost story.

Even hardened atheists like Stephen Fry and Stewart Lee have admitted their love for ghostly tales, engaging in the spectacle of spooky experiences that make us question our senses.[2] Through his writing and podcasting, Robins captures this universal fascination with the supernatural, creating spaces where fear, hope, and transcendence converge.

Throughout the *Uncanny* podcast, Robins navigates the delicate balance between belief and scepticism. Each episode presents chilling accounts of ghostly encounters, paired with expert insights that explore psychological, scientific, and cultural perspectives.

But Robins' real achievement lies in his inclusivity: believers and sceptics are equally welcome, and the podcast invites us to set aside the binary of true or false in favour of curiosity. For Robins, ghosts are not just about scares—they are a mirror to our fears of mortality, our longing for hope, and our need to connect with something beyond ourselves—ghost stories are another manifestation of our craving for transcendence.

D. Kelsey, *Transcendence and Collective Psychology*,
https://doi.org/10.1007/978-3-032-09495-7_9

Belief and Scepticism

This ethos carries through to Robins' theatrical work, such as *2:22: A Ghost Story*. The play captures social tensions between traditionalism and modernism, and existential debates between hard science and mystical experience.

2:22 cleverly situates itself in liminal spaces—between the old and the new, between belief and doubt—using the haunting of a newly gentrified house as a metaphor for the unresolved tensions of modernity. For Robins, the paranormal is a tool for examining deeper cultural anxieties: the fear of making mistakes, the inability to grow or change, and the societal pressure to choose a single, unwavering stance on complex issues.

What Robins offers is a model of popular culture that is contemplative and non-dual in nature, a rare space where believers and sceptics can engage in meaningful dialogue. It aligns with mystical themes of non-dualism, creating a bridge between seemingly opposing perspectives. By blurring the lines of reductive dichotomies between tradition and progress, or science and belief, Robins invites us to embrace the unresolved and to dwell in the liminal spaces where uncertainty reigns.

His work reminds us that transcendental cravings are not merely flights of fancy but deeply human desires that, when explored thoughtfully, can transcend divisions and create common ground. By valuing exploration over certainty, Robins exemplifies how we might navigate the mystical futures ahead—not by reducing everything to true or false, but by embracing the mystery and learning what it can teach us about ourselves.

Death and Transformation

Carl Jung viewed death as an archetype that represents not just the end of life, but a powerful symbol of transformation.[3] For Jung, death was not merely physical cessation but an essential part of the larger cycle of life—an archetypal process that calls for the shedding of the old self, making way for renewal and deeper self-understanding. Death, in this sense, is a psychological and spiritual boundary that, when encountered, forces us to confront the unknown and embrace the mysteries of existence.

Cultural conceptions of death reveal much about how we, as individuals and societies, grapple with the ultimate unknown. Culturally, our understandings of death are diverse—ranging from ancient mythologies that depict death as a gateway to another realm, to materialist secular views that regard it as the final end. The variations in these beliefs reflect humanity's attempts to make sense of death, whether through religious ritual, philosophical contemplation, or scientific inquiry.

In recent years, science has begun to revisit death in new ways, largely due to the growing body of research around Near-Death Experiences (NDEs). But the concept of NDEs is not a modern phenomenon. In Plato's *Myth of Er*, a soldier named Er is killed in battle but later revives on the funeral pyre. In his revived state, Er recounts a journey through the afterlife, witnessing the judgement of souls, their rewards and punishments, and the choosing of new lives, before returning with a message about moral responsibility and the consequences of one's way of living.[4]

Mystical experiences of life and death are also found in the lives of saints. Saint Francis of Assisi reported visions of Christ while praying on Mount La Verna, leading to his receiving the stigmata. He often described moments of spiritual ecstasy in which he felt connected to divine realms.[5] Likewise, Saint Teresa of Avila, a Spanish mystic, detailed her encounters with divine presence that often left her in a state of near-death, where she described profound visions of heaven during her ecstatic prayer experiences.[6]

Building on these historical accounts, the experiences reported during NDEs often involve a profound shift in self-perception, where individuals describe a loss of personal identity and a merging with a greater reality. The dissolution of the ego, which I've also referred to as "unselfing," mirrors the states described by mystics and those undergoing intense spiritual transformations.

In these moments, the boundaries between self and the external world appear to dissolve, leading to an overwhelming sense of interconnectedness, transcendence, and unity with a sense of universal consciousness.

Shared Inevitability

In his critique of the humanities as a discipline—and what he sees as its excessive preoccupation with human and cultural differences—Jeffrey Kripal instead draws attention to death as a universal reality we all share. And yet, a striking blind spot across the humanities is a widespread reluctance to engage with the possibility of human existence or experience beyond death.[7] The universality of death is a reality that transcends cultural and historical boundaries. How we understand death is another matter entirely.

This final case study invites us to consider the provocative questions Kripal poses: Do we all die in the same way? Does everything go blank at the moment of death, with consciousness dissolving into nothingness? Or, as Rupert Sheldrake also speculates, do we die into our imaginations—into the stories we've inherited, which provide culturally constructed maps to navigate the dying process?[8] Might there even be stages of death that move us from these culturally dependent imaginations into some form of cosmic universality?[9]

These are not just questions about the nature of dying. They are deep provocations—ones I will return to in the closing chapters—for how we understand the meaning of life, how we live, and how we prepare for the inevitability of death. Questions for everyone, across all cultures.

For Kripal, the reason we struggle with these questions in Western culture is because we don't tackle them commonly enough (especially in the academy) in robust, comparative, and systematic ways. This case study can only cover so much, but by drawing on medical science combined with the mystical foundation established so far, I aim to help initiate a deeper exploration of death in relation to transcendence and collective psychology.

Ego Dissolvement

As we shall see, what we learn from NDEs is that, like some psychedelic trips, an element of ego dissolvement provides insight to some other deeper or suppressed truth about the self. In NDEs especially, people describe what they sense to be their true self through a universal connection, divine love, and shared purpose that transcends the personal and experiential sense of self and ego in daily life.

Let's remind ourselves of Rohr's theological and psychological perspective here—particularly that *immortal diamond* he sees shining within each of us. For Rohr, the True Self is the soul: eternal, grounded in divine love, and created in the image of God. As discussed earlier, the false self is the ego-identity we build through fear, social conditioning, and external validation. It's not evil—it's a necessary container for navigating life—but it's not the whole truth of who we are. Rohr calls us to "die" to that ego-self so the deeper self can emerge.[10]

This deeper identity often comes into view through transformative experiences like NDEs, where people report a sense of divine clarity, detachment from material concerns, and a renewed sense of purpose. Rohr warns that, even for clergy, many religious roles can unintentionally reinforce the False Self. True spiritual maturity, he says, comes not from titles or status but from inner transformation and the guidance of those who've truly encountered their soul.

Integrating Death

While Jung did not make assertive claims on the afterlife, he saw death as a crucial part of the individuation process.[11] Individuation is the psychological process of integrating conscious and unconscious aspects of the self to achieve wholeness. Jung saw death as a meaningful horizon that individuation moves towards. Death, it seemed to Jung, was something the psyche seems to anticipate and prepare for, especially in the second half of life. Jung also viewed "mini-deaths" as pivotal moments of transformation throughout life, where old patterns, beliefs, or identities die off to make way for new growth.

These transformative experiences can be triggered by life events such as midlife crises, career changes, relationship breakups, personal growth, or a significant illness. By embracing these "mini-deaths" and integrating their lessons, individuals can move towards greater self-awareness and wholeness, making the "big death" less fearsome and more a natural culmination of life's journey. NDEs often take this principle to another level, revealing people to a realm of ultimate wholeness that enables the integration of self-learning.

As we see below, the common characteristics of NDEs expose people to such deep, meaningful, and divine experiences that they not only return with a sense of true self, but they no longer fear death. They claim to know what they are truly part of in this life, and they have a different perspective on the meaning of death when it arrives.

That's not to suggest they have no ego on return—this is not possible for anyone in any form—but they appreciate the difference between the False Self and True Self. This is a universal trait regardless of cultural or religious background.

Universal Experience

Modern research suggests that NDEs reflect a universal experience that is influenced by cultural conditioning, but pointing to a shared, transcendent reality. Even when marked by common phenomena, interpretations of NDEs are shaped by the individual's cultural and religious context.

Regardless, in *God and the Afterlife,* Jeffrey Long makes the point that thousands of independently reported encounters with a loving, conscious presence point not just to life beyond death, but to a universal experience of God.[12]

Drawing from the world's largest NDE database, Long emphasizes the extraordinary consistency of these accounts across geography, culture, age, religion, and even belief orientation—including atheists. Despite variations in language or symbolism, experiencers overwhelmingly describe a radiant being of light who embodies unconditional love, acceptance, and a profound sense of purpose.

This cross-cultural uniformity, Long suggests, cannot be explained by religious priming or neurological models alone; rather, it points to a shared human encounter with the divine. Unlike many researchers who avoid theological conclusions, Long interprets these convergent narratives as empirical evidence of a transcendent, benevolent God.[13]

Dr Bruce Greyson also makes the point that there are countless ways to approach the divine, and ultimately, the path one follows is unimportant. Upon reaching the summit, he says, all travellers encounter the same essence—love, light, peace, harmony, gratitude, wisdom, truth, and triumph. In the higher realms, distinctions between religions disappear, leaving only unity and joy. This is at least what Greyson takes from decades of systematic research on NDEs.[14]

NDEs raise profound questions about transcendental realms, the nature of consciousness, and the process of dying. While they cannot show us what lies beyond the point of no return, the scientific data we have on these experiences are challenging current paradigms and prompting a broader understanding of the mind and its relationship to reality. These profound, transformative events challenge our conventional understanding of death, suggesting that the moment of dying may not be the final severance from life, but rather an intricate process of transcendence.

A Tantalizing Taster?

While the ultimate nature of what lies beyond death remains a mystery, NDEs provide tantalizing glimpses of what *might* await us. They suggest either the continuation of consciousness in another realm or a profound (often euphoric) dissolution into nothingness. But NDEs are not just transformational portals for those who report having them. The data that has been recorded since the 1970s offers us personal and collective portals for transforming our cultural and scientific understanding of death and dying.

You should be well rehearsed now in my use of *strategic scepticism* to recognize, analyse, and integrate the awe and wonder of even the most dismissive and reductive readings of mysterious phenomena. This chapter requires strategic scepticism to find common ground in a shared appreciation of NDE research, regardless of what we believe (or not) about the afterlife. This research has come a long way since a young intern's pager went off during his lunchbreak in 1973.

The Spaghetti Incident

Dr. Bruce Greyson was sat in a cafeteria eating his lunch at the University of Virginia Medical Centre when he spilled spaghetti sauce on his tie. As he tried to wipe the stain off, his pager buzzed, calling him to patient who had overdosed. Embarrassed, and already trying to awkwardly evoke professionalism as a nervous intern, he quickly covered the stain with his lab coat and left the cafeteria to see the patient.[15]

The patient was completely unconscious when Greyson assessed her. After checking on her, he went to another room down the corridor to speak with the patient's roommate who brought her in, asking questions to understand the circumstances of the overdose. When he returned, the patient was still unconscious and was later sent to the Intensive Care Unit.

The next morning, Greyson visited the patient, who was now awake but drowsy. Before he could introduce himself, she told him she already knew who he was because she remembered him from the night before. Greyson was surprised, as she had been unconscious during his visit. She clarified that *she hadn't seen him in her room—she had seen him talking to her friend down the corridor.*

Greyson initially assumed the nurses had told her what had happened, but she insisted that she had seen it herself. She went on to accurately describe the conversation he had with her friend while pointing out one specific detail from that evening: the spaghetti sauce on his tie.

Beyond Belief

Raised in a scientific materialist household, Greyson had been taught that the physical world was all there is, and that death is the end. This worldview had guided him through college and medical school without question. However, he could not explain how the patient had described something she could not have physically witnessed unless she had somehow left her body.

As startling as the experience was, Greyson set it aside to focus on the patient's condition, particularly given the seriousness of her suicide attempt. He kept the incident to himself, wary of how others might react. That was until a new colleague joined Greyson at Virginia.

Enter, Raymond Moody.[16]

Like Greyson, Raymond Moody was a young medical student when he first encountered accounts from patients who had died and been resuscitated. They described experiences of a beautiful realm where they were greeted by deceased loved ones and "beings of light." Fascinated, Moody carefully listened to their stories and documented their accounts in detail.

Documenting the Afterlife

Moody compiled a notebook of these recollections, coining the term "near-death experiences" to describe them. In 1975, Moody published *Life After Life*, a book exploring the many experiences he had documented during his work. This was a phenomenon far more common than the medical profession was openly discussing—especially in the 70s and 80s when patients and medics feared ridicule if they told anyone what happened to them.

Moody noted common descriptions of a light that is like nothing we see in physical reality—it is described as a light of endless love and compassion. Experiencers often lose their fear of death because this destination is deemed to be so beautiful.

To Greyson, this was significant because he was used to working with suicidal patients and his initial fear was that the NDE would make them more suicidal because they knew there was a peaceful way out. But the opposite happened: by losing their fear of death, they lost their fear of life, and had a renewed sense of courage to confront life's challenges.

Moody's patients also frequently reported leaving their bodies, observing events from an elevated perspective, and traveling through a tunnel or canyon accompanied by loving guides. Other common features of NDEs include profound peace, encounters with a divine light. Some experience vivid life reviews—reliving events from the perspective of others and experiencing the joy or pain they had caused during the event.

Ineffable Experiences

While some patients recounted all these features, others described only a few. Yet, most shared a common sentiment: their NDEs were ineffable, filled with profound love, comfort, and awe that words could never fully express. For experiencers, this transcendental realm is often life-changing—the overwhelming feeling of wholeness and universal connection with the cosmos proving too powerful to return unaffected.

Moody speculated that death transitions us into a state of consciousness so vastly different from the spatial and temporal framework of physical reality that our language is insufficient to describe it. This belief emerged from his work with those patients who had been resuscitated after clinical death and shared remarkable stories of their experiences.

Individuals frequently report lasting changes in their values, attitudes, and beliefs, often becoming more empathetic, compassionate, and spiritually oriented. These transformations point to a profound human capacity for change and growth in the face of mortality. The recurring themes of love, unity, and interconnectedness in NDE accounts further highlight their potential to deepen our understanding of humanity's place in the cosmos.

Materialist Mindsets

Peter Fenwick is a neuropsychiatrist who admits that he once dismissed NDEs as utter nonsense. To him, they seemed like a whimsical Californian phenomenon, unlikely to gain any traction in "sensible" Britain. However, his perspective shifted when a patient recounted an NDE following a severe heart complication.[17]

Material science dictates that consciousness is entirely dependent on brain activity—yet Fenwick began to question this assumption. He argues that the very moments when the brain ceases to function are often when profound expansions of consciousness occur.

Fenwick's research, alongside Bruce Greyson's, reveals strikingly similar accounts of NDEs across cultures and continents. Many experiencers describe a distorted sense of time, encounters with a warm, radiant being of light, and the transmission of vast amounts of information through an otherworldly energy. Some mention celestial music, vibrant colours, and extraordinary scents.

Despite these varying sensory details, one pattern is consistent: upon returning, people are profoundly changed. During forty years of research, Greyson has found that even staunch atheists—those deeply cynical about anything spiritual—often come away with a belief in something greater, though its nature varies. Both researchers agree that science has yet to provide an adequate explanation for NDEs.

Several hypotheses have been proposed, but the data challenges them. Some suggest NDEs result from drugs administered during medical crises, yet studies indicate that fewer drugs actually increase the likelihood of an NDE, with sedatives often suppressing such experiences. Others argue that oxygen deprivation could trigger NDEs. However, Fenwick notes that the blissful nature of NDEs starkly contrasts with the confusion and distress typically associated with oxygen starvation.

The Case of Pam Reynolds

Greyson highlights the case of Pam Reynolds. During a complex brain operation, her blood was entirely drained from her body, her heart was stopped, and her brain was completely inactive for an hour. She was clinically flatlined, with no measurable brain activity. Yet Pam reported a vivid, detailed experience.

Pam described watching her surgery from above, recounting specific tools and procedures in detail. Her eyes had been taped shut, and moulded earpieces were inserted to block all sound, yet her descriptions were so accurate that the neurosurgeon admitted being baffled by her level of awareness.

For Greyson and Fenwick, cases like Pam challenge the materialist view that the brain generates consciousness. If the brain was completely non-functional, how could she have had the most vivid experience of her life? Fenwick suggests that such accounts require us to rethink our understanding of death. He raises a provocative question: is it possible that death involves an *expansion* of consciousness?

This line of inquiry leads back to an older idea—that the brain acts not as the creator of consciousness but as a filter or receiver for it. In this view, consciousness might exist beyond the brain, with death representing not an end but a transition to a broader, more expansive state of being in which our consciousness is released from the prohibitive filters of a receptive brain.

Gathering the Data

In 1983, Greyson created the NDE Scale. This was a standardized tool designed to evaluate the depth and features of NDEs. The sixteen-item questionnaire has become a cornerstone in the field, enabling researchers to differentiate NDEs from other phenomena. By integrating narrative descriptions with quantitative measurements, the scale provides a systematic and consistent framework for studying these experiences.[18]

A score of 7 or higher on the following questions is considered a near-death experience (NDE) for research purposes. The mean score among a large sample of NDEs is 15.

1. *Did time seem to speed up or slow down?*

   (0) *No*
   (1) *Time seemed to go faster or slower than usual*
   (2) *Everything seemed to be happening at once; or time stopped or lost all meaning*

2. *Were your thoughts speeded up?*

   (0) *No*
   (1) *Faster than usual*
   (2) *Incredibly fast*

3. *Did scenes from your past come back to you?*

   (0) *No*
   (1) *I remembered many past events*
   (2) *My past flashed before me, out of my control*

4. *Did you suddenly seem to understand everything?*

   (0) *No*
   (1) *Everything about myself or others*
   (2) *Everything about the universe*

5. *Did you have a feeling of peace or pleasantness?*

   (0) *No*
   (1) *Relief or calmness*
   (2) *Incredible peace or pleasantness*

6. *Did you have a feeling of joy?*

    (0) *No*
    (1) *Happiness*
    (2) *Incredible joy*

7. *Did you feel a sense of harmony or unity with the universe?*

    (0) *No*
    (1) *I felt no longer in conflict with nature*
    (2) *I felt united or one with the world*

8. *Did you see, or feel surrounded by, a brilliant light?*

    (0) *No*
    (1) *An unusually bright light*
    (2) *A light clearly of mystical or otherworldly origin*

9. *Were your senses more vivid than usual?*

    (0) *No*
    (1) *More vivid than usual*
    (2) *Incredibly more vivid*

10. *Did you seem to be aware of things going on elsewhere, as if by extra-sensory perception (ESP)?*

    (0) *No*
    (1) *Yes, but the facts have not been checked out*
    (2) *Yes, and the facts have been checked out*

11. *Did scenes from the future come to you?*

    (0) *No*
    (1) *Scenes from my personal future*
    (2) *Scenes from the world's future*

12. *Did you feel separated from your body?*

    (0) *No*
    (1) *I lost awareness of my body*
    (2) *I clearly left my body and existed outside it*

13. *Did you seem to enter some other, unearthly world?*

    (0) *No*

(1) *Some unfamiliar and strange place*
(2) *A clearly mystical or unearthly realm*

14. *Did you seem to encounter a mystical being or presence, or hear an unidentifiable voice?*

    (0) *No*
    (1) *I heard a voice I could not identify*
    (2) *I encountered a definite being, or a voice clearly of mystical or unearthly origin*

15. *Did you see deceased or religious spirits?*

    (0) *No*
    (1) *I sensed their presence*
    (2) *I actually saw them*

16. *Did you come to a border or point of no return?*

    (0) *No*
    (1) *I came to a definite conscious decision to "return" to life*
    (2) *I came to a barrier that I was not permitted to cross; or was "sent back" against my will*

* * *

Mystical Unselfing

The transcendental, unselfing, and mystical themes woven throughout this questionnaire highlight the profound shifts in consciousness often reported after NDEs. These themes align with the characteristics of cosmic consciousness discussed throughout this book, particularly in relation to the "otherworldly" or "unearthly" realms encountered through the arcane horizons explored in these case studies.

Altered Perception of Time (Questions 1 & 2): Experiencing time as non-linear—slowing, stopping, or losing meaning—points to transcendence over the constraints of ordinary reality. Incredibly fast thoughts reflect an expansion beyond the usual limitations of mental processing, opening to a sense of boundless understanding.

Expanded Knowledge (Questions 4 & 11): A sudden, profound comprehension of oneself, others, or the universe represents a transcendence of ordinary cognitive boundaries. Insights into the future suggest a connection to a realm beyond temporal limitations, bridging the past, present, and future into an integrated whole.

Union with the Universe (Question 7): Feeling one with the world or in harmony with the universe reveals a deep transcendence of self, where the boundaries between individual and cosmos dissolve into a unified experience of existence.

Mystical Light (Question 8): Encountering a brilliant, mystical light signifies a crossing into a realm of transcendence, often interpreted as divine or otherworldly. For experiencers, this light is seen as a symbol of divine truth, love, or enlightenment.

Separation from the Body (Question 12): The experience of leaving the physical form is a profound act of unselfing, detaching from bodily limitations and egoic identity. It often leads to a deeper recognition of self beyond the physical.

Experiencing Unity and Peace (Questions 5, 6 & 7): Feelings of incredible peace, joy, and unity dissolve personal anxieties and egoic concerns, shifting focus outward to connection and wholeness. This "unselfing" transcends individual desires, creating space for profound tranquillity and shared being.

Encounters with Beings or Presences (Questions 14 & 15): Mystical beings, unidentifiable voices, or deceased spirits challenge the ego's boundaries, inviting a broader identity that includes relationships with the unseen or spiritual dimensions.

Entering Otherworldly Realms (Question 13): Moving into a mystical, unearthly world reflects direct engagement with transcendent and mystical realities. These spaces are often perceived as sacred or deeply significant.

Extrasensory Awareness (Question 10): Awareness of events elsewhere or beyond ordinary sensory perception suggests a connection to a broader, non-material field of consciousness.

Encountering Borders or Barriers (Question 16): Coming to a border or being "sent back" against one's will often aligns with mystical traditions of liminality—a threshold between worlds where profound transformation or spiritual insights occur.

Life Review and Flashbacks (Question 3): Scenes from the past flashing uncontrollably often convey a mystical reckoning, reflecting on one's life as part of a larger cosmic or moral order.

These questions and themes collectively explore experiences that dissolve the boundaries of time, space, self, and reality. The altered perceptions, feelings of unity, and encounters with the mystical convey a sense of being part of something infinitely larger. The sense of an individual ego is temporarily set aside, allowing for transformative experiences of peace, understanding, and connection that reach beyond the self into a transcendent, mystical domain.

Monomythical Traits

NDEs reflect the essence of the monomyth, or hero's journey, where experiencers cross thresholds, face profound challenges, and return transformed. These experiences often begin with the crossing of a boundary into an unfamiliar realm, described as moving through a tunnel or a void towards a brilliant, all-encompassing light. For some, the initial threshold is harrowing, marked by fear or despair, mirroring the descent into the underworld in mythological narratives. Yet even the darkest experiences often evolve into moments of clarity, self-reflection, and transformation.[19]

Encounters with mystical beings or guides are common in NDEs. These entities, which may take the form of deceased loved ones, beings of light, or even unidentifiable presences, play a pivotal role in guiding individuals through their journey. And like the threshold guardians of classical mythology, experiencers often describe these beings in the form of guides or evaluators who decide or ask whether they will cross a point of no return or go back to their body.

The life review, a powerful aspect of many NDEs, allows individuals to relive past actions and relationships with emotional clarity, seeing the ripple effects of their choices through the lens of compassion and interconnectedness. These encounters serve not as judgement in the punitive sense, but as opportunities for growth and understanding, reinforcing the values of love, connection, and purpose.

A defining feature of NDEs is the moment of decision: whether to return to life or continue into the timeless realm they have entered. This timelessness, while suffused with peace, unity, and beauty, lacks the challenges, relationships, and opportunities for growth that earthly existence provides. According to experiencers, to stay is to transcend time, yet also to forgo the trials and tribulations that help create meaning in the universe.

The return to life is often framed as a negotiation, guided by the recognition that the soul's journey remains unfinished, and that life's struggles contribute to the creation of something greater. Death, in this sense, becomes less of a final destination and more of an ongoing dialogue until the moment when one is truly ready. Until then, experiencers often return to life with a sense of something greater than themselves, where they are less driven by selfish or material impulses and more by a sense of collective duty to others and a common good.

Regardless of NDEs, Carl Jung considered this transcendent state as an essential stage in life's journey for personal growth and a healthy psyche. For Jung, this was a point that we should all reach as we transition into the second half of life.[20]

Returning Transformed

As discussed, Jung described the second half of life as the transition from personal ambition or self-oriented action to a deeper sense of purpose. Here we see the embodiment of archetypes such as the mentor or wise elder who recognize and fulfil their responsibility to give something back to the community based on the lessons learned and knowledge gained on their journey.

Upon returning from an NDE, individuals frequently experience this profound transformation. They carry back messages of love, interconnectedness, and the imperative to live with purpose. Much like the mythological hero, who returns with the elixir to share with their community, after an NDE people often feel compelled to share their newfound wisdom.

However, the return is not without difficulty. Many struggle to articulate the ineffable nature of their experience or to reconcile their insights with the mundane realities of life. Some feel alienated, navigating the tension between the transcendent truths they have encountered and a world that may dismiss or misunderstand them.

As we shall see in the personal accounts covered in the next chapter, NDEs are deeply mythic in their structure, offering a modern expression of humanity's timeless quest for meaning and transcendence. They remind us that life's struggles and connections not only are necessary for growth but also contribute to a larger cosmic narrative, shaping the meaning we carry with us into whatever might lie beyond death.

Through this lens, death is no longer simply an end but a profound negotiation, a bridge between the trials of life and the timeless realms of eternity.

This echoes Jung. He believed that the second half of life should be devoted to exploring the depths of human experience and integrating the wisdom gained into a meaningful whole. Those who return from the brink often embody this shift, becoming guides for others as they navigate their own existential challenges. But these transformations do not come without their trials and tribulations—those common NDE troubles that I account for in Chap. 10.

Notes

1. Robins (2021, 2024).
2. Lee (2024); Fry (2021).
3. Jung (1969).
4. Plato (2007).
5. Pasulka (2019).
6. Teresa of Ávila (2008).
7. Kripal does not suggest that we shouldn't understand personal and cultural differences, but he does suggest these shouldn't become the absolute and exclusive lens of humanities research. He states: "I strongly suspect that the academy's overriding moral concern with difference and its near complete disinterest in ontological identity is very ... theistic. There is a deep theological program running behind the screen here, one that insists that human difference is fundamental and not illusory; that the Creator is separate for the creation (or does not exist at all); that every soul or person is distinct and special in some fundamental moral sense; and that the human being or self should be equated, full stop, with embodiment. All these claims, it turns out, are theological ones. They constitute a cultural reality posit that should be taken seriously but hardly absolutely" (2022: 73). To take the nuance of Kripal's point further, Richard Rohr himself makes the point that despite all our glorious differences and complexities as individuals, every single one of us is bound by the universal (incarnational) reality of being made in God's image.
8. Sheldrake (2012).
9. Kripal (2022: 73).
10. Rohr (2013).
11. Jung (1947, 1959c).

12. Long and Perry (2016). Long (2024). Jeffrey Long is also the founder of the Near-Death Experience Research Foundation (NDERF), established in 1998 to collect and analyse firsthand accounts of near-death experiences. The foundation hosts the world's largest publicly available NDE database. See: Near-Death Experience Research Foundation. Available at: https://www.nderf.org/
13. While critics challenge the scientific rigor of anecdotal data and the lack of medical corroboration, Long's work nonetheless deepens the conversation between spirituality and science. It reframes NDEs not just as altered states, but as encounters with a unifying source of consciousness that many call God.
14. Greyson (2020).
15. Greyson (2020, 2022).
16. Moody (1975, 1988).
17. Fenwick and Fenwick (1995); Stern (2021).
18. In the Summer 2007 edition of the University of Virginia Magazine, Lee Graves presented the NDE scale in the following article, titled, Altered States: Scientists analyze the near-death experience: https://iands.org/resources/education/greyson-nde-scale.html
19. Greyson (2020, 2022).
20. Jung (1933).

Bibliography

Fenwick, P., & Fenwick, E. (1995). *The Truth in the Light: An Investigation of Over 300 Near-Death Experiences.* Headline.

Fry, S. (2021). Stephen Fry's Victorian Secrets: Ghost Stories. [Audiobook] *Audible Originals.* Retrieved April 28, 2025, from https://www.audible.co.uk/pd/Stephen-Frys-Victorian-Secrets-Audiobook/B095JT86CJ

Greyson, B. (2020). *After: A Doctor Explores What Near-Death Experiences Reveal about Life and Beyond.* St. Martin's Press.

Greyson, B. (2022). Are Near-Death Experiences Real? Here's What Science Has to Say. *Big Think*, YouTube. Retrieved April 28, 2025, from https://www.youtube.com/watch?v=J5n2dzN1joU

Jung, C. G. (1933). *Modern Man in Search of a Soul* (W. S. Dell & C. F. Baynes, Trans.). Routledge.

Jung, C. G. (1969). *The Archetypes and the Collective Unconscious* (Vol. 9, Part 1 of the Collected Works of C.G. Jung). Princeton University Press.

Kripal, J. (2022). *Superhumanities: Historical Precedents, Moral Objections, and New Realities.* University of Chicago Press.

Lee, S. (2024). *Halloween: Trilogy of Terror.* [Podcast] BBC Radio 4. Retrieved April 28, 2025, from https://www.bbc.co.uk/sounds/play/m0024f6q

Long, J. (2024). *Near-Death Experience Expert Dr. Jeffrey Long | This Past Weekend w/Theo Von #479*. This Past Weekend with Theo Von. [Online video]. Retrieved July 25, 2025, from https://www.youtube.com/watch?v=RfOGrMfcMPg

Long, J., & Perry, P. (2016). *God and the Afterlife: The Groundbreaking New Evidence for God and Near-Death Experience*. HarperOne.

Moody, R. (1975). *Life After Life: The Investigation of a Phenomenon—Survival of Bodily Death*. Mockingbird Books.

Moody, R. (1988). *Coming Back: A Study of Resurrection and Immortality*. Mockingbird Books.

Pasulka, D. (2019). *American Cosmic: UFOs, Religion, Technology*. Oxford University Press.

Plato. (2007). *Republic* (D. Lee, Trans., 2nd ed.). Penguin Classics.

Robins, D. (2021). The UFO in the Playground. *Uncanny*, Series 1, Episode 8. BBC Sounds. Retrieved August 20, 2025, from https://www.bbc.co.uk/sounds/play/p0b8j7hx

Robins, D. (2024). *Into the Uncanny*. BBC Books.

Rohr, R. (2013). *Immortal Diamond: The Search for Our True Self*. Jossey-Bass.

Sheldrake, R. (2012). *Science Set Free: 10 Paths to New Discovery*. Deepak Chopra Books.

Stern, R. (2021). *Surviving Death: Episode 1—Near-Death Experience*. [TV series]. Netflix.

Teresa of Ávila. (2008). *The Book of My Life* (M. Starr, Trans.). Shambhala Publications.

CHAPTER 10

Troubles and Transformations

As an infant, David Ditchfield was happy, but his life changed upon starting school. Undiagnosed dyslexia made learning a struggle, and teachers unfairly labelled him lazy. Leaving school with few qualifications, he moved to London, hoping for a fresh start. However, he faced financial difficulties, identity struggles, and failed attempts to fit into professional circles. After losing his job and facing eviction, he sought solace with family.[1]

One day, while seeing off a friend at a train station, his coat got caught in a departing train. David found himself trapped as the automatic doors of the train station closed. His sheepskin coat caught in the corner, pinning him in place as the doors slammed shut. The train began to move with his friend Anna watching through the glass. He saw the terror on her face, and for a moment, he thought, "This is it. I'm going to die."

David lost his footing and was dragged along the platform's edge before being pulled between the platform and under the train. David was soon under the train being thrown around and mangled by what felt like a washing machine spinning him round and throwing him out. Suddenly, he was lying between the tracks as the train continued its journey. With his head down in the gravel, David feared the undercarriage might come down on him, but somehow it didn't.

As David laid on the tracks, he described deep, inexplicable joy at surviving—as if something bigger had saved him from death. David knew he

D. Kelsey, *Transcendence and Collective Psychology*,
https://doi.org/10.1007/978-3-032-09495-7_10

was badly injured. He could see the nerves and muscles inside of his arm, and the pain was unbearable.

David was rushed to hospital where a team of medical staff was already prepared for his arrival. As they worked on him, he could hear the fear in their voices. His family was there, and his mother, in tears, reassured him it wasn't his fault. He was concerned about Anna, who had witnessed the whole incident. When she told him they had announced his death over the loudspeakers, he was overwhelmed with relief to be alive.

Leaving the Body

But then things turned. At that point, David left his body. Now detached from the trauma and pain of his physical injuries, he entered a comforting, darkened space. Orbs of colour pulsated around him. He accepted that he might have died, but he didn't resist. The ordeal had been so horrific that he welcomed the peace he now felt.

As he rested in this awe-inspiring realm, David perceived a tunnel of brilliant white light approaching. He felt its energy before he saw it, a vibration that resonated through his being. The tunnel, surrounded by swirling flames, exuded an intense yet comforting power. Though such a sight might once have terrified him, he now understood what it was: the source of all creation.

This wasn't the God of childhood imagery, but an overwhelming presence of unconditional love and infinite energy. For David, it was both awe-inspiring and deeply familiar, an ultra-real experience of divinity that encompassed everything he had ever known.

As he adjusted to this new reality, he found himself lying on a large slate-like rock like a medieval altar, and he was surprised to discover that his injuries had vanished. His left arm was back in place, with no sign of injury, and he was covered by a satin-like blue sheet.

David felt as though the light was healing him, radiating warmth and goodness. He then became aware of a presence near him. At his feet stood a glowing figure with white-blond hair and skin that seemed to shine with an inner light. He felt as though he knew this being. He spoke, asking, "Who are you? I know you, don't I?" The figure smiled reassuringly, neither male nor female, a completely androgynous presence. David felt safe, guided by this being. He then relaxed, allowing himself to bask in the light.

He then sensed the presence of two female figures, standing on either side of him. They hovered their hands over his body, and he felt a powerful energy flowing from them, a sensation of love and healing. The energy vibrated through him, not just healing his physical wounds but also the emotional scars he had carried for years. His guilt, shame, and past traumas seemed to dissolve, leaving only the pure essence of his soul.

Peace and Healing

David's thoughts turned to his grieving family. Overcome with concern for their suffering, he tried to look down from the rock where he lay. Instead of Earth, he saw a cosmic waterfall of stars, akin to Niagara Falls, but with cascading galaxies instead of water. He gazed into its depths, marvelling at the vibrant colours of nebulas and the infinite expanse beyond. He felt deeply connected to the universe, part of something immeasurable and divine.

For the first time in his life, David experienced a profound sense of peace and healing. It was as if he had been cleansed, and he fully accepted the love and light that surrounded him. The experience was beyond anything he had ever known or imagined, and he knew, in that moment, he had been touched by something greater than himself.

Like many experiencers, David describes a revelation of infinite love and light that we are all a part of—a universal connection with the source of all creation, a loving God without judgement.

David was fortunate that his closest relatives understood his experience—even his church-going parents who saw no conflict between their faith and his encounter with divinity. His parents said they sensed a "glowing" that he had never radiated before in life.

However, like many experiencers, David went through a period of depression as he struggled to reintegrate into everyday life and communicate the depth of his experience to others. Having encountered a loving God and a profound sense of universal connection, he now saw the absurdities of life—and the unnecessary suffering caused by our false selves—as deeply tragic.

But David worked through it, and given he was desperate not to forget what he had seen and experienced, he began documenting his NDE.

Artistic Preservation

Despite no formal training, David began creating large-scale, emotionally charged paintings that depict the celestial imagery and spiritual themes of his NDE.

As described in his book *Shine On*, this experience also sparked a previously undiscovered musical and artistic talents. David felt a powerful urge to compose classical music, which ultimately led to *The Divine Light*—a symphony that premiered as a live orchestral performance.[2] He also began creating large-scale paintings that visually captured the vivid and otherworldly scenes he encountered during his NDE.

These artworks, like his music, emerged spontaneously despite having no formal training in either discipline. David's art and music now serve as a bridge between his experience and the world, reflecting his journey of healing, self-discovery, and a renewed sense of purpose.

David soon felt self-love and deep gratitude—no longer needing to live up to the expectations of his false self. His true self was expressed through the authentic voice of his artwork. David now encourages people to stop thinking about the past and future and accept that the present moment is fine. David describes how we act our way through life—faking what Rohr calls our False Self to navigate society and careers and meet the expectations of others to pursue status and material possessions.

David says that the love he now radiates and the deep contentment he feels in the present moment have allowed life's synchronicities to unfold naturally—leading to professional and social flourishing that seems to take care of itself. While he isn't opposed to ambition, his experience has taught him that such flourishing occurs in more authentic and beautiful ways when we stop trying to force new realities and instead learn to go with the flow.

The unlocking of unconscious creativity is not unique to David; many experiencers report a sudden surge of artistic or intuitive abilities following NDEs.[3]

The Case of Tony Cicoria

A grounded man of science, Tony Cicoria was an accomplished orthopaedic surgeon. However, a direct lightning strike during a family gathering in 1994 would soon change his perception of reality, selfhood, and the nature of existence.[4]

Tony's NDE began with a moment of pure shock. Struck in the face by a bolt of lightning while using a payphone, he was instantly thrown backwards. Yet rather than simply losing consciousness, he found himself standing upright, confused by the dissonance between what he had just experienced and where he now found himself. He quickly realized that he was outside his body, witnessing his own lifeless form on the ground while those around him frantically tried to revive him.

Tony's consciousness, completely intact, remained unbound by physical limitations. He could see, hear, and think clearly, yet no one could see or hear him. This realization led him to an overwhelming insight: death, as he had understood it, did not exist. He had not ceased to be, but he had transitioned into a new state of being, one where he felt liberated from his physical form.

Tony's Great Ascent

As he moved away from his lifeless body, Tony underwent a profound transformation. The boundaries of selfhood began to dissolve. Ascending a staircase, he found his legs disappearing, his form shifting into pure energy. Ego dissolution offered a state where the distinction between self and other vanishes. Tony no longer existed as a separate individual but as an awareness absorbed into a vast, formless presence.

This feeling intensified as he passed through physical barriers effortlessly, transcending material constraints. No longer bound by physicality, he entered what he later described as a "river of pure positive energy," carried by an unseen force. This transition was accompanied by an overwhelming sense of peace, love, and interconnectedness, similar to mystical states reported by meditators and psychedelic users.

As he moved upward, Tony found himself enveloped in a luminous, bluish-white light. The light radiated a presence, an intelligence composed entirely of love and peace. Like David Ditchfield, Tony identified this light as the "God energy," the source of all existence. Within this presence, he felt an indescribable sense of belonging, an ecstasy beyond anything he had ever known.

This moment marked the peak of his experience, where he felt fully absorbed into a higher consciousness. It was not a place, nor was it a being in any conventional sense—it was a state of being itself, an immersion into a fundamental source that transcended all distinctions between self and other. In this state, Tony encountered a rapid-life review, where flashes of key moments in his life appeared before him, unfolding without judgement but with deep clarity.

Tony's Painful Return

Just as he was settling into this blissful state, something abruptly changed. In an instant, the transcendent experience was ripped away. He was pulled back, not by choice, but by force. Pain surged through his body as he re-entered it, jolted into suffering and the harshness of physical existence. The contrast was staggering. Where he had just experienced boundless love and unity, he was now confined, limited, and once again bound by the constraints of the flesh.

His immediate reaction was one of deep frustration. He did not want to return—his soul resisted it. The transition from transcendence back into embodied life felt unnatural, a loss rather than a continuation. This reaction is a well-documented feature of NDEs: many experiencers report an intense reluctance to return, finding the earthly realm dull and painful in comparison to the ineffable beauty they encountered beyond.

The return to life did not simply restore Tony to his old self. The experience had permanently altered him, shifting his entire orientation towards existence. He no longer saw life as a mere physical process—he now understood it as a continuum, part of a much larger cycle of learning, evolution, and transcendence.

The Creative Urge

Tony's transformation did not stop at a change in worldview. Almost immediately after his return, an insatiable longing for classical piano music overtook him—a passion entirely foreign to his previous self. This was no casual interest. For Tony, much like David, it felt as if something within him had been activated. He soon found himself not only obsessively listening to classical music but also feeling an urgent need to compose it, despite never having played the piano before.

Then came the dreams. In vivid nocturnal visions, Tony saw himself performing a grand, celestial piece of music. Each time he dreamed, the composition became clearer, as though it were being dictated to him from another realm. The music would not leave him, playing in his head ceaselessly, until he finally surrendered to it. Teaching himself how to play,

Tony spent months transcribing the compositions from his dreams, as if he was channelling something beyond himself.

Tony came to see this newfound musical ability as a direct consequence of his NDE—like a gift or calling from the other side.

A Greater Continuum

For Tony, the near-death experience was not just a singular event but an initiation into a deeper understanding of existence. He came to believe that life does not end with death—it continues in another form, beyond the constraints of time and materiality. He saw human life as a journey of spiritual development, where each incarnation serves as a testing ground for the soul's evolution—like an arena for growth. To him, the path forward is about service, growth, and an eventual return to the source from which all things emerge.

His experience also reinforced a growing perspective among those who study NDEs: that consciousness is not merely a by-product of the brain but something that transcends physical life entirely. His story, like so many others, challenges conventional materialist assumptions and suggests that human beings are far more than biological machines. We are, as Tony came to see, eternal beings wearing temporary "costumes" of flesh.

Tony's transformation reveals a vision of human existence that is deeply mystical, one in which we are not just biological entities but spiritual travellers moving through cycles of learning and transformation. Whether one interprets his experience as a literal glimpse of the afterlife or as an altered state of consciousness, it remains a powerful reminder that reality is far more mysterious than we often assume.

In the end, Tony's NDE, like so many cases and accounts, was about so much more than a glimpse of what might lie beyond this life—it was about transformation and transcendence *within* this life.

The Case of Shawna Ristic

Shawna Ristic's NDE started her journey from trauma and disconnection to a higher understanding of love, consciousness, and the fabric of existence itself.[5] Her story shares those common NDE traits of ego dissolution, the encounter with luminous beings, the deep realization of interconnectedness, and the challenge of reintegration into ordinary life after glimpsing a greater reality.

Shawna's NDE began after a driving accident. Distracted by reaching for a phone, she swerved to avoid another vehicle, overcorrected, and lost control. Her car flipped multiple times, tumbling violently across two lanes of traffic. Thrown forty feet from the wreckage, her body was left broken and unresponsive, while her family kept vigil at the hospital, hoping for her survival.

But for Shawna, the experience was entirely different. While medical personnel and loved ones focused on her fragile body, her consciousness had already transitioned to another state, one where physical suffering no longer existed, and a new reality unfolded.

The Beings of Light

Shawna's first memory after the accident was waking in an overwhelmingly bright space, surrounded by six tall, luminous beings—three on each side. They radiated warmth and love unlike anything she had ever known. As they gently assisted her into an upright position, she realized that she was no longer inside her body. Yet rather than panic or fear, she felt an immense, all-encompassing love.

These beings were more than mere figures: they were expressions of pure acceptance. Shawna embraced them, feeling a profound sense of belonging—a sensation deeper and more real than any earthly relationship. There were no expectations, no judgement, only an infinite love that affirmed her worth beyond the roles and labels imposed upon her in earthly life.

This moment marked the first stage of ego dissolution. The weight of societal expectations, past mistakes, and external judgements all melted away. The beings conveyed an essential truth: she was not the sum of what she had been told she was—her value was intrinsic, woven into the very fabric of existence itself. The immortal diamond, as Rohr puts it.

Emotion and Connection

As the experience unfolded, Shawna was given a revelation about the interconnectedness of all life. Observing her mother in the hospital, grieving over her comatose body, she didn't just *see* her sorrow—she *felt* it. This was more than empathy: it was a direct, visceral experience of another person's emotions.

This deepened into an understanding of how every action, no matter how small, creates ripples through the web of existence. Her presence, her choices, and even her absence all had profound effects on others. The beings showed her that human lives are interwoven like the lights of a city viewed from above—each person a vital source of energy, interconnected with all others. If one light goes out, the surrounding ones dim. This realization transformed her perception of selfhood, reinforcing the idea that individual existence is not isolated but an intrinsic part of a vast, collective whole.

This perspective reframed the concept of *Judgment Day*. Rather than an external force condemning or rewarding souls, it became clear that judgement arises from within—when one fully *feels* the impact they have had on others. The pain or love people cause is not simply observed but *experienced*, creating an opportunity for deep, existential learning.

Later in her NDE, Shawna found herself in the presence of twelve luminous beings seated in a circle. These figures appeared to be debating her fate—whether she should return to her earthly existence or remain in that realm. For the first time, she sensed that her agency was limited and she had no control over the decision. This aligns with many reported NDEs where individuals feel their return to life is either guided or decided by a greater force or higher intelligence. For Shawna, the decision was made, and she returned.

Painful Transitions

Like so many experiencers, Shawna's return was neither seamless nor welcomed. Waking in the hospital, she found herself trapped once again in a broken body, unable to speak, surrounded by machines. The pain was overwhelming, the contrast between the love she had just experienced and the harshness of physical existence was devastating. She had been forced back into limitation, into a world governed by suffering, separation, and misunderstanding.

Yet, the love she had encountered on the other side remained. When her friend Patrick sat by her bedside, she could see it emanating from him—an invisible force that was now undeniably real to her. She began to recognize it in others as well, glimpsing the divine light within human beings, even when they themselves were unaware of it.

But integrating back into life was excruciating. The world felt harsh, fragmented, and oblivious to the love that underpinned everything.

Everyday interactions carried a weight of misunderstanding—people didn't see what she had seen, and they couldn't comprehend her experience. Her father, a rational-minded engineer, dismissed her vision of the council of beings as something she had simply absorbed from television. His explanation, though well-intended, only deepened her isolation.

This is a common struggle after NDEs as experiencers struggle to reconcile their encounter with a seemingly non-material reality when the world around them is anchored in materialist assumptions.

Integration and Identity

After her coma, Shawna felt compelled to embody the truth she had discovered—that life was fundamentally about love and that people were not their traumas, their failures, or the judgements placed upon them. But this didn't initially help her reintegration, as Shawna still struggled to find meaning and purpose while becoming disillusioned with the way people treated each other. War, violence, cruelty suddenly seemed unfathomable after experiencing the deep unity of all existence.

The transition was so difficult that Shawna contemplated ending her life. Having glimpsed the vast, luminous reality beyond, she felt alienated from the pettiness and suffering of earthly life. But the memory of her family's devotion during her recovery held her back. She could not betray their love.

Instead, Shawna turned to journaling, unknowingly entering a form of automatic writing. Through this practice, she re-established contact with the council of beings from her NDE. They became her guides once more, this time from within, helping her navigate her depression and confusion. Slowly, she found a new sense of purpose—not in career ambition, but in helping others remember their own divine essence.

A New Way of Living

Shawna's post-NDE transformation was radical. No longer drawn to her past lifestyle, she became deeply attuned to the subtleties of energy and consciousness. She developed an acute sensitivity to truth, learning to navigate life not through logic alone, but through expansion—following what made her heart open and her spirit lift.

Her greatest realization was the distinction between the *self* and the *mind-body complex*. She had directly experienced existence beyond the body, and she now understood that life in the physical realm was but a brief moment in the vast continuum of being. Her mission became clear. Shawna's purpose was to help others remember who they truly are—not flawed, limited beings subject to judgement and punishment, but luminous, eternal expressions of love.

Shawna's story offers a radical challenge to conventional understandings of life and death. It suggests that judgement is not imposed externally but arises from our own interconnectedness with others. It reaffirms the idea that death is not an end but a transition, and that the true nature of existence is boundless, radiant, and suffused with love.

For Shawna, the challenge is not in proving what she saw—it is in remembering it, embodying it, and helping others awaken to the same truth: that they, too, are made of light.

The Case of Mary Neal

Over twenty years ago, Dr Mary Neal, an orthopaedic surgeon, had an NDE that profoundly changed her perspective on life and death.[6] Mary wasn't someone who gave much thought to what might lie beyond this world. As a medical doctor and respected spinal surgeon, her outlook was rooted in science and the material. But in 1999, during a kayaking trip in Chile, Mary drowned and was resuscitated in circumstances that defied medical explanation.

Mary and her group were navigating a notoriously dangerous river known for its waterfalls. Initially, the trip went smoothly, but as they approached a particularly perilous waterfall, her kayak was caught in a powerful current and pinned underwater against rocks. Trapped beneath ten feet of water, her body was crushed by the force of the current, and her bones were breaking. Yet, she felt no pain, panic, or fear. Instead, she experienced a profound sense of peace and aliveness, far beyond anything she had ever known.

Released into the Heavens

Mary describes feeling her spirit separate from her body, as though it was being "released into the heavens." While her body remained trapped underwater, Mary says she was greeted by a group of beings—people, spirits, or something else. Consistent with the common traits of NDEs, Mary didn't recognize the beings, but she instinctively understood that they were deeply connected to her life, as if they had been watching over her. The beings radiated joy and love, welcoming her like family who had been waiting to reunite with her.

The beings guided her along a pathway lined with thousands of vivid flowers, emanating colours and aromas beyond anything on Earth. Another trait consistent with the vast data collected on NDEs, Mary said time and space dissolved, describing “all of eternity in every second, and every second expanding into all of eternity.” The pathway led to a vast dome, which she interpreted as heaven, or what she calls “God’s world.” Being there felt like coming home—a place of pure love, belonging, and peace.

At the same time, Mary remained aware of her physical body trapped underwater. Her fellow kayakers struggled desperately to free her, but after fifteen minutes, they assumed she was dead and shifted their focus from rescue to recovery. Mary had been submerged for over thirty minutes when they finally managed to pull her lifeless body to the surface.

The Reluctant Return

From Mary’s perspective, she was still in heaven, feeling completely at peace as the beings reassured her that everything was fine. She did not want to return to her body. However, the beings told her it wasn’t her time—she still had work to do on Earth. Reluctantly, she obeyed and re-entered her body as her friends attempted resuscitation.

As Mary explains, this wasn’t a simple case of grappling with divine beauty. Her reluctance to return to her body was another paradoxical characteristic of this transcendent realm. Seldom are experiencers keen to return to their bodies, often experiencing extreme guilt, frustration, and isolation upon return. They often have families they love and children they care about, and so the regret they feel upon returning is a difficult feeling to process.

Mary’s group carried her through the wilderness, expecting to face a long and difficult journey to find help. They discovered an ambulance waiting on a remote dirt track where they exited the forest. As Mary points out, for such an isolated location in southern Chile in 1999, the presence of the ambulance was inexplicable. Mary was rushed to hospital where doctors gave her no chance of survival. Even if she lived, they believed severe brain damage was inevitable. Yet, against all odds, she made a full recovery with no neurological impairment.

An Uncomfortable Warning

Mary's NDE and life afterward were far from easy. During her NDE, she received a message from the beings she encountered, warning of the unexpected death of her nine-year-old son. Though no specific timeline was given, Mary became convinced he wouldn't live past eighteen.

For years, she struggled with this forewarning, trying to find alternative explanations for her NDE to discount the message. Each day, she feared it might be the day her son would die. When her son turned eighteen, Mary felt relieved, believing his fate had changed. Tragically, two years later, Willie was hit by a car and died instantly.

Mary's NDE did not shield her from grief. She deeply loves her son and feels the pain of loss. However, her experience gave her solace, affirming that death is not the end but a transition to something greater. Despite the heartbreak, she finds comfort in the belief that she will see him again. As with so many NDEs, they might provide moments of divine ecstasy and love, but people's lives afterwards can be difficult, and experiencers often need support.[7]

The Seattle Support Group

Kimberly Sharp runs a support group in Seattle to help others navigate the challenges that often arise after such profound events.[8] While NDEs are often described as transformative and filled with love and light, Kimberly emphasizes that returning to the material world can be incredibly difficult.

The insights gained during an NDE often clash with everyday realities, including work, relationships, and societal norms. This disconnect can leave experiencers feeling isolated and misunderstood. Kimberly's group provides a space for people to connect, share, and find reassurance as they adjust to life after an NDE.

One of Kimberly's patients shared how the knowledge she gained during her NDE left her feeling completely alone. What she now understands feels impossible to explain to her loved ones. She avoids talking to her husband about it, fearing he'll think she's crazy. For people like Kimberly, the support group is a lifeline, offering a rare sense of connection with others who truly understand.

Jose Hernandez, a member of the group, shared his NDE story. A hardened atheist at the time, Jose was working as an electrician in an elevated bucket truck when an accident caused him to fall, cracking several ribs. Later, in hospital, he had an allergic reaction to painkillers, and his heart stopped.

During his NDE, Jose found himself falling into a tunnel that wrapped around him, filled with vibrant colours, whispering voices, and the sound of an ocean. In the water stood a man knee-deep. When the man turned, Jose recognized him—it was his father.

A Second Chance for Love

Jose and his father had a strained relationship during life. They had never been able to express love or affection, and his father had died with deep regret. But during the NDE, they were given a second chance. They embraced, shared words of love, and reconciled. Jose says this moment healed a deep wound in his spirit, as he finally knew how much his father cared for him.

Eventually, his father looked at him and said, "You need to go back." Jose didn't want to return, but they came to an agreement: when Jose's time came, his father would be there to guide him.

This experience profoundly changed Jose's life. He reflects that there may be things we can't say in this life, but there will be a time and place to say them elsewhere. Before his NDE, Jose felt like he was simply moving through life—going through the motions with minimal purpose. Afterwards, he felt truly alive, his spirit healed, and his perspective transformed. With a newfound sense of gratitude for life and an appreciation for a greater reality beyond the material world, Jose was no longer an atheist.

Resisting Hogwash

For Dr. Michael Sabom to start taking NDEs seriously, a major transformation was required.[9] When a medical colleague introduced him to Raymond Moody's *Life After Life*, he dismissed it as hogwash. As a cardiologist, Sabom initially approached NDEs with deep suspicion and assumed that the recurring accounts shared by patients after cardiac arrests could be easily debunked.

However, curiosity eventually compelled him to start recording accounts from his own patients. What he discovered challenged his preconceptions. Sabom notes that medically and scientifically, the precise point of death remains undefined—doctors resuscitate patients, they don't resurrect them. Nonetheless, he became convinced that NDEs do occur—at the very least during the *process of dying*—and should therefore be taken seriously. He argues that dying is a far more complex phenomenon than previously assumed, and one that modern medicine is only beginning to understand.

What ultimately transformed Sabom's perspective was his commitment to scientific verification. As a professional of strict scientific principles, he sought evidence to validate the NDEs his patients described. For Sabom, what he found was not definitive proof of life after death but rather compelling evidence that the process of dying might be accompanied by profound and meaningful experiences. These experiences, regardless of their ultimate implications, should be taken seriously.

There are lessons for us all to learn from these insights to death and dying. If accomplished materialists from respected scientific and medical backgrounds can see the importance of this phenomenon, then there's no reason why the rest of us can't rethink how we talk about death and dying.

Implications for Science

Returning to Bruce Greyson, his research has reshaped his understanding of reality and consciousness. He suggests that at our deepest level, we are energy beings of love and light, temporarily housed in physical bodies.

Greyson now advocates for a more harmonious relationship between science and spirituality, showing that embracing phenomena that are difficult to measure is not a rejection of science but rather an expansion of it. Science, he contends, is about exploring the unknown, and as Thomas Kuhn observed, progress often comes when new discoveries challenge existing paradigms.

Greyson critiques the idea that controlled experiments are the only valid form of scientific inquiry, noting that disciplines like astronomy and palaeontology rely primarily on observation rather than experimentation. He illustrates this point with the example of parachutes—where no randomized controlled trials exist—yet their effectiveness is universally accepted based on overwhelming observational evidence. For Greyson, the same logic applies to NDEs: although they resist conventional experimental design, they still offer meaningful insights into consciousness and the human condition.

Greyson addresses criticisms that NDEs are merely anecdotal by pointing out that all scientific inquiry begins with anecdotes. Over time, as patterns emerge and anecdotes accumulate, they transition into data, which can then be systematically observed and analysed. This process ultimately transforms anecdotal evidence into a foundation for scientific understanding, illustrating that dismissing experiences like NDEs outright overlooks the natural progression of scientific discovery.

Beyond the Brain?

Central to Greyson's findings is the suggestion that consciousness may not be entirely produced by the brain. He draws on clinical cases in which patients report vivid NDEs even after brain activity appears to cease within seconds of cardiac arrest, challenging the assumption that brain function is strictly necessary for conscious experience.

As Larry Dossey suggests, consciousness may persist not because of the brain but in spite of it. A former Chief of Staff at Medical City Dallas Hospital, Dossey has been instrumental in challenging materialist assumptions within mainstream medicine. Through works like *Healing Words* and *One Mind*, he blends medical insight with mysticism, suggesting that the mind is not confined to the brain but part of a shared, non-local field of consciousness—one that transcends space, time, and even physical death.[10]

NDEs, Bruce Greyson argues, reveal dimensions of experience that words cannot fully describe. As David Ditchfield found, music and art, with their unique abilities to convey emotions beyond language, can be a better medium for expressing the peace and transcendence often reported by experiencers.

Greyson also emphasizes the ethical implications of his research. Whether one believes in a "higher power" or not, he echoes the wisdom of writer Dinty Moore: living with kindness, compassion, and awareness benefits everyone. Similarly, his perspective aligns with the idea that all spiritual paths ultimately lead to the same mountaintop—an experience of love, light, and unity that transcends religious boundaries.

Through his work, Greyson invites us to rethink our assumptions about reality, consciousness, and our place in the universe. By embracing both the measurable and the ineffable, he envisions a more integrated approach to science and spirituality, one that honours the mystery of existence while seeking deeper understanding.

Panpsychism and Materialism

NDEs challenge our current understanding of consciousness and materialism. As the likes of Greyson have noted, there is compelling evidence suggesting that consciousness can persist even when brain activity appears to cease. While this does not necessarily confirm the existence of an afterlife, it does suggest that the process of dying is far more complex than the conventional materialist paradigm might assume.

Panpsychism offers a framework that accommodates these observations. As discussed earlier, panpsychism posits that consciousness is a fundamental aspect of reality, not merely a by-product of brain activity. If this is the case, consciousness might exert a form of agency that shapes matter, life, and biological structures, including the brain.

The brain, in this view, functions as a receiver or filter for a broader, universal consciousness, as researchers like Strassman, Greyson, and Goff have proposed. NDEs or psychedelic experiences may temporarily disrupt this filtering process, allowing individuals to access dimensions of consciousness that are ordinarily hidden from view.

I wish to avoid framing this as a strict dichotomy between materialism and panpsychism—debates that are valuable, but not essential here. If evidence emerged for a universal consciousness connecting all beings, materialists might interpret it as a new discovery about the physical properties of the universe. In that sense, what we call "material" may not be fixed, but evolving—potentially expanding to include phenomena once considered spiritual or non-material.

After all, materialism itself has undergone multiple transformations throughout scientific history—from the clockwork determinism of Newtonian physics, to the probabilistic fields of quantum mechanics, to the information-based models of contemporary cosmology. Rather than threatening to discard the materialist framework, we might instead encourage ongoing revisions to accommodate a more complex and layered understanding of reality. For both materialists and panpsychists, this line of inquiry could ultimately lead us towards a shared—but currently unknown—form of knowledge that lies beyond our present comprehension.

NDEs challenge us to reconsider the nature of consciousness and its role in the fabric of existence. Given we don't know whether NDEs lead into an eternal realm or not, we need to think about what meaning and memory provide us with in either scenario—whether it's a rich and complex process of dying or the beginning of another eternal realm altogether.

Meanings and Memories

Whether our journey ends in a peaceful fade into nothingness or continues into an eternal afterlife, one truth remains: the meanings, memories, and connections we form during our lives are profoundly important. These elements shape not only how we live but also how we approach the process of dying. They may even become central to the experience itself, offering comfort, closure, or transcendence as we transition from life to death.

In this view, the meanings and memories gather through life are crucial—whether they die along with our physical bodies or continue into another realm, they seemingly play a crucial role in the dying process. If NDEs are evidence of life after death, then those meanings, memories, and relationships we carry through life might accompany us into a greater reality—a return to an infinite source of consciousness.

Imagine this infinite source not as a physical place where we reunite with loved ones as we knew them, but as a realm where the love, meaning, and connections they left with us are the essence of our reunion. The relationships we shared in life transform into timeless experiences, carried by the emotions and significance they brought into our lives. Our loved ones, then, are present with us not as physical individuals per se, but as the enduring impact they had on our souls, and the meanings we take with us beyond this life. Whether those euphoric experiences described in NDEs are momentary or eternal, they are no less profound.

If NDEs do point to an eternal realm, the "afterlife" may not be a physical place like "heaven," but rather a state of universal consciousness where meaning, love, light, and connection are fundamental. If NDEs reflect something momentary in the dying process, then meaning still matters. Within this infinite cycle of life and death, the meanings and memories we create in life may serve, however briefly, as a bridge—connecting us to something greater and allowing us to feel complete. The love we shared on Earth becomes the foundation for a profound sense of reunion—regardless of those momentary or eternal potentials.

This idea resonates with the film *Jacob's Ladder*, in which a dying man sees his deceased son guiding him into the light. The scene suggests that love and connection are powerful enough to shape the transition from life to whatever lies beyond. While the film does not reveal where the man goes after death, it emphasizes that the bliss of reunion—however fleeting it might be—is real and meaningful, regardless of what follows.

Such possibilities underscore an enduring reality: the meanings, memories, and love we cultivate in life are not only vital to how we live but may also be essential to how we die.

Navigating Death

In Western society, we need to develop a healthier relationship with death. NDEs play a transformative role in helping us to navigate the complexities of dying, enabling us to approach those final moments—or transitions—with a sense of spiritual wholeness and intentionality. If NDEs encourage us to reflect on the nature of death and its profound psychological and existential dimensions, they might inspire a revolutionary paradigm shift in how we integrate death into our spiritual and psychological practices.

This does not mean cultivating an unhealthy obsession with death but rather fostering an awareness of its inevitability in ways that enhance both how we live and how we prepare for the moment of dying. Embracing this perspective could encourage a culture that values "dying well," just as much as "living well," by promoting practices of self-care, reflection, and connection that prepare us for life's ultimate transition—in accordance with our growing research and knowledge on NDEs.

Negative Experiences

Moreover, giving greater attention to the full spectrum of NDEs—including those that are perceived as negative or distressing—would allow us to create a more inclusive and compassionate dialogue around these experiences. By taking all accounts seriously, we could support individuals in processing their encounters and deepen our understanding of why such experiences occur. This openness could lead to richer interpretations of NDEs as tools for psychological growth, spiritual insight, and existential meaning.

Ultimately, normalizing conversations about death and dying could help dissolve the fear and taboo surrounding them, making space for a collective appreciation of life's fragility and mystery. This shift might not only transform our relationship with death but also redefine how we approach the broader questions of existence and consciousness.

Whether positive or negative, NDEs could offer profound opportunities for psychological and spiritual growth. If we can uncover why these different experiences occur, we may also be able to use them as catalysts for integrative post-NDE work. By making sense of the emotions and visions encountered during these episodes, individuals could engage in a process of healing and transformation akin to the Jungian concept of individuation—achieving greater wholeness by integrating the shadow and the light within themselves. Death is, after all, a conversational shadow in the West.

However, because we don't yet know whether all negative NDEs transition into positive states, it raises profound questions about the nature of these experiences and their potential parallels with concepts like purgatory. In religious and mythological terms, purgatory is often described as a transitional state where the soul undergoes purification to achieve divine union or eternal bliss.

Metaphors We Die by

Could this conception of purgatory be a metaphorical representation of psychological or spiritual transition that some individuals face during death? If negative NDEs reflect a transition from a state dominated by the shadow—fear, guilt, or unresolved conflict—into one where the psyche realizes its divine potential (the immortal diamond), they might serve as a transformative passage.

This process could mirror the spiritual journey from fragmentation to wholeness and transcendence, aligning with the idea of unlocking the "divine spark" within. As discussed earlier, metaphorical truths do not play down the magnificence of faith or divinity, they quite literally keep the meaning alive. Although we lack definitive answers, the questions and possibilities I raise here deserve serious consideration.

A mystical and contemplative grounding enables us to grapple with the hard science and experiential reflections to raise serious questions about the profound nature of such phenomena. This holds significant implications for how we understand the psychology of death and the broader human experience of transitioning from life to whatever else might exist—even if there's nothing at all, the process of dying appears to be significant and worth taking seriously.

Diana Walsh Pasulka's *Heaven Can Wait* explores purgatory not merely as a literal afterlife destination, but as a complex theological and symbolic concept shaped by historical and cultural factors.[11] Drawing on Catholic traditions, mystical accounts, and cultural representations, she frames purgatory as a liminal space of purification and transformation—operating both externally through religious doctrine and internally as a metaphor for psychological or spiritual transition.

Pasulka suggests that modern understandings often cast purgatory as a space of moral cleansing and hope for divine union. In this view, purgatory reflects an inner journey towards healing and wholeness—regardless of its referral to a metaphysical realm or not.

Developing a richer framework for interpreting all kinds of NDEs could help individuals approach the reality of death with more curiosity, courage, and preparation, ultimately enriching how we live and die. If nothing else, a closer understanding of our bodies and how our biology might assist in the process of dying is a worthy line of inquiry for research and public education.

The Fabric of our Biology?

Another bit of strategic scepticism comes in handy here. Let's go with the idea, for a moment, that NDEs do not offer a glimpse of an afterlife—they're purely material, within the brain, no afterlife, no other realm, just death and nothingness. Let's posit that NDEs occur through a release of chemicals from the body and brain that creates a euphoric experience that we cannot measure or detect with current technology.

With this hypothesis in mind, let's ask ourselves *why* our biology, in its final moments, orchestrates such beautiful experiences? From an evolutionary perspective, there seems to be no immediate advantage to a pleasant death. The fact that our bodies "know" they can provide this experience, and we carry the unconscious anatomical desire for a nice death is remarkable, regardless of our worldviews or philosophical speculations.

Perhaps these experiences are more than an anomaly; perhaps they reflect something deeply embedded in the architecture of our biology. Consciousness, intricately linked to our neurology, might possess an innate, incomprehensible wisdom—a drive to imbue the transition from life to death with meaning and peace. Could it be that our bodies or brains, in their final acts, release a cascade of chemicals designed not for survival, but for transcendence? These chemicals may evoke profound feelings of love, connection with deceased loved ones, and a sense of unity with existence itself.

Even if NDEs are not windows into an afterlife, they still reveal something profound about the human condition: the ability of our consciousness to turn death into an experience of extreme love and divine light. This is more than a biological quirk. Such poetic grace in our biological makeup ensures that death becomes a seamless and even harmonious part of the life cycle. Even if the materialists are right, that's still extraordinary.

Death and Renewal

As Richard Rohr reminds us, resurrection is not a singular event, but an ongoing pattern woven into the fabric of existence. As David Ditchfield has said since making sense of his NDE, he came to see the cosmos as a living, evolving force. He describes a profound realization that nothing in the universe is static; everything is in constant motion, unfolding creatively.[12]

This insight left David with a deep sense of connection to a dynamic and intelligent cosmos. He felt that we are all part of this ongoing evolution, contributing to its expansion like co-creators in a living artwork or symphony. His experience reframed life not as fixed or predetermined but as part of a sacred, ever-evolving process that invites active participation and transformation.

In life, death, and renewal, beauty and unity often mark the transitions—suggesting that even at the threshold of the unknown, our biology may be attuned to something profoundly transcendental. This perspective doesn't require belief in God, though for some (myself included), it reveals what feels like the work of God: a dynamic, loving source of all creation, intricately woven into the cycles of life and death.

Why Won't He Let Me Go?

While writing this chapter, my Nan is in a care home with dementia. She started on the top floor—cruelly aware of her condition, but no longer able to live independently or keep herself safe, well, and hydrated. She often says, *"Why won't the big fella upstairs just let me go?"* It's a cruel and torturous disease.

As the condition worsens, residents move down a floor. If they reach the ground floor, they remain there with the best care possible until they pass. Nan has just moved down one floor. She still has cruel days of knowing how sad she is—but there's an increasing absence of that knowing now, a strange unburdening that paradoxically feels like a kind of escape.

Nan hasn't lived in a culture where we commonly talk about and seek to understand death and dying—let alone challenge misconceptions of God. The monarchical God she grew up with seems to be torturing her, forcing her to stay longer than she wants to be here.

It's neither possible nor appropriate to tell her I'm researching NDEs or mystical understandings of divinity. And it would be absurd, in this context, to tell her that research on NDEs suggests she likely has a beautiful process ahead of her—one filled with light, peace, and divine love—where she meets lost loved ones again and it feels like home.

But it doesn't have to be absurd.

We should be able to have these conversations more openly long before the second floor of a care home. It could change so much for so many if this collective knowing were more prominent in our culture.

If such knowledge and conversation had been part of Nan's culture, this time might feel very different. Instead of feeling abandoned by a distant deity, she might recognize that God is already here—present in the relational love that holds all things together. Rohr's *vulnerable God*, revealed in the flow of the Trinity, is not separate from her suffering but intimately involved in it, gently accompanying her through this final chapter. She might be able to feel that love surrounding her now, preparing her for a release that is not abandonment, but reunion—into something luminous, kind, and beyond fear.

Demystifying Death

I would like to finish this case study by telling you about Julie McFadden. As a hospice nurse, public educator, and best-selling author, Julie has spent years witnessing and reflecting on the final moments of life. Her work, both in her book and across her YouTube channel, is dedicated to helping people approach death with more openness, understanding, and peace. Her mission is clear: to demystify the dying process—not by explaining it away, but by paying close attention to the patterns, moments, and mysteries that arise as life comes to a close.[13]

One of the most striking phenomena she explores is the widespread experience of what are often called *deathbed visions*. These are not isolated or rare occurrences. Drawing from both research and her own clinical experience, Julie notes that at least 50% of dying individuals report some kind of visitation or visionary experience.[14]

These visions are uncannily consistent. People nearing death often describe seeing bright lights, glowing figures, or beautiful landscapes. They may speak aloud to someone unseen in the room, reach upwards, or smile suddenly, often uttering phrases like, "They're here," or "I'm not alone." These experiences transcend individual belief systems—they occur across cultures, religions, and backgrounds, suggesting a shared human pattern at the threshold of death.

As Julie recalls, even Steve Jobs, despite his supposedly tech-minded rationalism, reportedly exclaimed, "Oh wow, oh wow, oh wow," just before his passing. Julie finds this unsurprising, noting that such expressions of awe and recognition are familiar in her work, which she believes is worthy of serious attention.

Julie tells another story about a woman who she expected to live only a few hours.[15] As the woman lay dying, Julie saw what she can only describe as a large, solid, human-like figure standing behind the bed. It did not match the ethereal, glowing image of angels she had grown up imagining. Instead, the being felt immense, powerful, and commanding, conveying silently but unmistakably: *"She is mine."*

At the time, Julie dismissed the vision, attributing it to fatigue or emotion. But the next morning, the woman—whose body had shown all the signs of imminent death—was awake, asking for pancakes. She went on to live three more months, with quality of life that, by all clinical logic, should have been impossible.

This event prompted Julie to reconsider what she had seen. The image she received, the recovery that followed, and the unexplainable nature of it all stayed with her. She began to wonder if what she had witnessed was in fact a kind of angel—though not the delicate, winged being of storybooks, but a different, more grounded expression of strength, presence, and care. She has since come to believe that angels may indeed appear in different forms and that such encounters are not to be dismissed or reduced but integrated into our understanding of death.

Julie has heard many other patients describe seeing angels. Whether or not these experiences fit neatly into religious categories is beside the point. What matters is their universality, the sense of comfort and continuity they often bring, and their role in helping people transition out of life. For Julie, these experiences are not just interesting anecdotes—they are a vital part of the dying process, deserving of conversation, respect, and reflection.

In this way, Julie's work challenges the cultural awkwardness around death. By inviting people to listen, share, and consider the possibility that more may be happening than we can currently explain, Julie offers a space where death is no longer something to fear or ignore. Instead, it becomes something to be witnessed—sometimes even with awe. Julie is helping to reshape how we talk about death by bringing honesty, compassion, and public understanding to end-of-life experiences, showing that the stories we tell about dying are inseparable from how we value life, meaning, and human flourishing—an ethos that lies at the heart of our mystical futures.

Notes

1. Ditchfield (2020, 2021).
2. *The Divine Light* premiered in 2011 in Ely Cathedral, Cambridgeshire, performed by a full orchestra and choir. The performance received a standing ovation, with audience members describing it as deeply moving and spiritually resonant.
3. Numerous studies and anecdotal accounts highlight a surge in creative or intuitive abilities following near-death experiences. NDE researcher, PMH. Atwater (2007) has documented cases where individuals report newfound artistic talents—ranging from painting and music to writing and healing—emerging spontaneously after an NDE. Similarly, Ring and Elsaesser-Valarino (2000) describe how many experiencers feel compelled to express their encounters through creative or spiritual channels, often as if a latent capacity has been unlocked.
4. Cicoria (2023).
5. Ristic (2024).
6. Neal (2018); Stern (2021).
7. Beyond what I discuss in the main body, provide references to cases and links where people struggle after.
8. Stern (2021).
9. Sabom (1982).
10. Dossey (1993, 2013).
11. Pasulka (2014).
12. Ditchfield (2021).
13. McFadden (2024).
14. McFadden (2025).
15. Ibid.

Bibliography

Atwater, P. M. H. (2007). *The Big Book of Near-Death Experiences: The Ultimate Guide to What Happens When We Die*. Hampton Roads Publishing.

Cicoria, T. (2023). *Surgeon Struck by Lightning: Discovers the God Energy (NDE)*. YouTube. Retrieved April 28, 2025, from https://www.youtube.com/watch?v=fCV7ayCLA1A

Ditchfield, D. (2020). *Shine On: The Remarkable Story of How I Fell Under a Moving Train, Journeyed to the Afterlife, and the Astonishing Proof I Brought Back*. O Books.

Ditchfield, D. (2021). *The Near Death Experience of David Ditchfield*. YouTube. Retrieved April 28, 2025, from https://www.youtube.com/watch?v=pRRJ3u6O2QI

Dossey, L. (1993). *Healing Words: The Power of Prayer and the Practice of Medicine*. HarperSanFrancisco (HarperCollins).

Dossey, L. (2013). *One Mind: How Our Individual Mind Is Part of a Greater Consciousness and Why It Matters*. Hay House.

McFadden, J. (2024). *Nothing to Fear: Demystifying Death to Live More Fully*. Vermilion.

McFadden, J. (2025). *My Experiences with Angels as a Hospice Nurse*. Retrieved May 2, 2025, from https://www.youtube.com/watch?v=LXH4wYfK3ZM

Neal, M. (2018). Death Brings Context to Life. *TEDxJacksonHole*. Retrieved April 28, 2025, from https://www.youtube.com/watch?v=C-M9zR17egA

Pasulka, D. (2014). *Heaven Can Wait: Purgatory in Catholic Devotional and Popular Culture*. Oxford University Press.

Ring, K., & Elsaesser-Valarino, E. (2000). *Lessons from the Light: What We Can Learn from the Near-Death Experience*. Moment Point Press.

Ristic, S. (2024). *Dancer Dies in Car Accident: Finds Unconditional Love on the Other Side (NDE)*. YouTube. Retrieved April 28, 2025, from https://www.youtube.com/watch?v=waNHxKi4iQQ

Sabom, M. (1982). *Recollections of Death: A Medical Investigation*. Harper & Row.

Stern, R. (2021). *Surviving Death: Episode 1—Near-Death Experience*. [TV series]. Netflix.

CHAPTER 11

Conclusion: Mystical Futures

What is it with our cosmic gaze? Whether we look to the stars, dive into the psyche, or seek truth from the tunnel of light in an NDE, we carry a celestial urge for going beyond. We keep looking up—not just with our eyes, but with something deeper. From ancient stargazers and medieval mystics to modern telescopes and space agencies, we remain captivated by the cosmos.

Perhaps we sense, more than we consciously know, that the story of the universe is the story of us. What Richard Rohr calls the Universal Christ is not confined to religious language. It points towards a divine presence woven through all of creation—what he describes as "another word for everything." This is more than theology; it is a way of seeing cosmic architecture.

Carl Sagan's famous claim that we are made of star stuff reminds us that the atoms in our bodies were forged in the hearts of ancient stars. So, when we peer into space, we are not merely indulging a curiosity about something other or distant—we are reaching towards the deepest part of ourselves. In doing so, we participate in an ancient psychological impulse: the drive to locate the self within a vast and mysterious whole.

This is the essence of cosmic consciousness—not the necessity for belief in aliens or science fiction fantasies, but a felt recognition that the universe is alive with meaning, and that our minds are tuned to seek it. We project

D. Kelsey, *Transcendence and Collective Psychology*,
https://doi.org/10.1007/978-3-032-09495-7_11

our transcendental longing onto the stars not because we are naïve or deluded, but because we are wired for wonder.

Wondrous and Weird

In *The Science of Weird Shit*, Chris French takes an empirical approach to debunking the kinds of phenomena explored in these case studies.[1] But rather than dismissing the "weird," French insists that it provides valuable insights into the workings of the human mind.

His scepticism is far from dismissive. French argues that we must take these topics seriously precisely because the *experiences are real*—whatever their causes. His scientific and psychological explanations, which he openly accepts could be challenged or disproved, are offered with respect for those who report anomalous encounters, emphasizing that such experiences reveal important truths about human perception, belief, and the workings of the psyche.

While our approaches differ, we share a commitment to understanding what these stories mean to us as humans. Where French interrogates the mechanisms behind anomalous experiences, I have explored their metaphorical and mythological dimensions, focusing less on proving or disproving and more on what such narratives express about our collective psychology.

It is no coincidence, then, that we both relate these phenomena back to themes and topics around transcendence. French highlights how the realness of anomalous experiences is often deeply transformative and appreciates that fundamental human needs are served by these phenomena: to find meaning, to process death, and to feel part of something beyond the self. French's materialist take may not affirm metaphysical realities, but it does aim to illuminate elements of the psychological architecture behind of our beliefs, perceptions, and identities.

Such provocations invite a new synthesis—one in which mysticism and science, psychology and cosmology, tradition and transformation are not in conflict but in conversation. Reaching this point has required a particular kind of doubt: not cynicism, but strategic scepticism—an openness that allows us to truly grasp the awe-inspiring wonder of what it means to be human, now and in the future. The journey through this book has been, above all, a contemplative one.

Contemplative Scepticism

Let's reflect on a tool I've used throughout the case studies in this book: strategic scepticism.

This is not to present the following as definitive conclusions, but to reflect on what they continue to signify, regardless of their "realness". If UFOs are "just imagined" encounters with non-human anomalies, if psychedelic trips are "simply illusions" of universal connection and alternative intelligences, if NDEs are "merely neurological" stimulations during the dying process, none of these topics are any less fascinating or transcendental. They all reflect patterns of revelation in the psyche.

Strategic scepticism keeps inquiry open. It recognizes that even attempts to explain away anomalous or transcendental experiences can reveal profound psychological, cultural, or metaphysical implications.

What began as strategic scepticism in my analytical line of inquiry offers an experiential state of mind beyond this book: contemplative scepticism. This is not just a method but a mode of being, one that sits comfortably with paradox, mystery, and unknowing. It aligns with the mystical and psychological traditions explored throughout this book, where expansive insight often begins where certainty ends.

For egos and worldviews, the phenomena covered in those case studies can be apocalyptic: *that's precisely why they are revelatory.* Whether it's the dissolution of a personal ego or collective intellectual paradigms, those endings create new beginnings, new possibilities, and portals to new truths and ways of knowing.

These experiences shed light on our shadows by providing messages and epiphanies that uncover our worst traits and greatest potentials—personally and collectively. They make us see and help us know by drawing our deepest fears, faults, and desires to the forefront of our consciousness. When such stories and experiences are collected and connected, something more than "mere" anecdotal evidence arises. They provoke more than they prove.

These are profound datasets. There's no place for dismissal on the premise that they are "just" psychological states of imagination, projection, and cultural mythology. There's no "just" required here. They are transcendental. Transcendence matters because when we stop to consider what these experiences say about our collective psychology, there are lessons to learn and states of being to take note of.

As the case studies have shown, transcendental realms are anything but easy matters, and paradigm shifts are daunting for our personal and collective egos.

Pursuing Wholeness

As Carl Jung observed, when the dominant values of consciousness begin to disintegrate, the archetype of the Self—representing wholeness and psychic totality—emerges from the unconscious in an attempt to restore balance.[2] This is especially relevant in our own era, shaped by a crisis of meaning, epidemic loneliness, mounting existential risks, and the fragmentation of collective identity.[3] The return of the "God hypothesis," the rise of spiritual but not religious (SBNR) movements, the renewed fascination with UFOs, psychedelics, NDEs, and even the cultural popularity of ghost stories—these are not isolated trends. They are symptoms of a deeper psychological and spiritual yearning.

In *The Surprising Rebirth of Belief in God*, Justin Brierley argues that despite the apparent decline of traditional religious affiliation, we are witnessing a resurgence of spiritual curiosity and a renewed openness to the divine.[4] As discussed earlier, his reference to the growing number of people who identify as SBNR suggests this trend reflects not a rejection of transcendence, but a shift in how individuals seek and express it.

For Brierley, this phenomenon signals a deep collective yearning for meaning, connection, and purpose in an increasingly disenchanted world. He observes that while institutional religion may no longer serve as the primary framework for belief, many continue to explore spiritual questions through alternative means—ranging from meditation and mystical practices to engagement with scientific wonder, philosophy, and the "paranormal."

Questions in Science

This is more than a social or cultural phenomenon. Scientists such as Stephen Meyer argue that mainstream science itself is increasingly revisiting questions once dismissed as metaphysical.

In *The Return of the God Hypothesis*, Meyer contends that developments in cosmology, physics, and biology are re-opening space for serious discussion of a transcendent cause behind the origins of the universe, life, and consciousness.[5] This intellectual shift suggests that belief in God is not simply persisting—it is being re-evaluated at existential, epistemological, and ontological levels.

Across these phenomena, we find a common thread: a collective search for coherence, transcendence, and relational wholeness in a world increasingly defined by fragmentation and tribalism. When believers and nonbelievers alike engage with these topics from a place of genuine curiosity, it underscores their power as shared symbols—ones that transcend binary categories of fact and fiction, science and spirituality.

In this light, these modern myths and anomalous experiences are not distractions from reality, but reflections of our deeper human longing: to reconnect, to integrate, and to find meaning in the midst of uncertainty. Like the circular shapes Jung associated with the archetype of wholeness, these cultural fascinations point to something more than themselves—they reveal a desire to make whole what has been divided, both within and beyond us.

Fear and Relief

If our explorations of human experience and interrogations of reality are to propel us into new realms—encouraging the paradigm shifts that thinkers like Richard Rohr and Thomas Kuhn have called for—then we cannot hold back. Perhaps Jake Barber, as quoted in Chap. 5, has a point: nonhuman intelligence and other radical revelations about consciousness and our place in the cosmos need not induce fear, but rather, ontological *relief*.

I am speculating on Barber's claims, of course. But it shows that we humans behave as if there is more to know—because there is. While we cannot predict what discoveries await us in the cosmos, our persistent search reflects something deeper: a collective intuition that learning never ends. The urge to know hums constantly in the collective psyche, reminding us that mystery is not a void to be feared, but a horizon to be explored.

Jeff Kripal argues that we in the humanities know this better than anyone. Kripal's account of the "superhumanities" is not a new proposition—it is a rediscovery and reconnection with the myths and mystical dimensions of reality that have historically formed an "occult side" to the "human sciences."[6] These disciplines once grappled comfortably with the so-called paranormal possibilities of existence before prohibiting the scope of their own investigative potentials. In recent history, those mystical dimensions of the humanities may have been momentarily subdued for a variety of reasons. But they've never disappeared.

Decolonizing Reality

Kripal argues that we cannot merely decolonize history, religion, literature, and society within the limited frameworks academia often prescribes. We must decolonize reality itself. As Kripal explains, his research endeavours have not just pursued the wonders of God, religion, and the soul—he's gone all in on the realms of space, time, and matter.[7]

Cognitive psychologist Donald Hoffman underscores the urgency of this ontological leap, arguing that our inherited paradigms—particularly materialist ones—are not just inadequate but misaligned with the nature of reality.[8] Mystical futures offer a vital space for the superhumanities to provoke and cultivate the questions and conversations necessary for humanity's evolution—physically, psychologically, and cosmically. As we familiarize ourselves with new realities, we will inevitably begin the process anew, once again questioning what lies beyond, expanding our understanding of what it means to be (super)human.

Kripal warns that current academic paradigms can only take us so far. He critiques the way certain scholars invoke decolonization in ways that often amount to reasserting familiar frameworks—such as Marxism, postcolonial materialism, or standard metaphysical critiques—without engaging the deeper ontological or mystical dimensions of human experience.

For Kripal, this represents not only an ethical shortcoming but also an intellectual impasse: a form of paradigm paralysis that limits new ways of knowing. Mysticism, by contrast, is grounded in lived, anomalous, or revelatory experiences. It refuses to retreat into theory alone and instead embraces direct empirical engagement with reality—often producing what he calls "ontological shocks," or, perhaps, "ontological relief."

Curious Entry Points

The phenomena covered in these case studies do not stand apart as isolated curiosities. What may seem disparate at first glance reveals a discrete coherence when viewed through a mystical lens.

One story illustrates this synthesis vividly: a young boy who, after an NDE, began to encounter cosmic beings throughout his life. His experiential journey echoes the core themes of this book—altered states of consciousness, spiritual awakening, mystery, divine light, and cosmic transformation. It is through stories like Dan Bowskill's that the full scope of transcendence becomes clear—not as a departure from reality, but as a deepening into its most intimate, mysterious, and expansive experiences.[9]

As a young boy, during his NDE, Dan recalls floating above his hospital room while doctors and nurses fought to save his life. In that moment, he entered a state of bliss, free from fear, content to remain in this luminous realm until an inner voice asked if he would return to his body. Hesitating, it was the sight of his mother's anguish that compelled him to re-enter the physical world.

This act of choosing love over bliss reflects a recurring pattern of transcendental experience. While we are drawn towards states of ultimate freedom, it is love that anchors us and connects us to others.

Yet this return to earthly life was not without struggle. As a child, Bowskill carried a deep sense of his eternal nature, sobbing at night because he longed to "go home" to the light. One night, he saw a being of light in his room, staring and smiling at him. He understood it as his future self, his light form, offering reassurance that everything would be fine.

Narrative Convergence

These experiences form part of that collage in which phenomena defy easy categorization, hinting at dimensions of existence that remain arcane and yet deeply resonant in the stories that will tell about them. Whether interpreted through theological, mystical, or extraterrestrial lenses, such encounters reveal shared archetypes: love as a universal force, light as a metaphor for eternal being, and the interwoven nature of self and reality—core concepts throughout each case study covered in this book.

Bowskill's account reveals how these phenomena challenge our frameworks for understanding transcendence. His story is a compelling reminder that the boundaries between the spiritual, psychological, and physical worlds *might* be more fluid than we imagine, pointing towards deeper realities we are only beginning to comprehend.

As with so many cases considered throughout this book, Bowskill's experience was as painful as it was divine. His transcendental knowing of a deeper truth beyond his lived and physical reality was frustrating, upsetting, and isolating.

Common Tensions

As I warned early on, transcendence isn't all sunshine and roses. There are forms of "unselfing" that can lead us astray into harmful or self-destructive behaviours, and even the most divine experiences can be profoundly challenging for those who go through them.

Take the journey of finding God after years of atheism—it's not without its hurdles. I am fully aware of the smirks, frowns, or even flippant comments from people you thought would be more supportive. Academia, for example, isn't exactly a place where professing a love of God feels welcome, given the lingering intellectual grip of seemingly dominant atheism.

Even within the church, the contemplative theology of a modern-day Franciscan mystic—one who sees truth through metaphor and understands the Trinity as a framework that unites religion and science—is often dismissed or even deemed heretical. Articulating such deeply held beliefs is no easy feat, whether you're speaking to friends, family, or a broader audience.

As we have seen, UFO experiencers, for instance, face similar challenges. They often risk ridicule, scepticism, or even patronizing doubts about their sanity. These reactions can fracture relationships or leave people isolated, struggling to reconcile their lives with the profound and arcane realities they've encountered, which many people may never experience.

Psychedelics have offered another striking example in this respect. The transcendental experiences they stimulate have historically been viewed as countercultural or even threatening to the establishment. Some psychedelic experiences can be profoundly traumatic, while certain spaces and practices surrounding them are vulnerable to exploitation by so-called "guides" acting with malicious intent.[10]

NDEs are often anything but blissful in their aftermath. Many experiencers return to this reality feeling deeply misunderstood and disconnected. They've touched a realm of pure divine love and light, only to find themselves longing to return to that timeless embrace. Those who have negative NDEs feel they should keep quiet due to moral judgement. Even though positive NDEs may fill experiencers with love and transform their inner lives, they often struggle to navigate relationships and daily life. Feelings of disillusionment, frustration, isolation, and loneliness are common.

Transcendence is, in a word, messy. From start to finish, it's a journey filled with tension, transformation, and the inescapable complexities of human experience.

But that's why I wrote this book: because we need to learn how we navigate transcendental realms and understand their cruciality to the human experience. How we manage our transcendental needs and cravings determines the health of our collective psychology—in our personal experiences, interpersonal relations, and communal agency.

The Cosmic Paradox

However, in looking to the stars (and beyond), we risk overlooking the mysteries unfolding right here, in the immediacy of our own existence. The mystics remind us that the divine is not only out there but also in the here and now, hidden in plain sight.

Arcane phenomena are not distant fantasies. They exist in the present, woven into the very fabric of our world. They offer transcendental potentials that are core to our collective and existential curiosities.

After all, humans have often mapped the cosmos and the surfaces of distant worlds more confidently than the hidden depths of our own planet. We are less reluctant to launch rockets into space than we are to launch psychedelic rockets through our collective states of consciousness. What lies beneath and beyond our typical states of consciousness is as much a mystery as the universe itself.

Scary New Knowledge

It's easy to forget just how deeply unsettling it was for people to accept that the Earth is not the centre of the universe, and that the sun does not revolve around us. What now feels like basic astronomy was once branded as heresy. Galileo was condemned by the Church, forced to recant under threat of torture. Giordano Bruno, who dared to suggest that stars were distant suns with their own planets—and that the universe might be infinite—was burned at the stake. These weren't isolated cases.

The suggestion that invisible forces like gravity could govern celestial motion seemed ludicrous before Newton. The idea that germs, too small to see, could cause disease was mocked before germ theory. The notion that continents drift across the Earth's surface was dismissed as fantasy before plate tectonics became scientific consensus.

In every case, those who introduced these "outrageous" ideas were ridiculed, punished, or ignored—not because they were wrong, but because their insights disrupted dominant worldviews and threatened entrenched power. Yet, over time, these heresies have become the bedrock of how we now understand reality. They didn't destroy our world, they expanded it.

Plato's allegory of the cave invites us to imagine a journey from the shadows of ignorance to the clarity of truth.[11] But what if we are constantly trapped in different kinds of caves, and currently one constructed via the rigid structures of materialism that are paradoxically illuminating and obscuring our sense of reality?

From Cave to Cave

This modern ontology, built on the assumption that matter is fundamental to reality, shapes how we think, perceive, and even dream. It narrows our gaze, tethering our understanding to what can be measured, observed, and quantified. Yet, as with the prisoners in Plato's cave, there are hints—shadows, if you will—that there may be something beyond the confines of this worldview.

History shows that the greatest discoveries often emerge from questions that defy prevailing paradigms. Perhaps by stepping out of the cave of current materialism, we can catch a glimpse of the true light, one that illuminates not only the nature of reality but our place within it.

The journey out of the cave is often framed as the triumph of enlightenment over ignorance—the awakening to a wider, more complex reality. Yet Plato's allegory also reveals a more difficult truth: the cost of awakening is often social rejection and psychological disorientation. When the freed prisoner returns to the cave to share news of another world, he is not welcomed as a visionary but mocked, ridiculed, even threatened by those still chained to the shadows. His new insights are not understood, they are feared.

This dynamic mirrors the fate of many who experience transcendent awakenings. Belief in God, in higher intelligences, or in the mere possibility of an afterlife is often met with suspicion or derision — dismissed as irrational, delusional, or naïve. Those who glimpse new dimensions of reality frequently face not only disbelief but also alienation from the communities they once belonged to. The price of insight is, all too often, exile.

Moreover, the world outside the cave is not simply more truthful—it is vast, unpredictable, and often overwhelming. Awakening is not a final arrival but the beginning of a deeper unravelling. Just as one begins to comprehend a previously unthinkable reality, further impossibilities arise that challenge even this new understanding. What initially appears as revelation can quickly become destabilization, as the mind struggles to integrate experiences that fracture established categories of truth. The light outside the cave does not simply banish the darkness; it casts new and more complicated shadows.

Ontological Shelter

In such moments, the temptation to retreat or find a new cave that becomes equally safe and familiar becomes almost irresistible. The familiar shadows on the wall, though illusory, offer a sense of comfort and certainty that the outside world lacks. This retreat is not necessarily a failure—it is a survival instinct, an attempt to reclaim the simplicity and clarity we once knew. Yet, it reveals a paradox: knowing more is not always the path to peace. The pursuit of knowledge and truth, while noble, can come at the expense of the blissful ignorance that shields us from existential fear and confusion.

As the likes of Jacques Vallee and Garry Nolan have pointed out, the temptation is to be drawn towards conclusions. We want clarity. But with phenomena such as UFOs and the potential for non-human intelligence—perhaps even co-inhabitants alongside us on Earth—all we can do is look at the data. We can speculate but we cannot yet conclude. And it might be the case that multiple conclusions are required to understand phenomena that aren't as monolithic as our conclusionary temptations urge us to believe.

Collective growth requires us to resist the pull of retreat, to remain outside the caves even when the world seems too vast and incomprehensible. It is in this space—between the desire for certainty and the confrontation with mystery—that transcendence becomes possible. Learning to dwell in this tension, as the mystics encourage, allows us to integrate the overwhelming complexity of the unknown without losing ourselves to it.

The question, then, is not whether we should leave the cave but how we navigate the disorientation that follows. Can we find meaning in the chaos without retreating into the comfort of illusion? Or is there a middle path, where we accept that some mysteries are beyond comprehension and embrace the humility that comes with it? This tension between enlightenment and retreat, knowledge and blissful ignorance, mirrors the broader human struggle with the unknown and our capacity to transcend it.

Perhaps, in this capacity, we offer more unique points for admiration in the cosmos than we typically appreciate. Let's contemplate for a moment the possibility that other lifeforms are trying to observe and understand us, as they struggle to comprehend those embodied aspects of human behaviours.

Those Ecstatic Humans

Imagine an extraterrestrial civilization that has mastered the art of technological advancement in ways that leave humanity awestruck—crafting machines capable of traversing dimensions, manipulating physics, and defying our understanding of reality. Yet, for all their technological progress, this civilization finds itself transfixed by us humans, not for our science or engineering, but for something far more elusive: our capacity for speech, song, music, sport, entertainment, and ecstatic experience—the craving for transcendence that gives us such rich and varied cultures, rituals, and belief systems.

What if these beings—visitors we call aliens, UFOs or NHI—only ever catch fleeting glimpses of these dimensions of human life? What if they speculate, as anthropologists of a kind, on the mysteries of emotion, creativity, and transcendence? Perhaps, to them, *humanity* embodies something arcane, an ancient and incomprehensible wisdom that eludes *their* grasp. We are fascinating not because we are technologically as advanced as them, but because we dwell in a realm of embodied or spiritual experience that is challenging for them to comprehend.

Just as we struggle to comprehend their mastery over matter and dimension, they might fail to fully access the depths of our sensory cultures and the shape of our collective consciousness. What we take for granted—shared states of ecstasy, communal rituals, and the boundless landscapes of art and spirituality—might appear to them as echoes from inaccessible realms or forgotten pasts.

For all their intelligence, they may seldom tap into the consciousness where such dimensions are possible. If it's true that psychedelics, for example, are a technology that unlocks access to another realm of non-localized (or even non-human) intelligence, then perhaps we are like the

UFOs, flying in for a fleeting DMT observation, before vanishing in the blink of a psychedelic jester's eye.

Of course, these are only provocations to ponder, but they help us to think about our transcendental ways and the meanings we create in this world. They also invite us to consider the possibility of a universe teeming with life and a multidimensional reality where consciousness and the cosmos are more entwined than we can currently comprehend.

In this light, both humanity and NHIs could represent complementary forms of ecstatic experience and consciousness, each limited and enriched by their respective pathways of evolution. To them, we offer a living archive of mysteries—our music and stories, our dances and prayers, our ability to transcend the self in moments of awe. To us, they hint at modes of being and knowing that stretch beyond the boundaries of our material and dimensional existence.

Perhaps this mutual incomprehension is the true arcane. Mystery lies not in their prospective machinery or our spiritual practices, but in the tantalizing possibility that intelligence, in all its forms, is far more diverse, interconnected, and boundless than we can imagine. Returning to those transcendental cravings in Chap. 2, when integrated in a healthy manner, they bring out the best of us as humans.

My Favourite Atheists

It might seem contradictory for a Church-going Catholic to have favourite atheists, but I do. In fact, like Rohr, I sometimes find my worldview more aligned with atheists than Christians. This is partly because some of the most thoughtful atheists call out the absurdities, hypocrisies, and excesses of religion—an important and necessary function that even religious people should appreciate. But more than that, I recognize in them a deep reverence for life, an appreciation of wonder, and a search for transcendence that, despite their rejection of God, reveals a profound engagement with meaning.

Take Ricky Gervais, for example. Known for his sharp critiques of organized religion, he is often mistaken for being hostile to all belief. Yet his work frequently reveals a deep humanism and a recognition of shared experience. In *The Invention of Lying*, his character comforts his dying mother with the idea of an afterlife and promises her that she's going to a wonderful place—not to mock belief, but to affirm the power of love, hope, and human connection. He wasn't attacking faith in that moment;

he was showing that, believer or not, we all navigate life's deepest questions with the same longing for comfort, meaning, and peace.

Gervais' love of animals and the natural world is another point of connection. He speaks passionately about kindness to animals, the sanctity of wildlife, and the beauty of nature. In this, he is not so different from St Francis of Assisi, who saw divinity reflected in every creature and called them his brothers and sisters. Whether one attributes that wonder to God or to the wonders of a Godless nature, the reverence does not diminish.

Even when Stephen Fry went on his famous rant against God in a conversation on the meaning of life with Gay Byrne, he was rejecting the conception of God that I have repeatedly distanced myself from in this book.[12] Fry passionately rejected the idea of a benevolent God, arguing that such a being, if real, would have much to answer for. He pointed to immense suffering, particularly diseases like bone cancer in children and parasitic infections that cause blindness, as evidence of a cruel and unjust universe.

That Stupid God

Fry described God as "capricious, mean-minded, and stupid," questioning why anyone should worship a deity that allows such horrors.[13] For Fry, the existence of suffering undermines the notion of divine justice, making a secular world—where humans take responsibility for alleviating suffering—far preferable. At its core, his argument rested on the classic problem of evil: how can an all-powerful, all-good God permit such suffering?

It would be easy for me to dismiss Fry by accusing him of literalizing the metaphor, and on one level that would be justified. But in fairness to Fry, he is rejecting the "almighty God" that the likes of Rohr and the mystics have traditionally sought to avoid—with the alternative conception I offered earlier pointing towards an "all vulnerable God." If religious authorities want to frame God as the omni presence of power and judgement who determines every outcome in a painfully cruel world while judging us like a tyrannical Santa Clause, then they perhaps they're asking for what the likes of Fry are ready to throw at them.

Like Dawkins, Fry recognizes the importance of stories and mythologies in what they tell us about what it means to be human. I do not doubt that the Trinitarian flow of God as a verb would be rejected and intellectually dismantled from Fry's personal perspective. But that's fine. I can sit comfortably with his justified ferocity and rejection of the same God that

I reject while also accepting that he would be no more interested in the God that I have come to know and love.

Such examples point to something important: belief and non-belief are not always the dividing lines we assume.

Existential Grappling

Regardless of our beliefs, we share the capacity to be deeply moral, profoundly moved by beauty, and engaged in existential questions of what it means to be human. In terms of those arcane topics covered throughout this book, transcendence may not always come from faith, but it arises nonetheless—in appreciations of art, science, nature, cosmos, and human connection. Such common ground is worth recognizing within the many truths of life, being, and meaning.

The diversity of phenomena covered in this book makes many authorities nervous across their respective fields. They disrupt the comfortable, structured reality we tend to rely on. But from a contemplative perspective, we can recognize that transcendence isn't necessarily about finding a single answer—it's about embracing the multiplicity of possibilities.

Confronting the mysteries of existence can be a daunting task. As the case studies in this book have shown, they offer deep insights and profound moments of spiritual revelation, cautionary tales about humanity, and bewildering experiences of fear and disorientation.

Given the plethora of personal insights and experiences I have covered, we are not pursuing a single, definitive answer in our quest to understand reality.

Messiness is fine. It's part of the adventure. But we should think about how we explore such mess and mystery. Through this lens, we can continue to expand our understanding of transcendence and the deeper layers of existence that connect us all and potentially determine our future as a species.

Breaking from Our Cocoon

Lawyer and political activist, Danny Sheehan suggests that advanced nonhuman intelligences, whatever they may be, are watching us—not just observing, but trying to understand whether we have the potential to flourish or if we'll collapse like so many failed species before us.[14]

Sheehan tells the story of a boy who collected butterflies. One day, he found a cocoon that held a monarch butterfly just beginning to emerge. The butterfly was nearly free, struggling against the last silken thread that held it. The boy, eager to help, carefully cut the final strand to set the butterfly free.

For a moment, the butterfly was perfect—its colours symmetrical with smooth and unbroken wings. But when it tried to fly, it couldn't. The struggle of breaking free from that final thread was necessary for those muscles in its wings to develop the strength to hold it aloft. Without that struggle, it was doomed.

We are that butterfly. Our world is the cocoon. The crises we face—climate change, tribal division, spiritual uncertainty—aren't just obstacles. They are the tests that will determine whether we rise into something greater or collapse under the weight of our own failures.

This struggle to save ourselves, our planet, and our species is something we must go through if we are to qualify for participation in life with those successful civilizations in the universe. If our struggles are futile and we falter or self-destruct, we won't be welcome at the table.

However, if we meet the challenge, we may earn our place in the unfolding story of life in the universe, shaping a future of connection and meaning. If we fail, our planet will go on without us, restoring itself in our absence.

Can we endure the struggle? Will it shape us into something stronger, or will we fall—never having truly taken flight?

Our future depends on the worlds we dare to imagine and the courage we find to build them. As Richard Rohr suggests, true courage lies in embracing the profound mystery of our own existence with humility.[15] Here, we can pursue new possibilities—within and beyond the scope of our current imaginations.

Notes

1. French (2024).
2. Jung (1959).
3. Kelsey (2022); Hari (2018).
4. Brierley (2023).
5. Meyer (2021).
6. Kripal (2022).
7. Kripal (2022).

8. Hoffman (1998, 2019, 2023).
9. Bowskill (2023).
10. At the time of writing, the Trump administration is actively advancing the federal legalisation of psychedelic therapies, prompting concern among some scientists and clinicians that the pace may be too rapid—or worse, driven by commercial or political interests rather than public health priorities (see Evans, 2025, 2025a, 2025b, 2025c).
11. Plato (2007).
12. Fry (2015).
13. Ibid.
14. Mazzola (2023).
15. Rohr (2019).

Bibliography

Bowskill, D. (2023). I Was Never Born and I Cannot Die. *Alien Kidnap Club*, 15 February. Retrieved May 15, 2025, from https://open.spotify.com/episode/6m3gwtnUqMsKOIT8j3yMNE

Brierley, J. (2023). *The Surprising Rebirth of Belief in God*. Tyndale Momentum.

Evans, J. (2025). Psychedelic Policy: Speed Up or Slow Down? *Ecstatic Integration*. Retrieved June 30, 2025, from https://www.ecstaticintegration.org/p/psychedelic-policy-speed-up-or-slow

Evans, J. (2025a). Fake UFOs in Congress, and Nine Other Stories I'm Following. *Ecstatic Integration*, 6 May. Retrieved June 16, 2025, from https://www.ecstaticintegration.org/p/fake-ufos-in-congress-and-nine-other

Evans, J. (2025b). Skinwalker Ranch and the Rise of UFO Political Religion. *Ecstatic Integration*, 17 April. Retrieved June 16, 2025, from https://www.ecstaticintegration.org/p/skinwalker-ranch-and-the-rise-of

Evans, J. (2025c). Nine Things You Should Know Before Entering the Psychedelic Industry. *Ecstatic Integration*, 22 April. Retrieved June 16, 2025, from https://www.ecstaticintegration.org/p/nine-things-you-should-know-before

French, C. (2024). *The Science of Weird Shit: Why Our Minds Conjure the Paranormal*. MIT Press.

Fry, S. (2015). *Stephen Fry on God | The Meaning Of Life | RTÉ One*. Retrieved May 7, 2025, from https://www.youtube.com/watch?v=-suvkwNYSQo

Hari, J. (2018). *Lost Connections: Uncovering the Real Causes of Depression—And the Unexpected Solutions*. Bloomsbury.

Hoffman, D. D. (1998). *Visual Intelligence: How We Create What We See*. W.W. Norton & Company.

Hoffman, D. D. (2019). *The Case Against Reality: How Evolution Hid the Truth from Our Eyes*. W.W. Norton & Company.

Hoffman, D. (2023). *Donald Hoffman: Reality is an Illusion—How Evolution Hid the Truth | Lex Fridman Podcast #293*. Retrieved May 15, 2025, from https://www.youtube.com/watch?v=reYdQYZ9Rj4&t=6417s

Jung, C. G. (1959). *Psychological Aspects of the Persona* (Vol. 6 of the Collected Works of C.G. Jung). Princeton University Press.

Kelsey, D. (2022). *Murmurations Podcast: Derren Brown: Illusion, Psychology, and the Art of Influence* [Podcast]. Retrieved September 10, 2024, from https://murmurationspodcast.com/derren-brown

Kripal, J. (2022). *Superhumanities: Historical Precedents, Moral Objections, and New Realities*. University of Chicago Press.

Mazzola, M. (2023). *We Are Not Alone* [Documentary Film]. Elysium Media/Uncork'd Entertainment. Retrieved July 1, 2025, from [streaming platforms, e.g., Prime Video].

Meyer, S. (2021). *The Return of the God Hypothesis: Three Scientific Discoveries That Reveal the Mind Behind the Universe*. HarperOne.

Plato. (2007). *Republic* (D. Lee, Trans., 2nd ed.). Penguin Classics.

Rohr, R. (2019). *The Universal Christ: How a Forgotten Reality Can Change Everything We See, Hope For, and Believe*. SPCK Publishing.

Postface: Mystical Journeys

For both narrative research and popular entertainment, one of my favourite YouTube channels is *Caspersight*. Its host, Ben Hendy, shares stories and footage of UFOs, hauntings, and supposed glimpses of the afterlife from a combination of humorous reaction and serious curiosity. What makes the channel distinctive is Ben himself: funny, communal, and engaging, yet also a rich source of recurring cultural narratives around the "paranormal."

While writing this book, I stumbled upon a video from Ben that struck me with a profound synchronicity.[1] Ben described an epiphany that echoed my own journey: a longing for more than resilience and self-growth, and a hunger for deeper connection with nature, spirituality, and transcendence. Watching him wrestle with this yearning felt like an affirmation of the very path I've been on.

Ben's reflections capture a wider cultural trend. Increasingly, people describe themselves as "spiritual but not religious," signalling a dissatisfaction with secularism's inability to meet our transcendental needs. As Justin Brierley notes, even as organised religion declines, the search for meaning endures. Ben is careful not to fall into New Age clichés or consumerist "spirituality," but his struggle reflects the same post-secular shift I explore in my research: the persistence of mystical longing in modern life.

D. Kelsey, *Transcendence and Collective Psychology*,
https://doi.org/10.1007/978-3-032-09495-7

Ben stresses the futility of worrying about others' opinions or things beyond our control—ideas Marcus Aurelius or Seneca would echo. As I argued in *Storytelling and Collective Psychology*, Stoicism and Cognitive Behavioural Therapy can foster resilience. But as I soon found, resilience alone is not enough. Ben describes his own journey through which he has moved beyond the anxieties of his younger years to stop worrying about what he cannot control. But like so many of us, Ben yearns for more—for awe, connection, and belonging within a greater whole.

Ben's growing interest in grounding, meditation, cold water therapy, and holistic health further reflects this shift. He describes an awareness to listen to his inner-self and the spirituality at his core—one that longs for connection with nature in a consciously physical and embodied sense. Such practices, often rooted in mystical traditions, suggest that spirituality today often unfolds outside institutional religion—through reconnecting with nature, the body, and the mystery of consciousness itself.

Here, "paranormal" culture becomes a fitting gateway. Stories of ghosts or UFOs are no longer just eerie entertainment; they are modern myths that open existential questions. If there is life after death, or intelligent life beyond us, then perhaps reality is more mysterious than we imagine. Carl Jung saw UFOs as archetypal symbols of humanity's yearning for wholeness. Whatever they might be, Ben's reflections show this same mystical impulse, not tied to dogma but alive in popular culture.

Ben's journey is personal, but it is also emblematic of a collective turn. Increasing numbers are not satisfied with reductive dismissal or merely coping our way through life. We are seeking experiences, meaningful stories, and practices that open mystical horizons, offering transcendence in a world where the old answers no longer suffice.

It's this premise that strikes me as I finish this book and turn towards the final instalment of a trilogy on collective psychology.

Across popular culture, there is a growing movement to take seriously the experiences and stories we share about humanity's most arcane anomalies and our place in the cosmos. Technology, for instance, is not only carrying us outward into space but also driving us deeper inward. It is stretching the boundaries of what we consider possible, hinting at truths beyond current understanding. In the process, even the very meaning of technology itself is being reimagined.

And here the mystical journey becomes technological. Even those who are sceptical of UFOs often suspect that new technologies are held back by economic interests that profit from delay. Others see plants, psychedelics, or breathwork as *neurotechnologies* for navigating the internal cosmos. Either way, what is unfolding is not only about machines, rockets, or other beings "out there." It is also about our *omega-minus* journey: the inward descent into our bodies, brains, and psyche, where our greatest technology may be discovered via consciousness itself.[2]

Philosophers have long argued that the figure of the inner engineer (archetype) is not incidental but a fundamental condition and expression of humanity.[3] This has struck me throughout several stages of this project on collective psychology. In *Storytelling and Collective Psychology*, I argued that we are narrative-building machines. In *Transcendence and Collective Psychology* I suggested we are collective weaving machines in the participatory make of a divine cosmos.

Now, I move towards what I call the *unified split*. It is a paradox. But as contemplatives, we are ready for paradox.

The unified split is where we look to the stars, launching ourselves, our technologies, and perhaps even our consciousness into the cosmos as an eternal trace of our being. But at the same time, we dive within, recognizing that our psychology itself may be the most profound technology and portal to reality that we possess. The next frontier is both outward and inward—from space missions to telepathic experiments, from AI to neuro-mystical practices, from material exploration to radical re-imaginings of what the "material" even is.

Such a premise was already stirring in me as I finished this book, especially while engaging with voices like Andrew Gallimore, Lisa Miller, and Tara Swart. Gallimore entertains radical neurotechnologies for exploring altered states. Miller highlights synchronicities as markers of spiritual attunement and collective prayer as a healing practice in modern psychiatry. Swart, a neuroscientist, now speaks openly of communicating with deceased loved ones and of seeing hidden patterns that shape our lives through signs and symbols that require engagement. Each, in their own way, is participating in what Jeffrey Kripal calls *authoring the impossible.*

Psychology itself continues to reveal distinct technological forms in its manipulations *and* instigations of new possibilities. And this is where the mystical journey continues. Expansive thinking and radical change are happening not only in popular culture but increasingly in science and academia. Telepathy, for instance, remains categorically unproven—yet it refuses to go away, and is gaining attention in research, popular culture, and arcane realms. Its persistence, whether as a hypothesis or a story, tells us something profound about who we are, how we think, and what we long for.[4]

This is why technology will be the focal point of my final instalment in this trilogy. Not technology in isolation, but technology as psychology and psychology as technology: the collective machinery of our biology, our longing, our connections, our creativity, our stories, and our transcendence. The unified split is underway: we are launching outward, and we are diving inward, and both are part of the same mystical journey.

Our next journey in collective psychology, via technomystical realms, has already begun. Watch this space.

Notes

1. Hendy (2024).
2. My reference to John Barrow's "omega-minus" model taken here draws from a conversation between Jesse Michels and Andrew Gallimore (2025). They held a wide-ranging conversation on topics such as quantum biology, consciousness, and the role of psychedelics in accessing hidden dimensions of reality. Michels begins by noting how quantum processes are increasingly recognized in biology: birds use quantum effects to navigate the Earth's magnetic field, enzymes exploit them in catalysis, and photosynthesis relies on quantum coherence. These examples suggest that quantum phenomena may underpin life at a fundamental level. From here, the conversation turns to physics. Gallimore recalls that many of the founders of quantum mechanics speculated that consciousness might play a role in the collapse of the wave function. Such speculation, once central to physics, has since been pushed to the margins, yet it remains a provocative way of thinking about the relationship between mind and matter. Both acknowledge how mainstream science resists these possibilities, often reducing them to hallucination, dream imagery, or archetypal symbolism. Gallimore argues that such explanations fail to account for the striking consistency of reports from DMT users. He proposes that these experiences may involve encounters with post-biological intelligences: civilizations that, rather than colonizing space in the Muskian sense, evolve inward, probing deeper structures of reality. Citing John Barrow's "omega-minus" model, Gallimore suggests that advanced civilizations may ultimately instantiate themselves at the fundamental computational substrate of spacetime itself, becoming "everywhere and nowhere." The implication, he continues, is that communication with such beings would not require physical manifestation but could occur directly through the brain—precisely what psychedelic states may make pos-

sible. Michels and Gallimore agree that if science can move beyond rigid materialism, it may begin to take seriously what DMT and similar experiences already hint at: that reality is not exhausted by its surface appearances. The future of exploration is not only about launching outward into the cosmos, but also about diving inward into the structures of mind, matter, and consciousness itself.

3. In 1958, philosopher Gilbert Simondon (2017) proposed that technical objects evolve and possess their own form of "concreteness." He argued that humans and technology are co-constitutive: the psyche and society are structured through their ongoing relations with technics. Bernard Stiegler (1998–2001) later took up and expanded Simondon's insights. In his multivolume work *Technics and Time*, Stiegler elaborated a philosophy of memory and individuation in which technology is not external to humanity but constitutive of human temporality itself.
4. While writing this book, *The Telepathy Tapes* held a significant stint at the top of the podcast charts, reflecting the renewed cultural appetite for such themes. Rupert Sheldrake has long argued for the serious consideration of telepathy through falsifiable studies, insisting that the topic belongs within scientific inquiry rather than outside it. Alongside my own attention to psionics and telepathy within ufology, these psychological capacities are gaining increasing attention across topics, genres, and disciplines in popular culture and academic research respectively.

Bibliography

Alcoholics Anonymous World Services (Ed.). (2001). *Alcoholics Anonymous: The Big Book* (4th ed.). Alcoholics Anonymous World Services.

Aurelius, M. (2006). *Meditations* (M. Hammond, Trans.). Penguin Books.

Brown, D. (2016). *Happy: Why More or Less Everything is Absolutely Fine.* Bantam Press.

Campbell, J. (1949). *The Hero with a Thousand Faces.* Princeton University Press.

Cox, B., & Cohen, A. (2021). *Universe: Exploring the Astronomical World.* William Collins.

Donlin-Smith, T., & Shafiq, M. (Eds.). (2023). *Mystical Traditions: Approaches to Peaceful Coexistence.* Palgrave Macmillan.

Eckhart, M. (1994). *Selected Writings* (O. Davies, Trans. and intro.). Penguin Classics.

Eckhart, M. (2009). *The Complete Mystical Works of Meister Eckhart* (M.O'C. Walshe, Ed. and Trans.). Crossroad Publishing Company.

Greene, B. (2003). *The Elegant Universe: Superstrings, Hidden Dimensions, and the Quest for the Ultimate Theory.* W.W. Norton & Company.

Hendy, B. (2024). We Must Be Connected to Earth... Right! [YouTube video]. *Caspersight.* Retrieved July 1, 2025, from https://www.youtube.com/watch?v=sLRtwTyyX1o

John of the Cross. (2010). *Dark Night of the Soul* (E. A. Peers, Trans.). Dover Publications.

D. Kelsey, *Transcendence and Collective Psychology*, https://doi.org/10.1007/978-3-032-09495-7

Kastrup, B. (2014). *Why Materialism Is Baloney: How True Skeptics Know There is No Death and Fathom Answers to Life, the Universe, and Everything* (Illustrated ed.). Iff Books.

Kastrup, B. (2021). *Decoding Jung's Metaphysics: The Structure and Content of the World as Will and Representation.* Iff Books.

Luke, D. (2011). *Otherworlds: Psychedelics and Exceptional Human Experience.* University of Exeter Press.

Maslow, A. H. (1968). *Toward a Psychology of Being* (2nd ed.). Van Nostrand Reinhold.

Menon, S., Sinha, A., & Sreekantan, B. V. (Eds.). (2014). *Interdisciplinary Perspectives on Consciousness and the Self.* Palgrave.

Michels, J., & Gallimore, A. (2025). Take DMT Like This, Aliens Show Up—Top Neuroscientist (Ft. Andrew Gallimore). *Jesse Michels.* Retrieved August 21, 2025, from https://www.youtube.com/watch?v=8XD1ZiuhXoY

Muedini, F. (2020). *Sponsoring Sufism: How Governments Promote "Mystical Islam" in Their Domestic and Foreign Policies.* I.B. Tauris.

Nutt, D. (2023). Psychedelics: The revolutionary drugs that could change your life – a guide from the expert. Yellow Kite.

Radin, P. (1956). *The Trickster: A Study in American Indian Mythology.* Routledge & Kegan Paul.

Rahner, K. (1965). *Theological Investigations, Volume I: The Relationship of the Church to Non-Christian Religions* (R. J. McInerny, Trans.). Darton, Longman and Todd.

Rahner, K. (1975). *Theological Investigations, Volume IV: More Recent Writings* (R. J. McInerny, Trans.). Darton, Longman and Todd.

Rahner, K. (1981). *Theological Investigations, Volume VI: The Church and the Sacraments* (R. J. McInerny, Trans.). Darton, Longman and Todd.

Rahner, K. (1996). *Foundations of Christian Faith: An Introduction to the Idea of Christianity* (W. V. Dych, Trans.). Crossroad.

Robins, D. (2021). *The Battersea Poltergeist.* [Podcast] BBC Radio 4. Retrieved April 28, 2025, from https://www.bbc.co.uk/programmes/p0940193

Rogan, J. (2017). *Joe Rogan Experience #989—Dorian Yates.* YouTube video, added by PowerfulJRE. Retrieved April 11, 2025, from https://www.youtube.com/watch?v=cu-7WSjaVyU

Saroglou, V. (2020). *The Psychology of Religion.* Routledge.

Simondon, G. (2017). *On the Mode of Existence of Technical Objects* (C. Malaspina & J. Rogove, Trans.). Univocal Publishing.

Smith, C. (2021). *Unknown: Cosmic Time Machine* [Documentary]. Directed by C. Smith. Netflix.

Stiegler, B. (1998–2001). *Technics and Time* (Vol. I–III). Stanford University Press.

Wasson, R. G. (1957). Seeking the Magic Mushroom. *Life, 49*(19), 100–102, 109–120.

West, M. (2023). Claims Made by 'UFO Whistleblower' David Grusch are Pure Science Fiction. *Forbes*, 13 June. Retrieved June 30, 2025, from https://www.forbes.com/sites/danidiplacido/2023/06/13/claims-made-by-ufo-whistleblower-david-grusch-are-pure-science-fiction

West, M. (2025). UFOs, Disclosures & What's Really Going On? *The Asa Park Podcast*. Retrieved May 13, 2025, from https://www.youtube.com/watch?v=j6xN3lfkZx8

Index[1]

[1] Note: Page numbers followed by 'n' refer to notes.

D. Kelsey, *Transcendence and Collective Psychology*,
https://doi.org/10.1007/978-3-032-09495-7

The manufacturer's authorised representative in the EU is Springer Nature Customer Service Centre GmbH, Europaplatz 3, 69115 Heidelberg, Germany. If you have any concerns regarding our products, please contact ProductSafety@springernature.com

Printed and bound by CPI Group (UK) Ltd, Croydon, CR0 4YY
12/08/2026
02194505-0001